Designing the BBC

Designing the BBC

A History of Motion Graphics

Edited by
Iain Macdonald & Paula Williams

BLOOMSBURY ACADEMIC
LONDON • NEW YORK • OXFORD • NEW DELHI • SYDNEY

BLOOMSBURY ACADEMIC
Bloomsbury Publishing Plc
50 Bedford Square, London, WC1B 3DP, UK
1385 Broadway, New York, NY 10018, USA
29 Earlsfort Terrace, Dublin 2, Ireland

BLOOMSBURY, BLOOMSBURY ACADEMIC and the Diana logo are trademarks of Bloomsbury Publishing Plc

First published in Great Britain 2025

Copyright © Iain Macdonald and Paula Williams, 2025

Iain Macdonald and Paula Williams have asserted their right under the Copyright, Designs and Patents Act, 1988, to be identified as Editor of this work.

For legal purposes the Acknowledgements on p. xvi constitute an extension of this copyright page.

Cover design: Jacob Capener

All rights reserved. No part of this publication may be reproduced or transmitted in any form or by any means, electronic or mechanical, including photocopying, recording, or any information storage or retrieval system, without prior permission in writing from the publishers.

Bloomsbury Publishing Plc does not have any control over, or responsibility for, any third-party websites referred to or in this book. All internet addresses given in this book were correct at the time of going to press. The author and publisher regret any inconvenience caused if addresses have changed or sites have ceased to exist, but can accept no responsibility for any such changes.

A catalogue record for this book is available from the British Library.

ISBN: HB: 978-1-3503-8226-8
PB: 978-1-3503-8225-1
ePDF: 978-1-3503-8228-2
eBook: 978-1-3503-8227-5

Typeset by Deanta Global Publishing Services, Chennai, India
Printed and bound in Great Britain

To find out more about our authors and books visit www.bloomsbury.com and sign up for our newsletters.

Contents

List of Illustrations — vii
List of Contributors — x
Foreword *Bernard Lodge* — xiv
Acknowledgements — xvi

Introduction *Iain Macdonald and Paula Williams* — 1

Section I

1 Branding the BBC: The cultural and creative impact of identity *Charlie Mawer and Paula Williams* — 9
2 Painting with sound: Musical improvizations in the creation of the BBC's idents *Melissa Morton* — 37
3 Consistency or change?: *Top of the Pops*' meandering journey towards a sense of self *Matthias Hillner* — 45
4 *Blue Peter*: 'Here's one I made earlier' *Iain Macdonald and Kevin Hill* — 57
5 A play in themselves: Drama titles and graphics *Iain Macdonald and Iain Greenway* — 67
6 *Doctor Who*: Motion graphics for a Time Lord *Iain Macdonald* — 77
7 Global circulations, national traditions: BBC Motion Graphics and Canadian television *Andrew Burke* — 85
8 The Old School Cool Youth Culture and Multiculturalism in Pre-2000s Britain *O Haruna* — 95

Section II

9 Revolutionary practices: No width, no speed *Graham McCallum* — 109
10 A hybrid creator's tool: The introduction of Quantel Paintbox *Margaret Harvey* — 115
11 Drawn to Paintbox *Morgan Almeida* — 121
12 The best technique for the job: Making the right choices for the right reasons *Liz Friedman* — 129
13 BBC Open University: Moving education design from analogue to digital *Haydon Young* — 137

14	Digital pathfinders: The BBC Computer Graphics Workshop 1980 to 1987 *Bill Gardner*	149
15	BBC Sport of dash and dare *Steven Aspinall*	157
16	'. . . and now for the News': Television, probably: The age of cardboard *Brian Eley*	169
17	*Breakfast Time*: To infinity and beyond *Terry Hylton*	177
18	News 24/7 *Chyas Buffett, Mark Chaudoir, Andy Davy, Ian Wormleighton and Iain Macdonald*	189
Epilogue	*For Michael Graham-Smith*	195

Appendix	197
References	199
Index	211

Illustrations

1.1	BBC (1953) first BBC 'Television Symbol' Bat's Wings Logo	10
1.2	BBC One (2006) Hippos Ident	11
1.3	BBC Two (1991) Martin Lambie-Nairn Idents	11
1.4	BBC Two (1991–2015) BBC '2' Ident compilation	12
1.5	BBC Two (1991, 1994, 1997, 1993, 1993, 2015) *Gardeners' World*, Moon Landing, Mars Weekend, Prison, Berlin Wall, India Idents	14
1.6	BBC Two (2005) Pedigree Comedy Ident	15
1.7	BBC One (2000, 2000, 2000, 2011, 2009, 2010) Sydney Olympics, Euro 2000, Walking with Dinosaurs, Planet Earth Live, Bang Goes the Theory, Strictly Come Dancing Idents	16
1.8	BBC One (2002) Rhythm and Movement Idents	16
1.9	BBC One (2006, 2006, 2006, 2007) Footballers, Hippos, Ring 'o' Roses, Mission Control Idents	17
1.10	BBC Two (2000) Dalek Ident	17
1.11	BBC Two (1994) Christmas Wallace and Gromit Idents	18
1.12	CBBC (2007) Shaun the Sheep Ident	18
1.13	BBC Four (2007) Charlie Brooker Idents	19
1.14	BBC (1991, 1985, 1981, 1969, 1974, 1968, 1964, 1964, 1963) BBC One Globe Idents	20
1.15	BBC One (1997–1998) Canary Wharf, Eilean Donan Castle, Angel of the North, St Michaels Mount Balloon Idents	21
1.16	BBC One (2002, 2012, 2017, 2018) Bollywood, Mirror, Swimmers, Footballers Idents	23
1.17	BBC One (2020–2021) Lockdown Idents	24
1.18	BBC Two (1998) Christmas Fairies Idents	25
1.19	BBC Two (1993) Christmas Tin Toy Ident	26
1.20	BBC One (1997) Christmas Balloon Santa Idents	27
1.21	BBC (1997, 1997, 2001, 2011) Reeves and Mortimer, Gary Rhodes, Toys, Gruffalo Christmas Idents	28
1.22	BBC One (2015) 'Doodle' Idents	29
1.23	BBC Two (1994) Bungee Ident	30
1.24	BBC One (1969–85) The machinery for generating the mirror ball globe	32
1.25	BBC One (2006, 2007) Magical Forest, Hippos	33
1.26	BBC Two (2018, 2018, 2019, 1974) Sharp, Escapist, Punchy, Cube Colour Idents	33
3.1	*Top of the Pops* (1983) Vinyl disc models	47
3.2	*Top of the Pops* (1981) title sequence	47
3.3	*Top of the Pops* (1983) title sequence	48
3.4	*Top of the Pops* (1998) Storyboard from title sequence	50
3.5	*Top of the Pops* (1988) title sequence	51
3.6	*Top of the Pops* (1995) title sequence	53

3.7	*Top of the Pops* (1998) title sequence	54
4.1	*Blue Peter* (1999) sketch	59
4.2	*Blue Peter* (1999) original 3D CGI render	59
4.3	*Blue Peter* (2004) silhouettes of crew in title sequence	61
4.4	*Blue Peter* (2004) refreshed ship based on Tony Hart original	62
5.1	*EastEnders* (1985) aerial photograph prints of London collaged on board for shoot	70
5.2	*A Sense of Guilt* (1990) inspired by M.C. Escher storyboard frame by Peter Parr	72
5.3	*Loves and Lives of a She-Devil* (1986) Mary Fisher book jacket prop roughs	73
6.1	*Doctor Who* (1963) titles created with howlround	78
6.2	*Doctor Who* (1974) titles created with slit-scan	80
7.1	*Maigret* (1961) title sequence logo	87
7.2	*The Forsythe Saga* (1967) title sequence logo	87
7.3	*Civilisation* (1969) title sequence logo	87
7.4	*I Claudius* (1976) title sequence logo	88
7.5	*The Barchester Chronicles* (1982) title sequence logo	88
7.6	*The Goodies* (1970) title sequence logo	89
7.7	*The Two Ronnies* (1977) title sequence logo	89
7.8	BBC 2 (1967) Ident	92
8.1	*The Lenny Henry Show* (1985) title sequence	96
8.2	*The Lenny Henry Show* (1988) title sequence	97
8.3	*DEF II* (1988) title sequence	99
8.4	*DEF II* (1990) title sequence	100
8.5	*Dance Energy Lift Off* (1993) title sequence	100
8.6	*Gardeners' World* (1993) title sequence	102
8.7	*QED* (1995) title sequence	102
8.8	*Sportsnight* (1990) title sequence	103
8.9	*Juke Box Jury* (1990) title sequence	104
10.1	*Reputations* (1998) by Tom Brookes, hybrid objects shot under rostrum and digitally composited	118
11.1	News graphics from drawings to Paintbox	122
11.2	*Sportsnight* (1990) Paintbox rough	126
11.3	*280 Useful Ideas from Japan* (1990) Sketchbook roughs for concept board	127
11.4	*280 Useful Ideas from Japan* (1990) title sequence	127
12.1	*Grange Hill* (1977) comic-style illustration by Bob Cosford	131
12.2	*Soldiers* (1985) end caption with animation cels by Dennis Sutton on a peg bar	133
12.3	*Chronicle* (1989) Liz Friedman on set with models made by Alan Kemp and motion control rig	136
13.1	*Sutton Hoo* (1987) title sequence logo	142
13.2	Open University (*c*. 1970) Maths faculty's illustration	142
13.3	Open University (1976) *Personality and Learning* title sequence	143
13.4	*Tomorrows World* (1976) title sequence	145
13.5	*Tomorrow's World* (1980) title sequence	145
13.6	*Tomorrow's World* (1984) Prosthetic makeup for the title sequence	146
13.7	*Tomorrows World* (1984) title sequence	147
14.1	BBC Computer Graphics Workshop mainframes, 1982	152
14.2	BBC Graphics Handbooks for Election 1979 and 1983	153
14.3	BBC Weather Presentation Apple Mac XL micro	155
15.1	Match of the Day (*c*. 1971) original artwork for cards shot for the title sequence	158
15.2	Sportsnight (1985) Storyboard and 3D images	159

15.3	BBC Sport (1996) Ident	162
15.4	Match of the day (1997, 1998) title sequence	163
15.5	*France '98 World Cup* (1998) logo	165
15.6	BBC Sport (1998) Jimmy Hill title sequence	165
15.7	BBC Sport (2006)	166
15.8	BBC Sport, *Olympic Games* (2004) title sequence	167
16.1	Playful visualizations of the United Kingdom using graphic materials of the day	172
16.2	*London Rock* (1977) image from title sequence	174
16.3	*Nationwide* (c. 1980) 35mm clip of computer-generated green grid and UK	176
17.1	*Breakfast Time* (1983) logo and on-screen clock with presenter Frank Bough	181
17.2	Designer John Martin adding Letraset to a news map 1985	183
17.3	Filling out a Graphics News Requisition, 1985	184
17.4	News Graphics rostrum with Ikegami camera, 1985	185
17.5	*Six O'Clock News* electronic graphics suite, 1985	186
18.1	*BBC News 24 Top the Hour Countdown* (2005) photos from shoot and tickets	194

Contributors

Iain Macdonald
Dr Iain Macdonald is an associate professor in the Department of Design Innovation, Maynooth University, Ireland. He was a motion designer at BBC Television from 1987 to 1996 and was a senior designer nominated for a BAFTA before a career as a commercials director at the Moving Picture Company. He has published on motion graphics in several journals and in a book *Hybrid Practices in Moving Image Design - Methods of Heritage and Digital Production in Motion Graphics* (2016).

Paula Williams
Paula Williams is Course Leader for Advertising and Brand Design at Ravensbourne University London. She is an internationally recognized and an awardee creative director working as part of the BBC's and RedBee Creative's brand team and, later, as co-founder of Wonder Creative. She is a founding member of the BBC Motion Graphics steering group, responsible for developing and establishing the permanent archive at Ravensbourne University.

Bernard Lodge
Bernard Lodge is an award-winning graphic designer who worked at BBC Television for fourteen years, joining in 1960, where he designed the iconic titles for *Dr Who*, for five series. He later formed a design company Lodge/Cheesman directing commercials and designing graphics and effects for movies, such as Alien and Bladerunner. He is now a printmaker and illustrator specializing in woodcuts.

Charlie Mawer
Charlie Mawer is the executive creative director at Red Bee Creative.
Charlie joined the BBC from JWT in 1994. He became the executive creative director in 2003 across all their creative output. A former chair of industry body Promax UK and Bafta nominee, he co-wrote *The TV Brand Builders* (2016) and *Broadcast Design* (2007). Chosen by *Broadcast* magazine as one of the industry's 100 most influential people after the creation of the BBC ONE 'Circles' identity. He has contributed to books by Professors Paul Grainge and Catherine Johnson on the promotional industries. He speaks around the world on developments within TV marketing.

Melissa Morton
Melissa Morton is Research Manager at creative music agency MassiveMusic, where she primarily works to measure and predict the impact of music for brands through research and testing. She was awarded her PhD in musicology from the University of Edinburgh in 2023, and her thesis examined TV channel idents and their production contexts. In addition, several papers on music and television branding presented at

international conferences such as *Music and the Moving Image* and in journals such as Critical Studies in Television (2022) and the Interdisciplinary Journal of Voice Studies (2023).

Matthias Hillner
Matthias Hillner is a professor at the SCADpro Department at the Savannah College of Art and Design in the United States. His role involves guiding interdisciplinary student teams who develop design innovations and start-ups in exchange with industry partners. He has received a range of awards including Awards of Excellence from the New York Type Directors Club in 2014 and in 2018. His research expertise spans across motion typography and design innovation. He holds three postgraduate degrees from the Royal College of Art and has authored two books: *Virtual Typography* (2009) and *Intellectual Property, Design Innovation, and Entrepreneurship* (2021).

Kevin Hill
Kevin Hill is a design consultant and worked as a motion designer at the BBC from 1994 to 2004. He started as a trainee in BBC News & Current Affairs, before moving to BBC Resources Graphic Design Department at Television Centre. He went on to become a design director within the department and eventually the group creative director of Identity at Red Bee Media. He won several awards including Design Week, D&AD in Book and Promax World Class, and designed the titles for *Blue Peter* in 1999 and again in 2004.

Iain Greenway
Iain Greenway teaches in the Communications Design Department at Pratt Institute, Brooklyn, NY, and teaches advertising and design at Adelphi University, Long Island, NY. After a long career in graphic design, branding and advertising and having launched NY-based branding and advertising agency the Brand Gallery in 2005 to 2016, he is now teaching as well as consulting for branding agencies in NY. He was made a fellow of the Royal Society of Designers in 1996 in recognition for his design work for the BBC and is the recipient of many prestigious awards including two BAFTA's and a D&AD Black Pencil.

Andrew Burke
Andrew Burke is a professor in the Department of English at the University of Winnipeg. His research focuses on television, cultural memory and visual archives. His most recent book is *Hinterland Remixed: Media, Memory and the Canadian 1970s* (2019).

Omeiza 'O' Haruna
Omeiza 'O' Haruna is a graphic design postgraduate university teacher at Loughborough University (UK) in the School of Design and Creative Arts. His practice-based PhD project investigates the experience of negotiating racial identity, and how such tensions can be represented through animation using a mixture of collaborative and autoethnographic practices. His broader research interests include horror, practice-based and practice-led research in animation, and narrative-oriented graphic communication.

Graham McCullum
Graham McCallum is a designer, director and co-owner of Kemistry, a creative agency and gallery. In the mid-1960s he joined the BBC as an illustrator in children's programmes before moving into the BBC Graphic Design Department. As one of the leading multi-award-winning motion designers in the industry, he formed MKD in the late 1980s with Paul D'Auria and John Kennedy, and then in 1996 established Kemistry.

Margaret Harvey

Margaret Harvey (Horrocks) works freelance as a storyboard artist for documentary film and moving image. She exhibits as a multimedia artist and illustrator, combining traditional techniques with digital and photographic processes. As an educator she devises inclusive cross curricular projects that combine art with music, science and literature to encourage flexible thinking and idea development drawn from diverse references.

Morgan Almeida

Morgan Almeida, creative director, works to transform business through creative strategies. After a world-class grounding at BBC, he helped relaunch global news networks CNN, Aljazeera, Bloomberg and US Telecoms, and other television broadcasting brands in Africa, China, Lebanon, Kuwait and India. He is drawn to enterprise, diversity and beauty in imperfection.

Liz Friedman

Liz Friedman is a multi-award-winning former BBC graphic designer. She was course director at Ravensbourne University, heading BA (Hons) Motion Graphics, Digital Advertising and MA Visual Effects courses and was instrumental in helping to launch the BBC Motion Graphics Archive. Her work has been published worldwide in magazines and books about design and typography. She has given seminars to the industry in London, Miami, Toronto, Frankfurt, Vienna and Berlin.

Haydon Young

Haydon Young was formerly graphic designer with the BBC Open University, and then senior graphic designer at BBC Television Centre. Haydon won a Churchill Fellowship Award in 1982 to research advanced computer graphic design technology and methodology. In 1987, together with Marc Ortmans, they set up the design company Ortmans Young. Over fifteen years the company produced award-winning work both in the United Kingdom and internationally.

Bill Gardner MBE

Bill Gardner MBE was the head of BBC Computer Graphics Workshop (1980 to 1987). He set up the Scottish Seabird Centre and in 1997 installed remote wildlife cameras on several offshore islands. He also worked as a senior fundraising manager for the Scottish Wildlife Trust and the National Trust for Scotland, and designed and installed remote video viewing systems in their visitor centres for Ospreys, Peregrines and Herons.

Steven Aspinall

Steven Aspinall is the head of design and brand management for the Labour Party.
Previously he was the lead graphic designer for BBC Sport. He recently created the branding for the seventieth anniversary of the publication of the first James Bond book, and the cover of Bond's most recent literary adventure *On His Majesty's Secret Service*. He also writes a popular creative blog *The Steven Aspinall Archive*.

Brian Eley

Brian Eley is a freelance writer living in London. He joined the BBC as a graphic design assistant in 1974. He was the creative director of Lambie-Nairn (1994–2003) and co-founder and creative director of Dunning Eley Jones (2003–9). He has an MA is Creative Writing (plays & screenplays) from City University. Since 2012 he has focused on writing for performance and was co-writer of documentary feature film *Red Trees* (2017).

Terry Hylton

Terry Hylton joined BBC Television in 1979, pioneering the use of computer animation. In 1984 he moved to CAL the UK's first Film and TV CGI company as creative director, followed by SVC Television in 1992. In 2000 he became graphics manager at LEGO Media. In recent years he has worked on various Chinese Theme Park projects. Terry currently divides his time as chief creative officer at Sunhouse Television, executive YouTube producer for the Davenport Film Collection and the Martin Lambie-Nairn Collection, Magic Historian, and Founder of Coslany Arts Community Gallery & Artists' Studios, based in Norwich.

Chyaz Buffett

Chyaz Buffett is the head of Brand for GREAT Britain and Northern Ireland at the Prime Minister's and Cabinet Office, UK government. Previously head of design at Sky, UK, design director at Red Bee Media and senior designer at BBC News, he presents on brand strategy at communication conferences around the world and advises international governments and creative studios on nation branding. He is interested in the history of typography in communication, the integration of brand design and platform in campaigns and is currently researching the history of nation branding around the world.

Mark Chaudoir

Mark Chaudoir is a freelance film director and lecturer. He worked at BBC Graphics from 1987 to 2000, including eleven years in BBC Presentation Graphics, then in 2000, as a director in BBC Creative Services. In 2009 he became a freelance director and lecturer. Mark has taught at the National Film and Television School, Brunel University, AUB, London College of Communication. He has won over fifty industry awards including D&AD Black Pencil for his work on BBC2 idents.

Andy Davy

Andy Davy works as a media consultant, most recently at Discovery, responsible for the worldwide launch of their online service, Discovery+. From 1983 he was a graphic designer in the BBC's News and Current Affairs Departments, where he redesigned all the corporation's national news bulletins before moving to Yorkshire Television as manager of their Graphics Department. Back at the BBC he led the News and Current Affairs Graphics and postproduction businesses before moving north to run all the BBC's facilities in Scotland, finally leaving the BBC in 2014 as its controller of Technology Operations.

Ian Wormleighton

Ian Wormleighton was a creative director at BBC Broadcast initially joining the BBC News team in 1989 from the Royal College of Art. In 2019 he became a creative partner at TWIN-Associates, which works with television channels internationally, and collaborated on the BBC rebrand that started to be rolled out in 2021.

Foreword

BERNARD LODGE

For me the history of motion graphics began in 1960. A great year, in which I was married, passed my driving test and landed a job at the BBC. Then in 1977 I finally left the BBC and became merely a viewer.

That's eighteen years, a relatively short period, but one in which the corporation was changing dramatically with the launch of BBC TWO. The graphic department felt those changes, but what was it like to work in that department? Graham McCallum (No Width, No Speed) gives a true picture of its varied characters, some trained at art colleges, some older artists unfairly called signwriters and a couple of photographers. Because of the new channel, five more designers were employed, and it was this group, now larger and more talented, who were inventing the grammar of tv graphics. This book, like previous books on television graphics, shows particular examples: title sequences and factual graphics, maps, idents and so on, but of course, its pages cannot display the daily pattern of work. We were hired to make title and credit captions, on a boring stream of 12×9 cards, roller captions or hand-lettered titles. But we were trying to do something extra. We were creating captions with images, and we were making title sequences that moved. This was due mainly to the influence of Saul Bass whose brilliant title sequences were spread across wide cinema screens. The book doesn't mention training, because at that time there was none. Although we had been schooled in aesthetics, we were untrained for many aspects of television: how to handle rostrum cameras, editing machines, how to synchronize soundtracks, how video mattes worked and so on, but we 'picked it up'. I remember the rostrum camera operator who was irritated by my ignorance, and a producer who came to brief me about titles for 16mm A rolls and B rolls, who laughed when he realized I knew nothing about the process. This was David Attenborough. Our relationship with directors and producers was crucial.

The book covers in detail my involvement with video experiments and 'slit-scan', though it doesn't (how could it?) mention the mistakes, the reshoots, the budget busting that luckily didn't show up.

In 1977 I left the BBC, and two years later the head of Graphic Design Department joined me to form Lodge/Cheesman. I was plunged into the world of advertising and cinema effects, which was complex and challenging, so I was hardly aware of the progress of motion graphics back at the Beeb, but this book now gives me a real insight into that progress. I've now learnt about some brilliantly designed effects due to new computer capabilities. I was handling similar techniques, but the BBC graphics were far more 'hands on'.

As an outsider, I was amazed when another outsider, Martin Lambie-Nairn, took over the branding of the corporation's identity. A cool refreshing redesign of those three little boxes. The book tells in enormous detail the psychology of the rebranding in 1991/1992 and the creative drive of the Lambie-Nairn team to explode the images of the two channels, especially the branding of BBC Two. I was amazed by the seductive number 2 floating in water, and I find the BBC News branding special, with its dynamic use of computer layers. If a spinning world globe is the greatest television news cliché, then this is a cliché that I admire every day at 6.00 pm.

This history isn't the work of one author. How accurate would that be? The BBC is so amazingly complex that its graphic designers, with their differing skills and talents, the growing technologies which they handled, would defeat a single author aiming for accuracy. But here you have chapters written mainly by the designers who were actually there, making the images. The history of motion graphics is told through the history of the designers' careers – a journey of excitement, puzzlement, experiment, setbacks and the development of ideas married often to new, seductive techniques.

The history is still growing.

Acknowledgements

For those who sought to break new ground.
For those who pushed the boundaries.
For those who crafted the analogue and pioneered technology.
For those who paved the way.
For those who gave their time and energy.

To all of those in design, who have worked across the BBC in the UK Nations and Regions.
Thank you.

Introduction

IAIN MACDONALD AND PAULA WILLIAMS

In the 2020s the multiplicity of viewing platforms and content channels has transformed audience viewing habits and the role of the British Broadcasting Corporation (BBC). The corporation's centenary in 2022 and the launch of the BBC Motion Graphics Archive have precipitated a fresh appraisal and retrospective in this, the first book to exclusively examine BBC Motion Graphics. This book aims to build on the historical foundations of Roy Laughton (1966), Douglas Merritt (1987 and 1993) and Martin Lambie-Nairn (1997), who have previously covered the early history of BBC Motion Graphics within a wider broadcasting context.

The editors of this book have brought together a collection of new essays that have been written in large part by ex-BBC designers, who write from first-hand experience and cover every decade of BBC broadcasting since the Graphic Design Department was formed in 1954 to the present day. Rarely does practice-led research in motion graphics have such a voice outside higher education lecture halls and studios, and occasional industry journal interviews. Other contributors come from the fields of graphic design, music and media studies to bring fresh perspectives in a field of design history that is still emerging and yet overlaps with many established academic disciplines.

Motion graphics in broadcasting and film is associated with opening titles and credits, content graphics and data visualization, channel idents and brand identity. The scope of this work encompasses animation, video, visual effects and computer science, as well as typographic design, illustration and photographic arts. Many of the creative principles of television advertising, in storytelling, as well as technical mastery, are evident in the design of opening titles. The art of communicating and preparing an audience in the opening twenty to thirty seconds is becoming increasingly examined by media courses beyond the practical design courses in universities and art colleges across the globe.

In 1967, Herdeg and Halas made an observation that is finally being rewritten today:

> Film and television graphics may have suffered from a feeling of inferiority in that they were outside the mighty mainstream of production output. The flow in the case of television has in fact become a flood with a tendency to sweep away the finer points of production, where the role of graphic arts lies. But gradually even in television good design is emerging. (1967: 187)

This book does not promise to contain all the very best in BBC Motion Graphics; that will be for the reader to judge when they have explored the online BBC Motion Graphics Archive, which is the source of nearly every example in this book.

> The influence of the Graphic Department at the BBC under various heads of the group cannot be over-estimated. The department can be seen to have set the standards in creative design, in aesthetic treatment and in developing technical methods since its inception. As the first graphic designers in a new industry with a privileged non-commercial ethos, all members of the department have tried to retain this special position. (Merritt 1993: 3)

A common thread through most, if not all, of the chapters is the effect of technological change and cultural working practices on the creative economy (Hesmondhalgh 2007; Macdonald 2014). The original handlettering artists and printers came from a similar tradition as print, predominantly male. Then as illustrators and designers graduated from art colleges into television graphics, the gender balance slowly changed, followed later by ethnic diversity. Ideas abounded in a new medium, and as resources multiplied and became more sophisticated, ambitions grew. For a time failure was tolerated (or at least afforded), and so experimentation and innovation flourished. Hendy (2022) remarks that 'making television, like making radio, had been an evolutionary process in which success was built on a tolerance of failure' (2022: 332), and several of our contributors generously, and amusingly, expose their early flops that led to steep learning curves, and none more so than when on air in front of millions of viewers.

> And just as an architect affects, through his design, the actual life of individuals, so graphic design has a much wider influence than its immediate object. As an opinion maker, a salesman, an educator, an entertainer, a humourist, an experimenter and a scientist, the graphic artist can fulfil, even if indirectly, one of the most basic communication functions of the present day. He can also be the first to influence the constant changes in these restless and dynamic media, where the evolution of styles and techniques demands analyses of cinematographic phenomena and deeper understanding of psychology and human behaviour. Mental alertness, ideas and high creativity are essential here. (Hedeg & Halas 1967: 187)

Peer-to-peer support was also matched with competition for wider industry recognition and award accolades. Sometimes it would take an award before a producer would sit up and take notice of the talent within the BBC. The exacting attention to detail – colour grading, letter spacing, lighting, pace of movement and editing – were all aspects of the art and craft of the motion graphic designer that were so often overlooked or taken for granted by television producer clients and the public who watched on their old television sets.

> The one distinctive element for the television graphic designer, is the ability to plan and produce images with *sound* and *movement*. Combining words, music and sound effects and then timing them precisely to pictures, frame-by-frame, is the essence of the craft, and this combination has proved to be one of the most compulsive ways of gaining attention. (Merritt 1987: 11; emphasis in the original text)

Real people with enormous creative talents are behind everything that appears in the archive and this book. It is too easy to assume all modern media is formulaic using computer-generated, generic software solutions. Where the real creative magic happens is through a designer's engagement with a script, conversations with producers, directors, writers, editors and sometimes composers. The BBC attracts the best talent and the brightest minds, which can often support a culture of creative excellence and ambition. Many found a permanent career there, while others left to seek fresh business or creative opportunities at home and abroad. As an export, ex-BBC design talent came with a world-leading brand status and caché.

Following the successful launch of the United Kingdom's fourth terrestrial channel in 1982, Martin Lambie-Nairn brought a new level of maturity to television brand communication as a professional service. His influence as an external commercial competitor prompted BBC Motion Designers to develop new skills and adapt their creative practice. Motion designers 'morphed' into brand consultants, art directors and film directors, often all in one, with the same obsession for visual detail and drive for new ideas.

The BBC has not always been a happy place to work for, and by its very nature television is a continuously evolving and transforming industry in terms of technology, management and commercial business models (Macdonald 2014). Constant change and variety from day-to-day can be both enormously stimulating and exciting, as well as exhausting, stressful and displacing. 'Everyone who has ever worked for the BBC will have a strong view as to its "true" history' (Hendy 2022: xvi).

We aim to take you on a journey that will inform, educate and in places entertain. Within the archive and this book, there will hopefully be some much-loved titles and idents, images and sounds that evoke memories and places in people's lives. How they were created and came to be broadcast can now be explained and revealed, hopefully without losing the mystique and glamour that sometimes cloak treasured memories.

The images and sounds the BBC has brought into our homes have been the portal to other worlds, other ideas, other times, 'the tissue of our dreams, the warp and weft of our memories, the staging posts of our lives'. (Higgins, 2015, p. 63–4)

(Hendy 2022: xii)

As an educational tool this book should appeal to design professionals and students alike: 'designers in all mediums must have a highly developed awareness of the past as well as the moods and mores of their own time' (Merritt 1993: 128).

Book contents

The book takes a thematic approach to the history of BBC Motion Graphics that covers technological development and the evolution of new creative approaches afforded by these advances. In this we examine different genres of programming such as drama, news, sport, children's, Open University and a comprehensive study of BBC idents and promos. We also bring in voices that deserve greater recognition and attention, from both an international perspective and a British Black and Asian viewpoint. A historical timeline of the BBC Graphic Design Department can be found in Appendix.

Presentation branding is at the very core of how the BBC is packaged and personified as a distinctive broadcaster in the United Kingdom and across the world. Paula Williams and Charlie Mawer reveal how a global brand established itself from the very first BBC 'Television Symbol', designed by Abram Games, the mechanical rotating globe of BBC1, to the iconic characterization of BBC2. Throughout this chapter, they will explore the unique role that the BBC idents played in the lives of the UK audience across a five-decade period – showcasing advances in technology, mirroring programming and viewer interests, reflecting larger shifts in representation of the audience themselves, celebrating changing talent and marking the very passing of the seasons themselves. These identities were loved and sometimes loathed, but they were never ignored.

Melissa Morton explores the aesthetic character of the music and sound design for idents, with examples including recent idents for BBC One, BBC Two and BBC Four. Chapter 1 observes continuities and shifts in the musical character of idents, comparing the evocative and often-mesmeric idents of the 1990s and 2000s to the short, striking mnemonics appearing on streaming platforms today. Overall, this chapter highlights the contribution of music and sound design to the brand identities of channels and services within the context of the current hybrid television landscape that bridges linear and digital spaces.

Music also features in Matthias Hillner's examination of Light Entertainment icon *Top of the Pops* (1964–2006). With its distinctive requirements for on-screen graphics, he investigates the different graphic and typographic approaches that defined generations of pop music and what led to its current form of cultural nostalgia.

Blue Peter is the longest-running children's TV series in the history of television. It has been broadcast every year since its launch in 1958. Chapter 4 looks at the last quarter century and examines how the programme refused to be ignored by waking up media attention to its radical new branding in 1999, and how the geographical move from London to Manchester in 2011, along with the competition from online media and changing viewer habits, were overcome.

BBC Drama has been another keystone in its creative output, and many title sequences, such as *EastEnders*, are indelibly linked to it. Iain Greenway and Iain Macdonald examine some case studies of the production process and relationship between designer and film producer/director and explore the different approaches to single drama, short-season serials and long-running series that have become household names. It explores how designers attempt to encapsulate the essence and mood of the drama about to be seen, in order to prepare the audience as well as inform them of the leading credits. Like all programme genres, the technical revolution of film, video and digital production have allowed greater sophistication in production and realize designers' ambitions to create new imagery, as well as having significantly improved clarity and resolution of text on screen.

Any history of the BBC would be remiss not to include *Doctor Who*, the longest-running sci-fi fantasy series in the world. Starting with Bernard Lodge, Chapter 6 charts from the beginning the sometimes extraordinary journeys of those who prepared audiences for an other worldliness to the modern-day enthusiasts and fans who have launched careers in motion graphics through their passion for the show on social media.

Canadian media studies academic Andrew Burke's chapter explores the conjunction of cultural memory and modern design by analyzing the circulation of BBC Motion Graphics worldwide in the 1960s and 1970s. Extensive overseas sales of BBC programming in these decades means the BBC Motion Graphics Archive has affective power and mnemonic purchase well beyond the United Kingdom. Thinking specifically about the Canadian situation first, it examines how the material collected in the BBC Motion Graphics Archive has significance for Canadian viewers, occupying a key place in national cultural memory. Second, it examines the role of motion graphics as a marker of both distinction and difference. Third, it compares BBC Motion Graphics Archive to the history of motion graphics in Canada, mobilizing Jan Hadlaw's concept of 'design nationalism' to argue that Burton Kramer's comprehensive 1974 redesign of the CBC's graphic identity was tied to the deliberate, state-led initiative to modernize Canada during the 1960s and 1970s.

The BBC holds a unique responsibility in championing and serving the multifaceted identities of its British audience through a variety of approaches to representation. Graphic design academic O Haruna examines off-screen representation through interviews with BBC motion designers and appraises their most innovative and memorable works. Locating on-screen multicultural representations in title sequences and idents, an oft-characterless endeavour, requires a greater level of sensitivity to unpick how objects, shapes and music may connote subcultures. As the future of public arts funding and BBC productions is challenged, questions of what will happen to the opportunities, visions of a unified nation's voice and growth in public acknowledgement of a Britishness hinged on more than whiteness become more palpable.

In Section II of the book, we have a collection of more personal first-hand accounts of different aspects and departments in BBC Graphic Design, written by the motion designers who witnessed the changes in technology, working practices and the era of brand consultant and international director.

Graham McCallum reflects on the changing skills and practices that occurred during the digital revolution of the 1980s, framing this in a broader review of the BBC Graphic Design Department witnessed from his personal experience spanning over three decades.

Margaret Harvey challenges the homogenization of digital applications and argues that the analogue and craft skills that many of her generation applied to the digital Quantel Paintbox allowed for a richer creative exploration.

Morgan Almeida examines the crossover of his drawing skills from pen and sketchpad to Quantel Paintbox to bring title sequences and branding concepts on the screen to life. He concludes with a speculative view of AI and what it might mean for creativity in the future.

Liz Friedman's chapter examines different animation techniques that she employed over several decades for documentaries and drama series. She considers how ideas for titles and content sequences forced innovations and advances in animation practices that were cutting edge at the time.

Haydon Young recalls his formative years working at Open University and how the technological advances of graphics came into play in delivering a 'university of the air' to provide accessible higher education to those who were not able to attend on campus – a concept model of delivery that has returned to prominence for the university establishment following the pandemic. Pre-digital methods of production are explained and illustrated.

The Computer Graphics Workshop was a research and engineering adjunct to BBC News Graphics and the main BBC Graphic Design Department. Bill Granger describes how his team contributed to the digital delivery innovations for the BBC presentation, weather and the election results.

Sport and the rise of a more competitive broadcasting landscape that led to more ambitious and arresting branding and data visualization are covered by Steven Aspinall. Milestone broadcasting moments, such as the Olympics and World Cup Football, are explained and examined alongside the weekly staples of *Grandstand* and *Match of the Day*.

Finally, we end with BBC News and Current Affairs, indisputable keystones of the corporation's global brand and daily output. The insatiable desire for design content that grew in the 1970s is detailed in the accounts of Brian Eley, Terry Hylton, Mark Chaudoir, Chyaz Buffet and others. They give personal accounts of their time at news, covering the changes to news programming and how they affected branding and graphics creation. This was the broadcasting crucible of the digital revolution, and its impact is explained in contributions from the next generation of post-digital designers.

Our intention is that future motion designers will find inspiration from the work discussed in this book to push the discipline and field into new, exciting spaces. Learning 'on the job' is part of the motivation and stimulation that comes with being a motion designer. But today's generation has the advantage of formal higher education in this field, largely taught in the United Kingdom by many who have worked in the industry, including some at the BBC.

Section I

1 Branding the BBC

The cultural and creative impact of identity

CHARLIE MAWER AND PAULA WILLIAMS

Introduction

The creation of the BBC Motion Graphic Archive marked the centenary of the BBC, which sits at a pivotal point in technology, global competition and change in the media sector. This offers a unique position of liminality from which to analyze the tone of voice, appearance, behaviours and cultural and creative impact of the BBC – brand identities, by those central to their creation. Branding by augmentation seeks to deliver on the purposes and values outlined in the BBC's Royal Charter. This chapter investigates the landmark shifts in the visual identity of the BBC. Using interviews with BBC Motion Designers, BBC Executives and members of the wider creative industry, idents and campaigns are explored through role, reflection of the nation, seasonality and the future of idents, as screen-watching experiences diversify and fragment across different modes of content delivery.

The first BBC 'Television Symbol' designed in 1953 by Abram Games (who had previously designed the iconic logo for the 1951 Festival of Britain) became an iconic representation of the BBC, as a modern, innovative and forward-thinking organization (see Figure 1.1).

It established a mode of visual identity for the company, encompassing broad concepts of the world and a vision of the broadcasting medium to come. The BBC issued an official description at that time:

> The abstract pattern consists of two intersecting eyes which scan the globe from north to south and east to west, symbolising vision and the power of vision. Flashes of lightning on either side represent electrical forces and the whole form takes the shape of wings which suggest the creative possibilities of television broadcasting. (BBC 1953)

The BBC's channel branding for the last seventy years has lived 'in-between' and is by definition 'non-programming'. However, the BBC's idents have not been peripheral to the experience of watching its content, but central to it, playing a fundamental role in the compounding, contextualizing and framing of the day's programming in a direct channel of communication with audiences. They are the 'connective tissue' of television (Moran 2013: 6), showing relative fusion of an essentially diverse set of elements in what Raymond Williams (1974) theorized in a pre-convergent era as 'television flow'.

The role of idents

Channel branding occupies an isolated timeslot in programming schedules; they are a clearly marked part of television, conceived not as separate objects but as having a formal relationship to the programmes, yet they are characteristically unalike. The BBC's Presentation Design team has been instrumental in creating

Figure 1.1 BBC (1953) first BBC 'Television Symbol' Bat's Wings Logo. Courtesy BBC.

codes of practice that have informed many of today's broadcast identities. Nevertheless, those inner rules and modes of operation are not fixed. In their durations, idents are brief and conversely need to possess a 'living hold' in visual and audio terms, allowing specific live continuity to frame the programmes. Although possessed of this uneasy and indistinct status, this storytelling medium delights and encourages audiences to engage with the BBC's content, through design rich in visual imagery, creativity and technical innovation. Far from insignificant and statistically negligible, the BBC's idents occupy a volume of output comparable to a genre such as drama. When explaining the value for money in the production of the 'Circles' era idents, the BBC One team calculated that the previous set of idents had been aired 43,000 times over a 4.5-year period (on average, around 30 times a day).

However, for over fifty years the prevailing visual manifestation between the programmes on BBC Television (TV) and, as it was called after the launch of BBC Two in 1964, BBC One was a ticking clock and/or a single rotating globe. The graphic design of the globes and clocks evolved over the years, but they became such a permanent and familiar fixture on the United Kingdom's TV screens that it is no surprise that BBC Television's former head of graphic design, John Aston, described the BBC One identity as 'where angels feared to tread' and a subject that 'everyone had an opinion about' (in Lambie-Nairn 1997: 128). Over time their role developed to incorporate a wide variety of uses in their seemingly simple five to fifteen seconds.

In many ways to their creators, they are a uniquely challenging creative puzzle – Nobody knows how long it will last (duration), what someone else will be saying over the top of it or indeed what will come before or after it. The music has to be designed to be of indeterminate duration, and any sense of reveal or story arc must be followed by a holding pattern.

They serve as a familiar and reassuring presence to indicate a sense of place or home for viewers, marketing message, a gear shift between different moods of programmes – particularly needed on general entertainment channels such as the BBC's where you might be going from a situation comedy into a hard-hitting drama or current affairs show. They provide a moment for a voice of the channel to alert viewers to any sensitivity or language warnings in the incoming show and, in a live schedule, to update any time changes. All of this over a piece of film that at its best will visually entrance and engage when seen 3,000 times over a 10-year period. Much like the artist Tracey Emin commented in 2006:

> Have you seen the BBC hippos? Every time I watch them . . . I'm lulled into a whole sense of enchantment. It's probably one of my favourites, most comforting things of the year. And what's strange is when I mention it to other people, their faces light up with glee. (Emin 2006) (See Figure 1.2)

The BBC has always been a leader in the development of both form and function of channel idents, but there have been three landmark shifts in their overall creative role. The first was marked by the emergence of the moving globe in the early 1970s. The second by the groundbreaking BBC2s as designed by the influential Martin Lambie-Nairn (see Figure 1.3) and the in-house Presentation Design team through the mid- to late 1990s (see Figure 1.4). The third was in the explosion of digital brands.

Figure 1.2 BBC One (2006) Hippos Ident. Courtesy BBC.

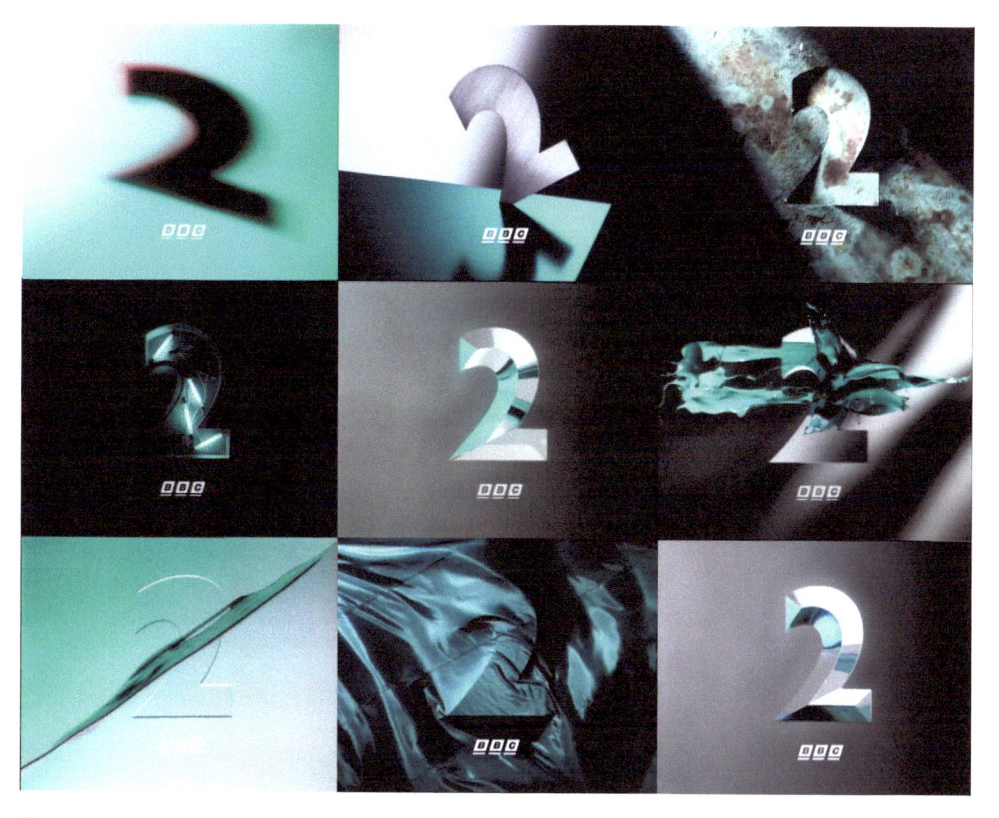

Figure 1.3 BBC Two (1991) Martin Lambie-Nairn Idents.

Figure 1.4 BBC Two (1991–2015) BBC '2' Ident compilation. Courtesy BBC.

12 Designing the BBC

Consistency from confusion

Taking the second landmark moment – the channel and corporate rebranding in 1991 and 1997 by Lambie-Nairn. Before the move there was 'creative anarchy' within the channel presentation teams, with, as Pam Masters recalls, 'each week's rota'd team choosing whichever colour, font, layout they saw fit for information graphics' (Pam Masters 2023). Lambie-Nairn brought in a desire for 'layout consistency as provided in magazines' (Sarah Davies 2023). Despite some ferocious internal resistance – coming as ever from the BBC in the form of 'Stiff memos', it was clearly time for the shackles to be put onto 'the Pres teams'. The hiring of Masters from Channel 4 by Sir Paul Fox in 1987 was the inciting act of the rebrand. Channel 4 under her stewardship had redefined the nature of channel branding. For the next twenty years she was a crucial point of sign off on all the channel identities. Masters had high standards of craft which drove the creative and technical aspects of the hand-picked team to new heights.

> I think I've always had an eye for what I think would work, although I have no graphic design experience. But I do have a feel for creatively what might look good . . . and I suppose I knew I had that editorial side of it as well, I knew to be aware of how the audience might react to some of these things. (Masters 2023)

Sarah Davies, account director at Lambie-Nairn, articulates the need for proper accreditation and attribution – the professional marketing of broadcasters as driven by 'deregulation within the industry – the sudden plethora of competitive channels' (Davies 2023).

> When I went to work on the BBC brand I discovered that it owned over 150 different logos or brands. They were producing them at a rate of two a month. It seemed that anybody with a budget could commission a version of the brand . . . and did. The result was expensive chaos in the organisation and confusion in the market. If one is serious about having an effective global brand it must be directed from the centre. That doesn't mean that the centre ignores the needs of specific parts of the business. It means that one devises a system that delivers flexibility, that fits in an overall 'one company' brand scheme. (Creative Review 2015)

TV channel brands are not the only heuristics we use to guide us on what to watch, as we will see later, but they still play a very important role. Magnus Willis, co-founder of the insight and strategy consultancy Sparkler, is one of the best thinkers and researchers in the television world and introduced the concept of 'flag channels' and 'frame channels'.

> The analogy I always had in my head was: if you're standing on a plain, there are things that are nearby that you can see because you have been looking at them for a while, you kind of understand them. Meanwhile there are things in the distance that you can't even contemplate because they are so far away. Therefore, what is the best way to get people to see things that are far away? That's where the whole flag thing came from. . . . On the horizon, you are basically going to have to put a stake in the ground with a flag on top of it and you have to wave your flag like a maniac to get people to go there. (Willis in Bryant and Mawer 2016: 47)

Willis describes how the 'frame' concept works like this in the context of channels:

> It borrows from the world of terrestrial TV where in essence everyone was a generalist and what united the channel was not something at its centre . . . but something that encapsulated and framed everything. (Willis in Bryant and Mawer 2016: 69)

Idents as a marketing tool

A third defining period of innovation during the rapid proliferation of digital channels was the development of idents as a marketing tool to help audiences attribute programmes to the right channel and give credit back to the BBC for those loved properties. Beyond standard marketing campaigns, this was an opportunity to indelibly and creatively link a show with the channel that had invested in its commissioning and development. New BBC idents were conceived to be adaptable to promote themed programming while retaining brand integrity.

Early markers that the idents could play this role were, as ever, seen within the 'test tube' of creativity at BBC2. During the 1990s controller Alan Yentob sought to change perceptions and make BBC2s idents a better representation of the channel's content. BBC2 would often create evenings of content around themes. Controller Michael Jackson saw a value in super serving fans of particular passions with whole 'nights' dedicated to *Doctor Who*, or horror, or natural history programming – in an early example of what transmedia pioneer Andrea Philips called sending 'love letters to the audience' (Philips 2012). Idents were also commissioned with a short-lived lifespan to play throughout the evening.

> For me, what was interesting, was that you suddenly had this flexible system of design that had an ability to wrap the brand and content in a way that had not been done before as a national broadcaster. We used the language of the '2' being a playful chameleon and character to do that. (Williams 2023)

The quantity and quality of ideas allowed the channel, over twenty-five years, to create idents for themes as diverse as *Gardeners' World*, Moon Landing, Mars Weekend, Prison, Wimbledon, Berlin Wall and Seasons such as India (Figure 1.5). 'They were just really well thought out, well executed, fun ideas that had the essence of each theme. It was simple, unique inventiveness' (Chaudoir 2023).

The idents were also increasingly used to help shift audience perceptions of the brand. BBC2 felt in early 2005 that it was deemed serious and worthy in audience research, despite creating and nurturing some of the most groundbreaking comedy in the country. Red Bee's (formerly BBC Broadcast) creative response was the 'Pedigree Comedy' campaign, which once again saw the beloved 'fluffy BBC2 dog' starring in a series of sketches and 'meta' idents (see Figure 1.6). Charlie Mawer recalls:

Figure 1.5 BBC Two (1991, 1994, 1997, 1993, 1993, 2015) *Gardeners' World*, Moon Landing, Mars Weekend, Prison, Berlin Wall, India Idents. Courtesy BBC.

Figure 1.6 BBC Two (2005) Pedigree Comedy Ident. Courtesy BBC.

In writing the sketches we had to pass a spectacularly high bar of being deemed funny enough not just by the director Mark Mylod – (sometime before he became lead director on Game of Thrones and Succession), but also the talent who ranged from Catherine Tate and Rob Brydon to Jon Culshaw and Stephen Fry. The joy of the 2 'fluffy dog' was that while not speaking, he has such a defined comedy character that we could persuade stars to act alongside a living brand marker for the channel itself. (Mawer 2023)

Meanwhile, on BBC One, as the competitive pressures and increased professionalism of marketing as a function with the organization took hold, the idents were no longer subtly informed by landmark programming – they actively embraced it. The balloon flew over Sydney Opera House for the Olympic Games, soared behind a goalkeeper in the Brussels night sky for *Euro 2000*, and, indeed memorabe moment, appeared gloriously anachronistically behind a herd of dinosaurs to celebrate the truly innovative launch of *Walking with Dinosaurs* (see Figure 1.7).

The BBC One 'Circles' identity was created with the need for greater flexibility and adaptability in embracing shows and talent, compared to what had been afforded by the 'Rhythm and Movement' era (2002–5) (see Figure 1.8) it replaced. While the launch idents had broad genres within their codification – Hippos – Natural History, Footballers – Sport, Mission Control – Sci-Fi, Ring-O-Roses – Childrens' and so on (Figure 1.9), over time programme-specific iterations began to be commissioned to match the role played by the '2' over a longer period. Dramas like *Ashes to Ashes*, landmark factual like *Planet Earth Live* and *Africa*, entertainment megabrands like *Strictly Come Dancing* and new factual launches like *Bang Goes the Theory* all gained their own 'Circle' idents. *Bang Goes the Theory* even launched its ident with a live multi-experiment chain reaction stunt in the junction (see Figure 1.7).

Branding the BBC 15

Figure 1.7 BBC One (2000, 2000, 2000, 2011, 2009, 2010) Sydney Olympics, Euro 2000, Walking with Dinosaurs, Planet Earth Live, Bang Goes the Theory, Strictly Come Dancing Idents. Courtesy BBC.

Figure 1.8 BBC One (2002) Rhythm and Movement Idents. Courtesy BBC.

Doctor Who has become one of the most valuable properties for the BBC both domestically and internationally. Back in 1999, BBC2 leveraged this with a Dr Who Night, complete with a bespoke ident (see Figure 1.10).

> Dr Who had cult status and by that time so did the BBC2 idents, it was a gift. . . . We brought them together and created a '2 Dalek', a radio-controlled practical model about two feet high, built by model makers Complete Fabrication . . . the ident we shot was so popular, that the model was eventually auctioned through BBC Children in Need and raised a huge amount of money. (Platt 2023)

Figure 1.9 BBC One (2006, 2006, 2006, 2007) Footballers, Hippos, Ring 'o' Roses, Mission Control Idents. Courtesy BBC.

Figure 1.10 BBC Two (2000) Dalek Ident. Courtesy BBC.

In 2009 David Tennant's Doctor was persuaded to hook his Tardis to a string of reindeer and fly them into the northern sky for another circular ident. Perhaps most iconically, *Albert Square,* the most resolutely non-circular of shapes, was bent into an unfamiliar sphere for a celebration of *EastEnders'* twenty-fifth anniversary week.

Occasionally existing idents got playful modifications to herald new programming on the network. A chameleon, which caught and ate a fairy, was added to the Magic Forest ident to promote *Life in Cold Blood* in 2008. Red noses appeared on the Hippos to celebrate *Comic Relief* in 2007 and 2009. Mission Control was amended to play into a *Doctor Who* episode as if it had been hacked (see Figure 1.25).

Aardman Animations' long involvement in BBC idents took them from CBBC to BBC2 to BBC One as their own shows took centre stage. In BAFTA-winning Christmas idents on BBC2 in 1995 (see Figure 1.11), Jane Wyatt-Brooks recalls their inception:

'A Close Shave' was scheduled on BBC2. Michael Jackson, the then Controller, wanted to bring the two together. The obvious answer was to link the two iconic characters the '2' and Gromit. The '2' was almost like the cheeky nephew that comes for Christmas and messes things up. . . . A lot of time was spent at Aardmans with Nick Park being incredibly generous with his time and very collaborative. Scenarios were brainstormed and honed down to a final set. Their antics needed to be true to both characters, with the most successful ideas based on either Gromit or the '2' getting the upper hand. Getting the comic timing and expressions right was vital, with sequences blocked out in rough animation form before the final shoot over 3 weeks. Everything had to be squashed into those three ident seconds. (Wyatt-Brooks 2023)

Figure 1.11 BBC Two (1994) Christmas Wallace and Gromit Idents. Courtesy BBC.

Figure 1.12 CBBC (2007) Shaun the Sheep Ident. Courtesy BBC.

Figure 1.13 BBC Four (2007) Charlie Brooker Idents. Courtesy BBC.

This first success then extended to *Wallace and Gromit's World of Invention* on BBC One, and *Shaun the Sheep* starred chaotically in idents for the children's channel CBBC (see Figure 1.12).

While the BBC's digital channels did not have the same level of investment to create bespoke idents for their talent on most occasions, one example deserves highlighting. For years Charlie Brooker had mocked and ridiculed continuity announcers talking over the end credits of his savagely satirical BBC4 masterpiece *Screenwipe*, so it was with great glee that he was persuaded by Ollie Harnett and Susan Ayton to appear in front of a series of BBC4 idents, clutching a megaphone as he stalked the library background while shouting over the harassed continuity announcer, 'See you don't like it when I do it to you' (see Figure 1.13).

Reflecting the nation

There are innumerable challenges for a public service broadcaster to be relevant to the nation in an increasingly atomized world. Today amplified competition means audiences have never enjoyed more choice – none more challenging than for BBC One.

The early BBC onscreen graphic tuning symbol served as an initial and urgent need to mark the channel and signal to the public who was providing the service. These marker designs focused singularly on the provider.

> Until 1955, with only one transmission from the BBC in this country (UK), there was little sign that design was regarded as a necessity in the new medium. Nor was there the clear vision to see that design (not merely graphics) should become an essential factor rather than an optional 'artistic' activity. (Merritt 1993: vi)

From the 1960s transition to BBC TV and then BBC 1, the focus from an identity perspective was demonstrating that the BBC, as a modern organization in a new commercial landscape, was well placed to serve nations, regions and the world. The BBC's in-house Presentation Design team led by Sid Sutton created the Globe design logo, which came to be synonymous with the BBC in several iterations driven by changes in broadcasting, colour and technological innovations (see Figure 1.14).

Figure 1.14 BBC (1991, 1985, 1981, 1969, 1974, 1968, 1964, 1964, 1963) BBC One Globe Idents. Courtesy BBC.

Joe Moran talks about television's relationship with audiences as 'Participatory rituals' in programming that speak of a 'virtual community', an extended family brought together 'part of the same armchair nation'.

> Much of the television meant for adults also seemed to share this incantatory quality, this rhetorical conjuring up of collective life. . . . As magazine programmes act as 'Britain's nightly mirror' to the face of Britain. (Moran 2013: 3)

Television performed a mostly benign confidence trick, convincing us that we believed the same things and were part of the same armchair nation. (Moran 2013: 4)

Through ident storytelling, there is a transformative experience from passive to cultural, seasonal and national engagement semiosis. Roland Barthes described 'the verbal language as always providing the definitive meaning for the image' (Seiter 1987: 20). The BBC's idents have been the language to provide the definitive meaning for its images. Their designs have been the most visual representation of the BBC itself, its fourth public purpose, that the corporation 'should accurately and authentically represent and portray the lives of the people of the United Kingdom' (BBC 2023a).

The BBC's brand values and emotional relationship with its audience profoundly differ from other broadcasters. The BBC had historically benefitted from an inheritance of viewers, but as the market changed with the proliferation of digital channels in the late 1990s and with the launch of several new BBC digital channels, the need to differentiate, reflect purpose and actively seek out audience investment and retention was even more paramount. BBC One's identities were seen to capture this most prominently in an age Davenport and Beck (2001) described as the 'attention economy'.

There was an institutional understanding of the power that branding could have on the internal viewing of a channel and its programming beyond a marker and for channel identities to be seen as an integral part of broadcast culture and perception by the audience. 'Brands, of course, are the ultimate heuristic: mental shortcuts that make potentially complex decisions simple for consumers. They speak to the "cognitive miser" in all of us' (Green 2010).

To some extent, the BBC's branding pivot to audiences paralleled what Jonathan Ive articulates about Apple around that time. 'It marked the beginning of moving away from what was general purpose to something that was specific in what it did and specific in who it did it for' (WIRED 2021).

Jane Fielder remembered how audiences used to send in ideas for '2's', including one persistent writer who had mocked up a 2 as a car 'L'-plate.

> Janice Beale, the Presentation Design team Producer (and wrangler), religiously kept a folder of viewers correspondence, which we always responded to. . . . It was simple ideas and inventive storytelling we all brought to the '2', like any kind of development of a character. The idents evolved into pieces of micro entertainment in themselves, the audience became invested in them and wanted to create their own versions. (Williams 2023)

In response to audiences and a solidified marketing positioning of 'Our BBC1', Martin Lambie-Nairn reimagined the BBC One globe, which had stood relatively unchanged since the 1960s, as an iconic hot air balloon (see Figure 1.15). It was a channel identity with an authentic voice with the kind of impact that captured the nation's imagination and mood, entered the public consciousness and sparked a national

Figure 1.15 BBC One (1997–8) Canary Wharf, Eilean Donan Castle, Angel of the North, St Michaels Mount Balloon Idents. Courtesy BBC.

conversation. In terms of reflecting the audience, Pam Masters recalls the importance of involving the BBC Nations in any identity developments:

> We achieved it through constant visits, you know Martin (Lambie-Nairn) and Celia Chapman. We used to go to all the nations to take them with us on the journey, because it was important that they had buy-in, and we involved them so that they felt part of it. (Masters 2023)

The Balloon initially resonated with audiences. The idents had a physicality, with the BBC Balloon as part of the fabric of the UK's landscape – a sense of place in, and part of, the nation. Nigel Cole, creative director of BBC One Promotions at the time, recollects the creative driver behind BBC One Balloon identity.

> It was the notion of BBC One bringing the world to every place in the UK. And that was not that revolutionary in some respects because BBC One's image was the world and always had been for 20-30 years. But it was the notion of actually doing it, in such an awe-inspiring way, and in such an ambitious way. That simple concept of the BBC world coming to everywhere in the UK. (Cole 2023)

The BBC One Balloon had taken flight, tapping into the fabric of British life and the national psyche – a floating icon above recognizable UK locations, giving the channel personality and resonance. Jonathan Ive again, 'A design can assume as you know, a momentum where it assumes a cultural gravity and significance – referred to as an icon' (WIRED 2021).

There was, in part, criticism that the idents were one-note in terms of pace, and they inherently didn't have the ability to flex with the variety of BBC One content or events. Mawer recalls how market research at the time 'suggested that viewers still perceived the balloon idents as "removed" and "distant"'. The representation of a 'distant' globe gliding above everything delivered the wrong message and led to new approaches that sought to link the globe more closely with the audience emotionally. New Idents featured low-angle shots from ground level, with the globe viewed through various people, from football players by the Angel of the North to walking by St Michaels Mount (see Figure 1.15).

With the arrival of a new channel controller, Lorraine Heggessey in 2002, a new set of idents were commissioned. These retained the red brand colour but were a huge departure from the globe icon, which had stood for nearly forty years – a concept that was entirely people-focused, with a universal theme of dance that hoped to engage the nation through 'Rhythm and Movement' (see Figure 1.16). 'Designed to reflect life in contemporary Britain, the idents were short films featuring diverse groups of people dancing, often in unexpected locations; styles included capoeira, hip-hop and Bollywood' costumes' (BBC 2023b).

The thematic approach and coherent codes meant that these idents could flex with the content and the audience. They could also match the programming mood and tone of voice as brand storytelling pieces. Paul Grainge elaborates on this:

> While promotional content can certainly be crass, boring, and uninspired, it can also be beautiful, funny, and thoughtful. Picking up this theme, the cultural historian Joe Moran likens modern television idents to 'visual poems'. (Grainge 2021: 184)

By 2005, BBC One's identity had, in some respects, gone full circle. Peter Fincham, who had taken over as controller from Heggessey, changed the image of BBC One once again. With BBC One as one of the many established providers of broad entertainment content and news, Mawer recalled Fincham's decision at the time, 'counterintuitively, in an era of fragmentation, with more and more and more channels, you need a place to bring people together, and that's what BBC One should be' (Mawer 2023).

Figure 1.16 BBC One (2002, 2012, 2017, 2018) Bollywood, Mirror, Swimmers, Footballers Idents. Courtesy BBC.

The new identity had a simplicity and duality that has resonated with audiences in various evolved forms for nearly eighteen years. Mark Ritson would attribute this to 'the foremost key to success in branding is to create a tight positioning statement. A positioning that captures the essence of the offering in a way that is accessible to all members of the organisation and appeals to consumers' (Ritson 2004). The simple core positioning at the heart of BBC One then, and today, is 'Together', visualized through the purity of a circle, with a circular motion that has brought the various forms within the idents, channel content and nation together (see Figure 1.16).

However, it could also be said that success has been due to a historical and inherited shared television experience of the BBC One identities, a deeply codified understanding of the globe, which has been retained and in tune with its audience's notion that we are part of BBC One's 'television as a gathering place' (Adams 1992: 117). The BBC One idents evolved from the first television symbol, which projected concepts of the world and a vision of the broadcasting medium to come, to today's inner world of our nation as a community.

The idents also crucially reflected a changing picture of what togetherness meant in the British Isles. Demographics were constantly changing, and the idents needed to be in lockstep with the licence fee payers themselves. Active decisions to be visibly inclusive were often hugely controversial, but were felt by all the creative teams over the years to be important. From the casting of Ade Adepitan and the wheelchair basketball team in the 'Rhythm and Movement' idents, to the 'Bollywood' dancers within the same campaign – which the *Guardian* even announced with a headline 'BBC1 Drops Balloon in multi-cultural branding exercise' (Hodgson 2002) – through to a blind lead actor in the 'Windows' Circles ident, and Martin Parr's portraits of Britain today during the 'Oneness' era (see Figure 1.16). The BBC message board would often be as full as the Daily Mail leader columns with complaints about political correctness, but unquestionably it was a truer reflection of the nation. Mark Thompson speaking in 2004 highlights this moment of change.

Branding the BBC

Figure 1.17 BBC One (2020–1) Lockdown Idents. Courtesy BBC.

Sometime in the early Nineties, strategists inside the Corporation began to use the word 'under-served' and suddenly, all over the BBC, commissioners and producers found themselves staring with ashen faces at bar charts showing how this or that audience was using a given BBC service less than the average: the young, the less well-off, members of ethnic minorities, the North and so on. Now there is a very important and positive idea behind all this. The BBC is paid for by everyone and should offer value to everyone, the young as well as the old. It has a particular responsibility to reach poorer audiences who may not be able to afford other audio-visual products. It has a special responsibility, too, to draw on the talent and reflect the experience of all of Britain's many minorities. (Thompson 2004)

Perhaps the most clear-cut example of the BBC reflecting the lives of its audience was seen during the Covid-19 pandemic, when a series of 'lockdown idents' were user generated by the public themselves. The films showed simultaneous isolated tea breaks, a Sunday league football team still practising together while staying safe in their respective homes and an 'isolation disco' attended every night by many Brits – filmed by the participants and edited together by BBC Creative (see Figure 1.17).

Seasonality

To reflect the nation requires, above all, to demonstrate that you 'wake up on the same day as the audience' (Mawer 2022), and one way that was achieved was through seasonal packaging and refreshes. It remains a huge advantage over both cable channels initially with pre-recorded continuity and imported schedules, and then increasingly non-linear streaming brands, that Public Service Broadcasters (PSBs) can demonstrate agility to the mood, weather, audience mindset, in a way that a Netflix or Disney+ are unable to do. A core element of that, retained to this day, were Christmas idents, and across BBC One and BBC Two they became a totemic symbol of the arrival of Christmas every bit as important as the bumper *Radio Times*.

The initial commissioning of seasonal idents or stings had a very practical function. They were created as signifiers of fresh content and heralds of 'newness' at the three or four seasonal press launches then held every year by the channel controllers. Press officers of the time like Keith Samuel and Sally Osman would stage elaborate events in places like the *British Film Institute*, *Royal Opera House* and *The Victoria and Albert Museum*. Needing graphic design interstitials to open the event and intercut often strongly contrasting genres, the events were months in the planning and accorded budgets to match. The controllers themselves quickly saw these new symbols as a way of showcasing the very best in new animation techniques and creative thinking and put them onto their channels.

Christmas magic

The first Christmas idents actually appeared on BBC One in 1967 as minor modifications to the 'Noddy system' rotating globe. They evolved utilizing the same basic technical framework of a rotating platform in front of a locked-off camera. But the BBC Presentation Graphics team in the late 1980s and early 1990s began to flex away from the globe. In 1990, the last BBC One Christmas ident, before the complete rebranding of BBC One and BBC Two by Martin Lambie-Nairn, saw a stop-frame animation Wizard wrap the junctions. The idents increasingly played a role in providing additional material to top and tail promos for Christmas special shows, wrapping a coherent brand narrative around the whole season. Long before characters from specially commissioned landmark shows like the Gruffalo appeared in Christmas idents, inventive characters were employed to spread Christmas sparkle or to create mischief. As in 1998, a group of wicked fairies, each up to no good inside a cracker, a Christmas pudding and glass, echoed the cheeky spirit and strategic positioning of BBC2 – 'The power to surprise' (see Figure 1.18).

Figure 1.18 BBC Two (1998) Christmas Fairies Idents. Courtesy BBC.

Christmas idents could be seen as the precursor for what, in recent years, was known as the John Lewis Christmas advert 'phenomenon'. Paula Williams and Maylin Gouldie recall their significance:

> You felt you knew how much the BBC was central to the nation and you felt that these were part of the Christmas television experience. (Gouldie 2023)

People would wait and see what the actual Christmas Ident was going to be. The Idents were under embargo and didn't get released till Christmas Eve. I remember there was a real sense of anticipation and it's that point where you feel like you're talking to the audience more directly, because you were all in the same place at the same time. It was 'appointment to view' television (Williams 2023).

The Christmas idents began to outdo the idents shown during the rest of the year in their inventiveness and elaborate production values – idents such as BAFTA-winning BBC Two 'Tin Toy' created by Jane Fielder and Iain Greenway in 1993 (see Figure 1.19). The narrative followed the journey of a tin '2' decoration to the top of a Christmas tree, aided by a host of Victorian characters. This Christmas campaign involved a complex stop-frame animation shoot on a physical set. The articulated puppets and live effects were filmed in 35mm. Although lit by a large tent-like golden reflective cyclorama, the main lighting came from practical candles, which can be seen burning down through the sequence. Jane Fielder recalls that the model build was the work of animators 3Peach, and after five days of stop-frame shooting, it became the first-ever '20-second-long idents film'.

> At the last minute, the little 'fire lady' on top of the tree actually caught alight on a candle, so if you look carefully in her last frames, she's got shorter hair. We literally mugged the fireman who had stood next to us for the five days and grabbed his fire extinguisher as we were half a day from finishing the longest sequence ever and he wanted to squirt foam all over it. (Fielder 2023)

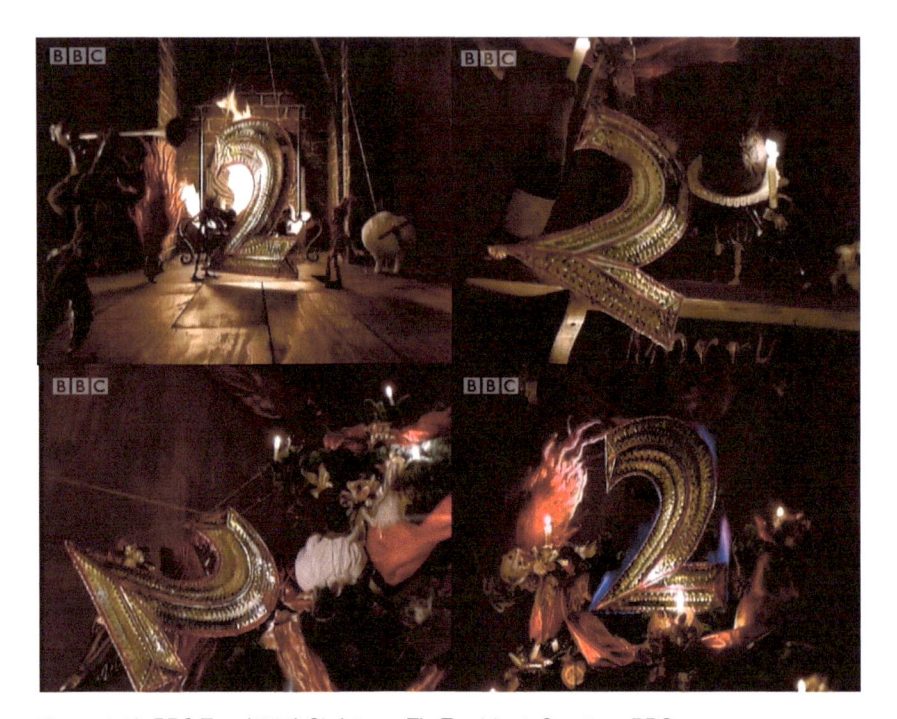

Figure 1.19 BBC Two (1993) Christmas Tin Toy Ident. Courtesy BBC.

With the arrival of the BBC One balloon, the designers of the seasonal iterations faced a new creative challenge but one that was met with a range of increasingly playful 3D solutions, where the scale and role of the balloon could be played with to match the entertainment value of Christmas programming.

> Christmas 2000 was a pre-streaming era. A lot of money was still invested in high profile films and content within the schedule. We wanted to try and capture the cinematic feel of the classic Christmas Day film. I remember thinking this has to feel monumental. So, we tried to do something cinematic within the constraints of Christmas, the channel identity and the budget. It was a huge responsibility to capture the scale and magic of the movies and content, I looked to Spielberg for inspiration. We brought together Santa and the BBC One Balloon to deliver the Christmas magic. This was the first and only time the audience would see someone flying in the balloon. It involved quite a production, an actor in full costume, hair and make-up, shot in a large green screen studio, sat in a life-sized hot air balloon basket, with ropes and a flaming Christmas Pudding. The practical burner was also shot against green screen and composited in post-production with VFX night sky, moon, snow and flame lighting. (Williams 2023) (See Figure 1.20).

Later BBC One idents overtly referenced key pieces of seasonal programming, beginning with an *Aardman Animations* CG animated BBC One Balloon era piece in which the balloon hovered outside a window. Inside a Christmas tree provided the setting for adventures featuring the *Only Fools and Horses*' iconic van, a *Walking with Dinosaurs* T-Rex and a robot dog steering as legally close as allowed to representing the year's premiere linear screening of *Toy Story*. Meanwhile, on BBC Two designers Tim Platt and Mark Chaudoir were directing talent – Reeves and Mortimer, Jeremy Clarkson, Julian Clary and Gary Rhodes in imaginative stories of mischief, with the '2' as a co-star (see Figure 1.21).

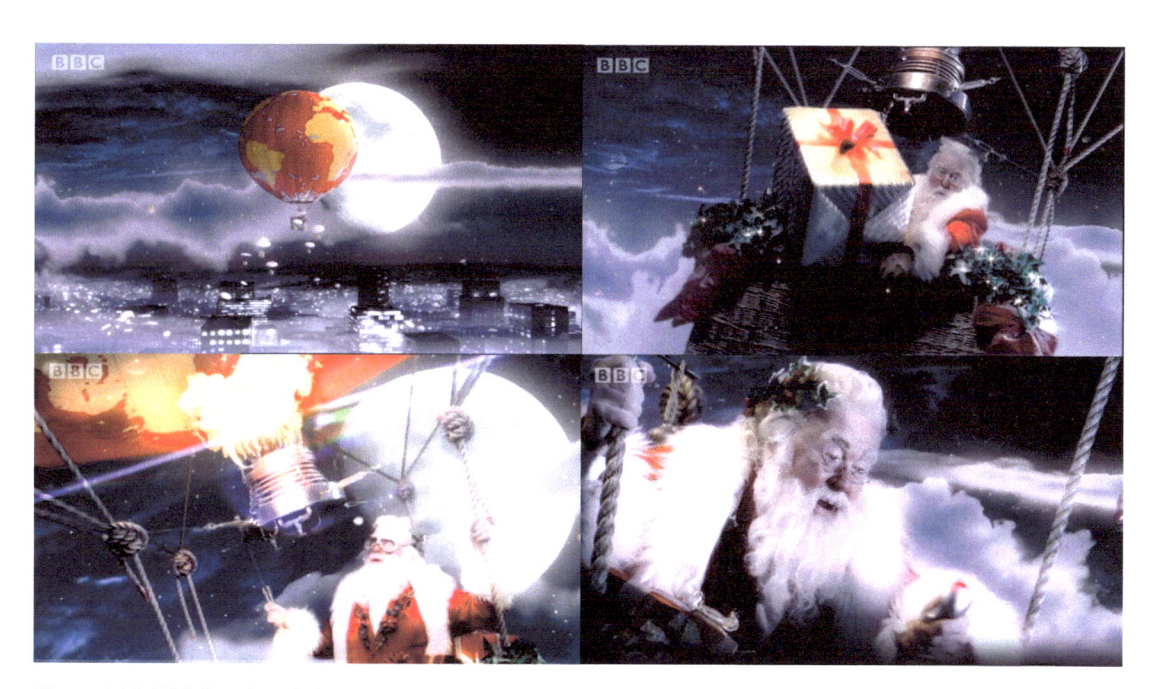

Figure 1.20 BBC One (1997) Christmas Balloon Santa Idents. Courtesy BBC.

Figure 1.21 BBC (1997, 1997, 2001, 2011) Reeves and Mortimer, Gary Rhodes, Toys, Gruffalo Christmas Idents. Courtesy BBC.

Later from the circle identity onwards, direct nods to seasonal specials were incorporated – in one Christmas forest, trees were decorated in homage to *Doctor Who*, *The Great British Bake Off* and *Strictly Come Dancing*. Exciting collaborations between Red Bee Creative and the 'signature animation house of the year' saw *Wallace and Gromit*, *The Gruffalo* (see Figure 1.21) and others produce new bespoke branding films. This approach eventually transmogrified into the Christmas idents merely being short pieces of additional or de-contextualized content, badged with the logo as the BBC moved into masterbrand marker territory. Examples from this phase include BBC Creative working with *Magic Light Pictures for Zog* (2020), and with *Bad Robot* and *Apple TV* on animated special sequences from Charlie Macksey's *The Boy, The Mole, The Fox and the Horse* (2022).

Beyond Christmas

While Christmas saw the largest budgets and most concerted seasonal branding, autumn, winter and a spring/summer would also see new 'campaigns' as the idents and promo wrapping were christened.

Flagship programmes could be leveraged as inspiration for designers, and perhaps it was an industrial setting like Newcastle upon Tyne for the popular *Spender* series (1991) that was the trigger for an ident 'Crate', dramatically delivering a new season BBC1 symbol in 1992.

Within the archive these are some of the most numerous and imaginative creations of the '2' ident. While Martin Lambie-Nairn had created the iconic launch set of idents, it is actually within the seasonal idents created by the Presentation Design team that many of the most loved versions first appeared (see Figure 1.4).

For 10 years, this group of young designers stayed together, people came in, people came out, but it was a bit like a really successful football team. People from different design, illustration or fine art backgrounds, that was its success. . . . We'd all gone to art school, and we worked through a very traditional way of ideating, which was communicated through simple drawings. You were forced into a sort of a marriage with another designer on a seasonal campaign. . . . I think that's what created great design. . . . As a team we understood that we had to produce the best work. We always felt that creative pressure. . . . Those idents in that period became iconic and we even won a D&AD Black Pencil. (Chaudoir 2023)

Seasonality and topicality remained important elements in the arsenal of demonstrating that the channel 'woke up on the same day as your audience' through into the BBC1 Circles identity. A series of flash animation bumpers were commissioned that could reflect daily events with the almost disposability of the Google Doodle. From 'the first day of snow' to 'hoovering up pine needles on the 12th night' (see Figure 1.22).

The whole point was to be super reactive with these bumpers, to be current and to strategically hit the junctions but the practicalities of that were very challenging. Everything had to be turned around in a day, from creative sign-ff, to animation, to delivery to playout. (Wyatt-Brooks 2023)

Meanwhile the nations could flex their own seasonal notes, with BBC Wales creating Daffodil circles idents for St David's Day, or BBC Scotland for Burns Night.

Figure 1.22 BBC One (2015) 'Doodle' Idents. Courtesy BBC.

Branding the BBC 29

Technology

There are fewer or better timelines of how technology has shaped creative thinking over the last five decades than in the story of BBC idents.

Technology has facilitated the evolution of a special language of visual communication. The development of post-production, software and graphic technology has informed the codes, visual vocabulary and creative face of innovation. Such technical changes have radically influenced the tools and options available to design creatives, contributing to the shift in status, function, influence and its development into such a dynamic design field.

There is often the pushback that technology and the quest for newness, from motion control to Computer Graphics (CG) to Artificial Intelligence (AI), has removed a layer of humanity and tactility from the idents, but conversely the very best exemplars often feel impossible to decode whether they were hand puppetry as with one iteration of the fluffy 2, craft-driven stop motion as with another or entirely computer generated as with another iteration of the same basic idea.

> The 'Bungee' ident was influenced by the CGI in the Terminator2 film, and I was really into the idea of creating a '2' that was made of liquid metal. . . . The campaign set of idents we were making were all real and had one simple action around the '2'. . . . At that point there was no way we could have either filmed a metal model doing what we wanted because it was soft, or creating it in 3D from scratch, so in conjunction with Cell Animation, the suggestion was to shoot a high speed, thin rubberised '2' filled with water as a reference for the falling and landing. . . . Cell took that footage and used it almost frame by frame, to create a gold metal '2' in 3D . . . it had great visual impact. (Gouldie 2023) (See Figure 1.23)

The BBC Presentation design team from early pioneers have had the ability to link their concepts to new procedures and materials, embracing the advancement of technology and collaborative craft. Great enterprise can be seen in the work of those designers, who applied intuitive creative craft skills to the forward surge of technology. They determined its applications and have worked beyond technical constraints in the experimentation and creation of new imagery.

Matthew Losasso, Mark Chaudoir and Jane Fielder were designers in the Presentation team in the 1990s and reflect on the technological changes.

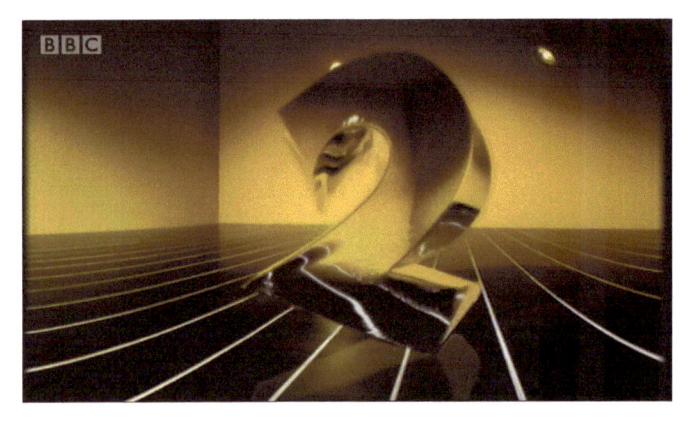

Figure 1.23 BBC Two (1994) Bungee Ident. Courtesy BBC.

Broadcast graphics – and television generally – were on a cusp: digital technology was beginning to supersede the tactile techniques that had been in use for decades. But, like the corridors of TV Centre, traces of the BBC's analogue past were ever present. I remember a colleague stumbling across Liz Friedman's iconic *Grange Hill* title sequence – Pop Art sausage and all – and how strange it was to see those familiar images frozen as a hand-drawn artefact. By today's standards, the cutting-edge technology of the 1990s would look antique: the Quantel Paintbox and HAL video design suite – the go-to effects systems in the post industry at the time – had to be housed in dedicated dark rooms. Today, much of what the Paintbox and HAL could do could probably be done on an iPhone. But this meeting of old and new – this collision of very different processes – was tremendously exciting and inspiring at the time. We were still cutting things out by hand and playing around with material techniques – but we were also experimenting with the brand-new technology at our fingertips. We were standing on the brink of a whole new era for motion graphics. (Losasso 2023)

We were obsessed with quality and were driven by Pam Masters to keep standards incredibly high. We honed down the trusted D.O.Ps to a small handful of people like Doug Foster and Karl Watkins, who along with Artem and 3Peach were trusted to produce quality live action results. We also sought out the most talented young animators every year from the RCA, like with my Magritte 2 ident. We were patrons of the best new animators coming through. (Fielder 2023)

We were ideas driven and drew on different methods to make those BBC TWO ideas happen. . . . At the beginning of the 90s, there was a reaction against 3D logos that had emerged after Channel 4. People started to employ more live action and model making. I think there are happy accidents that come from a camera. . . . The BBC TWOs were almost entirely in camera effects, and the idents which heralded the new Millennium, were shot using a Phantom Camera, at 5000 frames a second, which obviously you had no idea what that would look like until you got the film rushes back the next day. (Chaudoir 2023)

Ident designers have always been problem solvers. We only need to look at the 'Noddy' camera system, used for capturing and transmitting BBC One and BBC Two idents from late 1963 to February 1985. The 'Noddy' video camera was controlled by a *servomotor* to pan and tilt (or 'nod', hence the name Noddy) across a set of pre-arranged physical objects, captions and mechanical models – most notably the rotating globe or indeed the channel's clocks. The camera was black-and-white, with colour electronically added to its output. This system eliminated the delay associated with swapping graphics upon a conventional 'Copy Stand'.

In 1969 BBC1 began broadcasting a full schedule in colour and Presentation Senior Designer Sid Sutton was commissioned by Paul Fox, the Controller of BBC1, to create a BBC Globe for the colour era (See Figure 1.24). NODD (Nexus Orthicon Display Device), universally known as Noddy by the BBC, was the mechanical means by which TV channel idents had been displayed on air since 1963, with the device rotating the globe and a dedicated monochrome camera filming the result in real time. With the introduction of colour television in 1967, an electronic process had been added to colourize the camera's output. In order to pitch his new idea, Sid Sutton made a cardboard mock-up, using a section of polished steel borrowed from the Photographic Department's dry mounting machine. He turned a small model globe by hand and persuaded Fox to put his head inside the blacked-out cardboard box. He emerged impressed by the potential of what he had seen and convinced by Sid Sutton's rationale for the design concept, namely that television showed not only the world as it was through news, documentaries and sport but also reflected it through fictional drama and comedy. The concept of the Mirrored Globe series was born.

The next great technical evolution of the BBC ONE globe came with the introduction of the computer-animated Virtual Globe in 1991. But unlike the development of the Channel 4 idents, the challenge was

Figure 1.24 BBC One (1969-85) The machinery for generating the mirror ball globe. Courtesy BBC.

less the animation itself and more the transmission. Martin Lambie-Nairn wanted it to be played off a laserdisc to ensure colour consistency across all transmissions and asked if this was possible. On hearing that it wasn't possible, Davies recalls how 'Pam Masters pulled in a crack team from the BBC's technology development unit at Kingswood Warren along with Sony's own experts and within weeks a system had been devised to enable the high-quality image to be played out as Martin had wished' (Davies 2023).

New technology was often an enabler. The original set of twelve BBC One balloon idents, shot as live action (see Figure 1.15), were not without production challenges, and the use of 3D technology offered tangible benefits practically – and for the audience. Nigel Cole reflects on the inflexibility of the production techniques that led to a reappraisal for the successive iterations of the identity.

> The practicality of those shoots was somewhat different; I don't think anyone quite realised just how sensitive the balloon was. Even on a calm and sunny day with great light – no, no, the wind is blowing in the wrong direction. . . . You were often stuck waiting for the right conditions. Well, that was me when we were filming the Eileen Dunluce Castle ident. . . . The team managed to get composed shots where the balloon was close to the ground, but then the pilots just said no, we can't do a thing because of the wind. . . . Eventually the balloon actually blew away and had to be rescued. (Cole 2023)

Technically, new 3D renderings of the globe could now be combined digitally with pre-shot activities of people, on location, on the ground. Postproduction allowed flexibility and fantasy in where the globe could be taken (see Figure 1.7).

A stated ambition at the outset of the BBC One 'Circles' idents was to show things that have never been seen on television before – capturing that elusive magic in the bottle of genuine originality. For 'Circles', a key collaborator was the London postproduction company *Framestore*. Fresh from breaking new technical ground with *Walking with Dinosaurs*, Creative Director Mike McGee was ideally suited to create lifelike synchronized swimming hippos, ice skating penguins and indeed the fairies that flew in Losasso's direction of a 'Fairy Circle' ident. Green-screen acrobats, and 3D wing animations were painstakingly composed over plates shot in an Italian wood (see Figure 1.25).

Further technical mastery was on display in SuperUnion's updating of the classic '2' shape in 2018 'Curve' (see Figure 1.26). Working with BBC Creative and a range of London's pre-eminent motion graphics studios – FutureDeluxe, Buck Design, The Mill and More and More – the idents showcased the very best

Figure 1.25 BBC One (2006, 2007) Magical Forest, Hippos. Courtesy BBC.

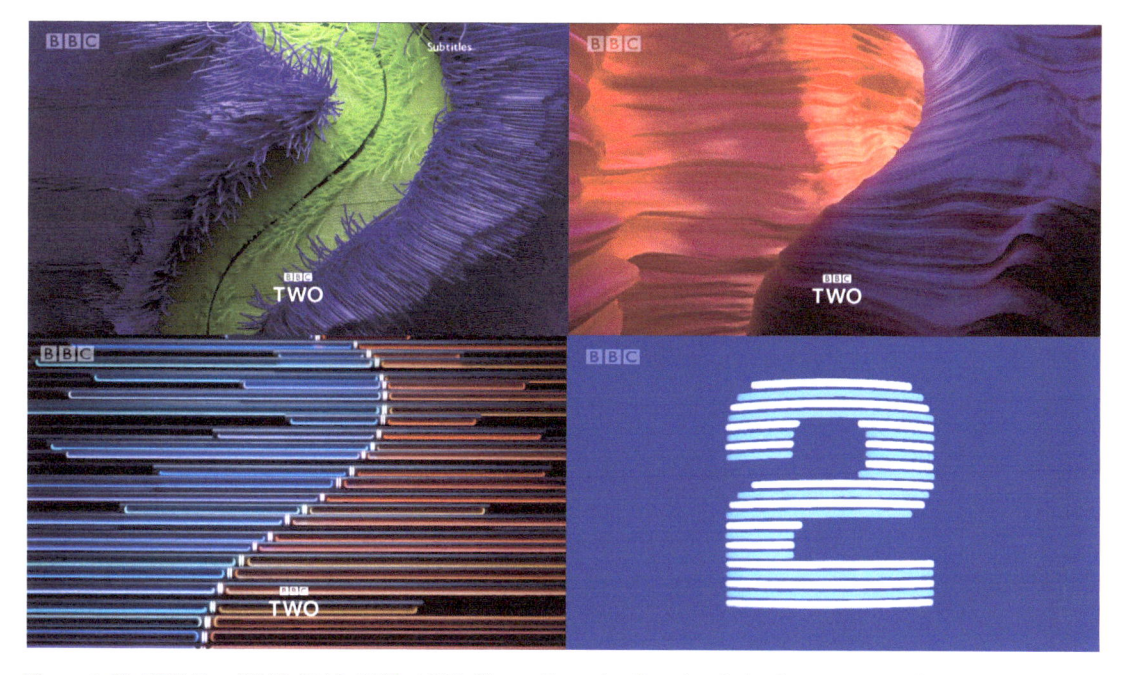

Figure 1.26 BBC Two (2018, 2018, 2019, 1974) Sharp, Escapist, Punchy, Cube Colour Idents. Courtesy BBC.

textural, fluid motion and detailed rendering available in dazzling high definition. BBC2's colour ident from 1975, created using analogue techniques by the late great Sid Sutton, even received a contemporary 3D update in 'Punchy' (see Figure 1.26).

In recent years we have seen an acceleration of styles; identities have to be repositioned, reinvented against a tide of change. There are some voices that question whether the widespread availability of technology to create has complicated design. Do designers now merely faithfully replicate the latest advances in motion graphics and Cinema 4D plugins, to a point that, rather than channel idents driving forward the creative community, they simply mirror what developers make possible? 'There is a resulting danger that beneath the welter of effects and gloss that the content fades and the medium itself looms large' (McLuhan 1969: 136). Or are they simply a response to rapidly changing audience tastes and a reflection of our wider exposure to visual language and information?

The future of idents

We have seen throughout this chapter the unique role that the BBC idents played in the lives of the UK audience across a five-decade period – showcasing advances in technology, mirroring programming and viewer interests, reflecting larger shifts in representation of the audience themselves, celebrating changing talent and marking the very passing of the seasons. Idents created by a team of art-schooled designers were loved and sometimes loathed, but they were never ignored.

As we write the very role of channel, idents is facing an existential crisis with the inevitable move towards mainstream non-linear viewing. As broadcasters shift towards predominantly masterbrand led strategies, as evidenced within all the major European PSBs including the BBC itself, will the idents return to being fundamentally a watermark or ownership stamp at the introduction to programmes, signifying little other than attribution at its most basic? In many ways, this represents a full circle back to the 1950s, when the first BBC idents mimicked the heraldic openings to theatrical films. If we examine the branding of Netflix, Disney+, Apple TV+, we see many of the same hallmarks – sonic mnemonics, bold logo animation and so on, a sense of drawing back the curtains at the start of a show.

Branding occupies the space 'in between' the content and the audience, and that relationship is always moving and evolving. It is difficult to assess whether, like any relationship, the loyalty and trust established through BBC One and BBC Two identities, discussed in this chapter, will be retained. In a landscape full of similar content and services, with little to distinguish between them, can simple graphic descriptors as opposed to dynamic identities communicating brand experience still hold the power to change perceptions and influence behaviours?

> Branding arose to inject a little personality into the abstraction of corporate identity. After all, a logo is just a name, while a brand is an experience. Branding today is a narrative-driven enterprise. A logo was a mark of ownership, while a brand is a story, which is the most compelling form of communication and the most personal. (Blauvelt 2011)

What we don't see compared to the golden age of idents described in this chapter are the sense of connection to viewers' lives, the range or versatility, the ownership of programme properties, the gear shift of mood or the sheer creative vitality. It is truly 'branding', solely as a mark of ownership. Perhaps as streaming brands discover that audiences want more than just a vast reservoir of content, the role for curatorial sub-brands will emerge again. At that moment it is hard not to believe that idents will have another chance to shine.

At the time of going to press, the design and advertising industry is in a defining period of innovation, with the rapid advancement of AI tools. Such tools are transforming and facilitating the creative process from strategy to production – all through meticulously curated commands.

As seen earlier in this chapter, the BBC's design teams, as problem solvers, have always embraced the advancement of technology and collaborative craft within this wholly human-centric design field.

While AI technology undeniably offers practical benefits by harnessing speed, real-time adaptation and data-driven insights for personalization, it also raises ethical questions. As we debate the best practices for using AI, should those responsible for the future of BBC graphics, or any other broadcasters, be concerned or elated? Is the allure of the affordable price of entry of high-level craft skills a sufficient trade-off against the potential pitfalls of AI?

One example of practice is the production of 'Hippos' swimming in a circle for BBC One, which AI could produce in minutes rather than months with a production quality that would almost certainly pass the casual eye test. However, AI is currently unable to make that leap of creativity to generate the idea in the first place.

To understand that representing the spirit of togetherness inherent in the brand could be captured with the magical realism of these lumbering beasts behaving balletically underwater; we are several generations off that being a step that AI can make. If ever. Designers' powers of human observation, the randomness of connections that influence their creative thought process and the people they meet daily propel their thinking in any particular path – a machine can simulate that but never actually live it. It is for this reason, in the lived experience of designers, creatives and audience, that the future of branding should remain a resolutely human one.

2 Painting with sound

Musical improvizations in the creation of the BBC's idents

MELISSA MORTON

Throughout its 100-year history, the BBC has been central to the development of a particular form of motion graphic design – the channel ident. The word 'ident' is short for 'station identification' and refers to the brief logos that appear between the programmes on television. Until the establishment of ITV in 1955, UK viewers were provided with a single channel: the BBC Television Service. Intervals between programmes were lengthy, often featuring silent test cards or short 'interval films' that featured natural scenes accompanied by light orchestral music.[1] In 1953, the BBC was faced with the prospect of competition for the first time, and poster designer Abram Games was hired to create a memorable and unifying symbol to replace the more generic-looking test cards. Games's design featured 'two intersecting eyes' to symbolize the power of the BBC's reach, surrounded by flashes of lightening that take the form of wings ((see Figure 1.1)).[2] The soundtrack was improvised by BBC Symphony Orchestra harpist Sidonie Goossens. Visually, the harsh wire and brass 'wings' recalled the Abrams' work as Official Poster Artist during the Second World War; some criticized the image as 'Germanic' and 'threatening' (Ibid.). Musically, however, the ident reflected the sedate pace of early BBC Television, with restful and reflective pauses between each gentle harp chord.

As competition increased, with the launch of Channel 4 in 1982, and then an explosion of new channels in the digital era, the BBC played a unique role in the aesthetic development of onscreen channel branding. Whereas the United Kingdom's commercial public service broadcasters ITV, Channel 4 and Channel 5 rely on selling airtime to advertisers, the BBC's publicly funded channels do not air advertisements and instead possess greater creative and editorial control on the spaces between the programmes. Additionally, this interstitial material served an important branding role for public service channels; as Catherine Johnson notes, public service channels were historically required to air a 'wider range of programmes and genres, to cater for a range of needs and tastes, and thus faced a stronger need to create an overarching authorial identity' (Johnson 2013a: 275). Beginning with the creation of the BBC's Graphic Design Department in 1953, the BBC remained at the centre of innovation and experimentation in channel branding (Macdonald 2014; Laughton 1966; Crook 1986). As non-narrative spaces between programmes, idents provided designers with a testing ground for new technology and creative approaches. For example, in 1979 BBC designer Oliver Elmes used a Logica graphics generator to create an ident for BBC Two – the first ident to use computer animation.[3] The extensive variety of the BBC's past and present idents form ideal case studies for understanding the role of motion graphics and sound in the construction of a television brand identity.

The visual aspects of idents have been explored by academics in graphic design (Brownie 2013; Macdonald 2014, 2015), but the sonic aspects have been relatively unexplored, despite the centrality of sound to television motion graphic design (Brownrigg and Meech 1999, 2002, 2011; Morton 2022, 2023). This chapter examines three case studies: the BBC Two idents created in the 1990s, the BBC Four idents created in 2002 and returning to BBC Two to explore the most recent iteration of the channel's identity, created in 2018. Whereas the flagship channel, BBC One, is required to have 'broad appeal' (Born 2005: 251), BBC Two and BBC Four have typically been assigned with more narrow remits. The designers and composers creating the idents were often therefore accorded more artistic licence to experiment. Through analysing idents for BBC Two and BBC Four, this chapter argues that the BBC's idents have constituted a uniquely rich space for close synchronization and interaction between images and sound.

Case study 1: BBC Two

In 1991, TV branding pioneer Martin Lambie-Nairn collaborated with composers Tony and Gaynor Sadler to create the United Kingdom's longest-running series of idents. Market research had revealed that BBC Two was struggling with unfavourable impressions of its identity, considered 'dull', 'worthy' and 'snobbish' (Lambie-Nairn 1997: 122). Aiming to combat this problem, Lambie-Nairn's visual design consisted of nine different variations. The visuals were produced first, consisting of live-action films of a wooden model of a Gill Sans '2', shot on 35mm film. The idents featured ordinary materials that act in unusual and impossible ways: paint moving sideways in slow motion, silk rippling like water and water moving diagonally across the screen (see Figure 1.3).

The composers were provided with the finished films and only a simple brief from Lambie-Nairn – to create a 'sense of Two-ness'. The first ident was *Paint*, in which the wooden '2' model is filmed sideways, and slow-motion paint appears to fly in sideways to hit the '2'.[4] The composers closely examined the visuals, recalling: 'I particularly liked the big splashes: there were two big splashes as the paint hit the "2", two big ones, "tik-dum"' (2020). The composers decided to sonically 'render' the slow movement of the paint as an extended or delayed gong splash.[5] This effect was created by manipulating the recording of a wind gong being hit with a soft mallet. A typical gong hit makes a loud, crashing sound when hit with a mallet, and the sound naturally decreases in volume, or 'decays', as the gong reverberates. In this ident, however, the composers reversed and delayed the recording of the gong hit, so that instead of decaying, the sound increases in volume until the point at which the mallet hits the gong. In this way, both the image and the sound play with the viewer's sense of space and time. Like the paint that falls in from the side, the sound also appears to move in the 'wrong' direction. After recording the gong, the Sadlers continued examining the film for details noting that 'then the paint came on and trickled and splashed on the two, and I thought, okay, I'm getting wind chimes' (2020). They decided to use twinkling wind chimes and crotales (a collection of small, tuned cymbals) to represent the smaller droplets of paint. The composers concluded:

> In essence, the paint coming on to that figure '2' was like an action painting, a moving action painting. And our reaction to that was to throw these percussion sounds at the image. It was a natural partnership, really. (Sadler and Sadler 2020)

In *Paint*, the Sadlers had created a structure that functioned as a template for the many other BBC Two idents the partners were to create over the next twenty years. For *Paint*, the guiding idea behind the compositional process was a form of improvisational synaesthetic correspondence – metaphorically painting with sounds.

In another version of the '2' ident, *Silk*, the wooden '2' is hidden beneath rippling viridian green silk. The composers noted that the visuals

> looked to us like a sunken ship or a sunken submarine and the silk to us was a billowing sea. So we created a kind of sunken wreck complete with ship's bells. The 'diddly-dee-da-da-da' that we did on

the [wind chimes in *Paint*], we put that on a ship's pipe [in *Silk*]. Very, very ghostly – that was the ghost captain being piped aboard the ghost ship. (Sadler and Sadler 2020)

The music in *Silk* begins with a repeating harp motif, oscillating between two empty-sounding perfect fifths.[6] The buoyant rhythm of the harp seems to complement the rapidly rippling silk 'waves', while also recalling the rhythm of the crotales in *Paint,* creating a musical link amongst the ident variations. The harmony makes use of added-note chords and non-resolving dissonant harmonies, creating a dream-like and evocative sound-world redolent of the work of Impressionist compositions in early twentieth-century France such as Claude Debussy and Maurice Ravel, who often used music to describe the natural world (Pasler 2001). The abovementioned harp motif was recorded by submerging the microphone in a bucket of water, sonically evoking the image of a sunken shipwreck. Additional percussion instruments were layered on top of the harp pattern: a tin whistle, a ship's bell and a rare percussion instrument called a waterphone, which combine to create a rich and ethereal soundscape.[7] In this ident, the visual and musical elements tell complementary yet divergent stories: the flowing silk moves in a way that mimics water, and the sound hints at activity that the viewer cannot see: shipwrecks, bells and whales.

In a third variation, *Water,* the composers decided to create a soundscape that conflicted with the image.[8] Here, a diagonal line of water hovers across the screen and a translucent figure '2'. Rather than creating an interpretation based on water, they instead perceived the diagonal line as a 'tattered flag' and created the 'dry' environment of a 'desert outpost':

The water one, we looked at it and actually, it looks a bit like, if you are in a desert outpost and it had been deserted. This is just the remnants of your flag – this line of water is a flag – and it's tattered. So we made it very dry, we put some Moroccan pots on it. (2020)

The waterphone is again used, but is bowed much more slowly than in *Silk*, creating a smoother, whistle-like timbre. When the waterphone enters, we also hear a gentle sandy percussion noise, created by a rain-maker or shaker, which evokes the sound of waves breaking on the shore. Towards the end of the ident, livelier rhythmic patterns are played on Moroccan pots. Also known as *tbilat*, the pots are a percussion instrument consisting of a pair of decorated pottery drums. Here, the dry, hollow sound of the drums contrast with the echoing reverberations of the harp, the disparity of timbres creating an intriguing soundscape. The emptiness of the texture, the use of stark-sounding parallel 5ths and the hollow sound of the Moroccan pots all afford an interpretation of an empty 'desert' scene that conflict with the watery image. Some elements of the music could be interpreted as complementing the image, however, through their associations with the seascape music of *Silk* – such as the watery treatment of the harp motif.

The composers continued to apply their process to other variations in the series, sometimes complementing the visual details, as in *Paint*, and at other times deliberately creating a mismatch, as in *Water*. The Sadlers' compositional process was highly methodical and yet also intuitive and improvisational, taking the visual material as an inspirational cue, creating an imagined world for the channel through sound.

Case study 2: BBC Four

The idents for the digital channel BBC Four, launched in 2002, followed in the example of BBC Two in continuing to explore interrelations between visuals and sound. The BBC launched its first digital channels – BBC Choice and BBC Knowledge – in the late 1990s, when the evolution of satellite, cable and digital technology led to a proliferation of new television channels. BBC Choice and BBC Knowledge were soon renamed BBC Three and BBC Four in the early 2000s, and the channels needed to be rebranded to differentiate their identities in an increasingly competitive landscape. It was decided that BBC Three was to target young audiences with a focus on entertainment and drama genres, whereas BBC Four was positioned as a 'rich mix of intelligent, enriching, and diverse programming' (Light 2004). In response, the brand identity of BBC Two needed to adapt, and the channel's controller Jane Root led a shift to target a more mainstream, younger, audience. Replacing the idents created in 1991, BBC Two adopted a new yellow look with fresh variations of the music composed again by Tony and Gaynor Sadler incorporating more playful sound design and elements of dance music.[9]

During this transitional period, Johnson argues, the experience of watching television was increasingly 'framed through a set of spatial, as well as temporal, metaphors' (2013b: 35). With increasing competition and more demands on viewers' attention, television channels were depicted as enticing 'spaces' for viewers to inhabit, and the junctions between the programmes were further elevated as pieces of entertainment in their own right (Ibid.: 39). The use of music and sound in the launch idents for BBC Four exemplifies this shift towards a 'spatial' understanding of television channels.[10] The brief for the channel's launch idents was given by the channel's controller, Roly Keating, who asked 'to ensure that the channel's visual identity reflected the sophistication of British culture, drawing on influences from artistic landmarks such as the Tate Modern' (Bashford 2002). Taking their cue from this brief, designers Lambie-Nairn and Jason Keeley envisaged the ident as a 'mini art installation' (Keeley 2020). The idea of a metaphorical space reflects the wider branding of the channel, which was launched with the tagline 'Everyone needs a place to think'.

In the field of broadcast design, some designers discourage work that is deemed too 'arty' or creatively indulgent without a strategic reasoning behind it (Lambie-Nairn 2020). A more 'artistic' approach was appropriate for BBC Four, however, due to its educational focus on the arts, and specifically on classical music programming. Keeley noted, 'it could be quite stripped down because it was an arts channel. You wouldn't get away with it for BBC One, it's a bit cold for that channel' (2020). The idents were highly unusual in that they were generated in real time during the breaks between programmes by computer graphics that were programmed to react visually to the music and voice-over. The music and visuals consisted of prerecorded cells that were programmed to play in a random sequence. Different instantiations of the ident show different combinations of sounds and shapes. For example, a guitar might be accompanied with vibrating rectangles, a saxophone with cylinders and a flute with angular triangles. No two versions of the ident were ever the same – both visually and sonically. Lambie-Nairn recalled:

> On this occasion we thought we'd produce a piece of video art which couldn't be produced in another way. And we devised a system that was never an ident repeated. It didn't exist in video form – it was in the ether. (2020)

Aptly labelled 'Improvisation', this series of idents highlighted the fact that live broadcast television is in a perpetual state of evolution. As non-narrative pieces of motion graphics, idents visually and sonically tell the story of a channel brand over time. Idents go through large-scale changes during a rebrand, but they also change every time they are seen. They are purposely designed for flexibility – to be cut in and out of at different lengths. According to Keeley, it was especially important that the visuals were made to react to the continuity announcer's voice: 'if it only reacts to music, it could be pre-recorded. The voice always seems live even if it was recorded last week' (2020). Composer Joe Glasman worked in close collaboration with Keeley to design and coordinate the various musical cells. A wide range of musical instruments were recorded, including a piano, a violin, a saxophone, a guitar, a flute and a digeridoo. The project's Creative Director Keeley recalls:

> We found certain instruments, in sound terms, have more attack. So, if you plink a piano key, it's got quite a strong attack. When you see that in visual terms, that means it's a bigger trigger. We did a

lot of testing to see how it would react, and then broke the sounds into higher frequencies and bass frequencies. (2020)

Through improvising with the computer programme, Keeley and Glasman were experimenting with ways of visualizing different aspects of musical sounds. They analytically broke down the musical recordings into different elements, including attack, pitch, vibrato, timbre and volume. Over time, Glasman and Keeley established certain fixed structural connections between the visuals and sonic elements. For example, the shapes in the idents jump up higher for a loud or high note, whereas smaller movements are paired with lower pitches and quieter volumes.

The work of Keeley and Glasman can be considered a form of 'visual music', a practice pioneered by early animators such as Oskar Fischinger (1900–1967) and Norman McLaren (1914–87), who designed graphics to visually depict the 'mental forms' conjured by pre-existing pieces of classical music.[11] For example, Fischinger's *An Optical Poem* (1938) is a piece of multimedia art based on an orchestration of Franz Liszt's *Second Hungarian Rhapsody* (1847). Fischinger represented the dramatic string opening with pink circles that appear to fall away from the screen, with darker shades of pink depicting lower frequencies, whereas woodwind instruments were depicted by pale blue squares and rectangles. Representing music in visual form is necessarily a creative and interpretive undertaking; while visuals and music may share certain structural similarities, there is no way to directly 'translate' from one medium to another. The artist must make certain decisions, choosing which melodic lines to highlight, which shapes, colour, shades and movements to use to depict them. This creative connection between visual and sonic arts lies at the root of motion graphic design as a discipline. As Michael Betancourt notes, the field emerged from an 'aspiration to create a visual art comparable to music: literally a "visual music"' (2013: 11). As a form of live improvisation between live continuity announcer and the computer, the BBC 4 idents extend the concept of 'visual music', by using computer algorithms that can create unanticipated combinations of sounds and images. The idents therefore provided viewers with a 'space to think' about the connections and disparity between hearing and seeing, exemplifying the channel's 'intelligent' and challenging brand identity.

Case study 3: BBC Two

In the current era of streaming, the idents for the BBC's linear public service channels continue to push creative boundaries and allow composers and graphic designers opportunities to explore the relationship between sound and images. In 2018, branding agency Superunion and composer Alex Baranowski collaborated to create a new series of award-winning BBC Two idents, the biggest rebrand of the channel since 1991. Adapting the channel to the age of streaming, the channel executives wanted the idents to represent different 'moods' of programming, akin to Netflix's categorization of content on the streaming platform. BBC Two executives sorted the channel's programmes into categories, eventually settling on seven moods (neutral, pleasurable, fascinating, lively, eye-opening, non-conformist and challenging) containing twenty-five sub-moods. A separate ident was created for each of the twenty-five sub-moods, and Superunion commissioned sixteen different animators to create the different 'moods', thus incorporating variety into the production process. The idents themselves signalled a drastic departure from the past, dispensing with the Gill Sans '2' logo that Lambie-Nairn had devised in 1991. Instead, the designers created a concept based on the curved shape of the '2' that runs vertically through the entire television screen. The idents are not only used to cut in and out of programmes, but they also frame trailers and teasers within the breaks in order to create a 'fluid viewing experience' (see Figure 1.26).

To unify the set of idents, Baranowski included an arresting chime and harp chord at the start, and all are based on the tonal centre of D. Unlike the Sadlers, Baranowski was working in the age of non-linear editing, meaning that elements of the visuals and the music could be moved around and edited in real time. Baranowski recalled, 'we'd check in every couple of days and I'd send them my most recent work to their most recent animations, and all the feedback was very much like: "I really like this", "could we bring out this a bit more", or "maybe that's a bit too much"' (2020). He explained that while the animations were in their early stages, he would begin to form a 'palette' of sounds based on the moodboards:

> Animation is quite a slow process. They have an idea of the movements, especially with CGI. There are very early stages where it's all sort of cuboids. And so you can start to put a sound palette together.

Much like a piece of visual art, Baranowski selected sounds and instruments that would serve as his palette. He noted,

> I very much had to take the lead on what they were doing. And because I really wanted the sound to originate from the movement, I had to wait for it to be formed enough for me to play. Very often I worked to quite rough images and then it would all be rendered beautifully, and I'd think: 'This sound doesn't work. I've done quite hard sounds and actually rendered it's much softer and more beautiful.' If the lighting is different, the sound is different. So yeah, it needed to be at a certain place before it can really click. (2020)

The language Baranowski uses to describe the music reflects an approach that prioritizes sounds and textures over melodies and instruments, noting 'lighter moods have lighter instruments like a triangle; darker moods would perhaps use a darker cowbell pitched down' (2018). Baranowski's idents involve complex layers of instruments and sound effects, and his ident compositions create an effect analogous to walking around an object and viewing (or hearing) it from different angles.

In one variation, *Charged*, small clouds of purple smoke float in from each side of the screen. When the clouds meet, a bright white line flashes in the shape of the curve of the two.[12] The clouds flurry back and forth throughout the ident. Sonically, it begins with a 'chime' sound on an open fifth, a high and bright timbre that creates a 'hit point' with the flash of light emerging from the two curve.[13] Then, a low-pitched windy sound effect enters as the clouds of smoke begin to unfurl. The clouds join again, and the bright light of the curved line is accompanied by crackling sounds that conjure images of electrical sparks. The harmony is based on a floating and uplifting D major chord, with an added seventh. Different pitches within the chord stand out at different moments, creating a sense of forward momentum while the graphics loop continuously. The heavy use of reverb and delay on the harp and piano create a sense of rhythm in this ethereal ident, as we hear the attack of the strings in the harp and piano reverberate, repeat and fade away. Combinations of deep, reverberating sounds of 'underwater rumbles' and wind are contrasted with the higher and more energetic layers of bubbles and electricity. Overall, the ident possesses a conflicting and ambiguous quality, due to the juxtaposition of contrasting sound effects, as well as the visual contrast between the dark clouds and the bright white light in the centre.

Another ident, *Gripping*, is used to introduce 'gripping drama'.[14] The images are based on a metallic rope-like material that continuously twists around in knots, making contorted and disjunct movements. The visuals for this ident were created by designers at Mainframe, who also created the idents for *Sharp Satire* and *Offbeat*. With fewer rhythmic tape delays, the sound effects for this ident are more visceral and immediate, contrasting with the ethereality of *Charged*. Although *Charged* begins with an empty and ambiguous-sounding open fifth, the chord here is D minor, instantly establishing a dark and sombre mood. As the D minor chime chord continues to echo, low and metallic scraping sounds are added to convey the kinetic feeling of the metal being wound into the knot. The harsh metallic sounds inform the viewer that this animated material is heavy, solid and requires great strength to move and twist. In one use of the ident, the continuity announcer seems to reproduce the tension and friction conveyed in the sounds and images. The announcer almost whispers, with a high degree of harsh breathiness in their voice, matching the crunching and scraping sound effects: 'the film premiere from BBC films now on 2. [*sharp exhale*] With some strong language, happiness comes at a price.'[15] The close relationship between the graphics and Baranowski's evocative and detailed scores evidently created a sense of cohesion and integration that allows the live continuity announcer to establish a mood that matches the programme that follows. Baranowski reveals that he considered the idents as virtual spaces, perceiving his role as composer and sound designer, to make these spaces seem realistic:

> When we were making the idents, any time it felt like that instrument is sticking out, there's a violin playing here, it was like no, get rid of the violin. . . . That was the thing, everything had to come from the environment. (2020)

In designing the BBC Four idents discussed earlier, the Creative Director Keeley was determined to create the illusion that the moving images were somehow generated announcer's voice. Here, Baranowski aspired to create the impression that the sounds emanated from the visual environment. Similarly, the Sadlers used the visual material as inspiration for imagined worlds of shipwrecks and deserts. In all three of these projects, therefore, the creatives aimed to craft an impression of a direct relationship between visuals and sound. An exploration of the production processes, however, illustrates the intricate human labour that goes into creating an apparently seamless piece of audio-visual media.

Conclusion

This chapter has argued that idents provide unique opportunities for creative collaboration and improvisation. Creativity scholar Min Tang notes, 'interdisciplinary communication and collaboration is a creative process, as people of different disciplines need to apply creativity to bridge gaps and create new combinations' (2020: 678). As this chapter has illustrated, the creation of motion graphics and music for idents is inherently collaborative and involves bridging gaps between disciplines and between sensory modes. Creating music and sound for idents requires a synaesthetic frame of mind: an openness to imagining new connections between visuals and sounds. This chapter has shown how composers can characterize or 'render' the visuals in musical and sonic terms, a highly creative and imaginative process (Chion 1994: 110). These interpretations are often based on individualized responses to the graphics. For example, when composing music for the BBC Two idents in 1991, Tony and Gaynor Sadler interpreted *Silk* as a shipwreck and *Water* as a 'tattered flag'. For Baranowski, the lighting and colours of the animations had a direct impact on the instruments he would choose for each variation.

In focusing on BBC Two and BBC Four, this chapter examined some of the most ground-breaking and experimental of the BBC's idents; each of the examples discussed were awarded multiple industry awards, including D&AD Pencils, Cannes Lions awards and a BAFTA. It is apparent that constructing idents can stimulate invention, improvisation and creativity in and between visual and musical disciplines. The rich history of the BBC's channel brands evidently continues to provide creative inspiration for the designers and composers who work in this field.

Notes

1. The BBC's interval films can be viewed at: https://www.bbc.co.uk/archive/interludes/zjkk382.
2. The 1953 BBC Television Service ident can be viewed at: https://www.ravensbourne.ac.uk/bbc-motion-graphics-archive/1953-bbc-bats-wings-identity.

3. The 1979 BBC2 ident can be viewed at: <https://www.ravensbourne.ac.uk/bbc-motion-graphics-archive/1979-bbc2-computer-animated-ident>.
4. BBC2 ident, *Paint*. 1991. https://www.ravensbourne.ac.uk/bbc-motion-graphics-archive/1991-bbc2-rebrand-paint-ident.
5. The term 'render' refers to film scholar Michel Chion's concept of rendering, defined as the 'effect whereby the spectator recognizes a sound as true, fitting, and proper. The point is not to reproduce the sound that the source makes in reality in the same kind of situation but to render (express, translate) the not specifically auditory sensations associated with this source or with the circumstances evoked in the scene' (1994: 210).
6. BBC2 ident, Silk, 1991. https://www.ravensbourne.ac.uk/bbc-motion-graphics-archive/1991-bbc2-rebrand-silk-ident. (Accessed Aug 15, 2022).
7. For a demonstration of this instrument, see: https://www.youtube.com/watch?v=Pnbuv5MnN3E. (Accessed June 7, 2022).
8. BBC2 ident, Water. 1991. https://www.youtube.com/watch?v=eEqUYhpCeR0. (Accessed June 17, 2022).
9. The BBC Two 'Personality' idents can be viewed at: https://www.ravensbourne.ac.uk/bbc-motion-graphics-archive/bbc-archive-search?querybbc=BBC2+personality.
10. The BBC Four idents can be viewed at: https://www.ravensbourne.ac.uk/bbc-motion-graphics-archive/bbc-four-sound-reactive-rings-ident-2002.
11. In her book-length study of 'visual music films', Mollaghan defines the term as a film 'in which visual presentations are given musical attributes such as rhythmical form, structure and harmony' (2015: 1).
12. BBC Two, Charged, 2018. https://theident.gallery/player.php/BBC2-2018-ID-SMOKE-1. (Accessed Aug 23, 2022).
13. 'Hit points' or 'synch points' describe moments where the music or sound seems to align with the visual movement on screen (see Chion 1994; Davison 2013).
14. BBC Two, Gripping 2019. https://www.ravensbourne.ac.uk/bbc-motion-graphics-archive/bbc-two-curve-gripping-ident-2018.
15. This version of Gripping can be viewed at: https://www.youtube.com/watch?v=L89ETEqCF9I. (Accessed Jun 17, 2022).

3 **Consistency or change?**

Top of the Pops' meandering journey towards a sense of self
MATTHIAS HILLNER

It [your true self] probably does change over time. You are going down your path and you come to a fork and you choose left or right, and you make that decision. And sometimes that decision at the time may feel absolutely correct to you. But then you may find yourself well down the road, and it is difficult to get back because you have lost something of yourself. (Midge Ure 2023)

Introduction

BBC's *Top of the Pops* was born in 1964. Remarkably, it lived for over forty years, before it succumbed to the likes of iTunes and Spotify, mobile phone apps which introduced revolutionary changes to the way in the way music was consumed and enjoyed. The popularity of pop songs, on the other hand, does not tend to last. Monitoring fluctuations in popularity was precisely at the heart of BBC's *Top of the Pops* programme. It was a ranking-based programme built around the songs that secured the highest sales of singles. This focus on single sales was upheld even after the CD had superseded vinyl and album sales became a more significant measure for the popularity of bands in the late 1980s, and also when online music distribution introduced downloads as a new measure for the popularity of tracks in the early 2000s.

Despite being so rigorous (perhaps a little too rigorous?) in its fundamental product definition, *Top of the Pops* evolved throughout the decades, and the changes are reflected in the way in which the programme was packaged. This chapter tells the story of *Top of the Pops* focusing on some of the title sequences that introduced the show in the 1980s and 1990s. It discusses how the design and production of the title sequences reflected the spirit of the times. While *Top of the Pops* was light entertainment aimed at a mass audience and despite the fact that it re-enforced the status quo within the music industry through promoting what was already popular, it was also on the lookout for that which was new. The designers involved in packaging the programme were likewise in search of state-of-the-art solutions and of possibilities to push the boundaries of visual expression. The evolution of *Top of the Pops* titles forms almost a kind of microcosm that is reflective of the changes in British mainstream music, technology and culture in general.

Ray of light

Marc Ortmans's title sequence for *Top of the Pops* coincided with MTV's introduction in 1981. The latter gave little rise for concerns at the time, since the BBC show was already a well-established asset with strong viewing figures that had peaked at 19 million in 1979 (The Guardian 2004). Like some of the other designers and producers discussed in this chapter, Ortmans joined the BBC early in his career. He had just left Southampton College of Art (now part of Solent University Southampton), where he had specialized in film and television graphics. Ortmans has always maintained a strong passion for music, although this was by no means limited to pop music. He redesigned the preexisting logo which was an arrangement of the letters of the programme title within a circle. Instead of relying on the old and dated drop shadow effects to simulate three-dimensionality, he had the logo crafted physically. With the stroke ends rounded, the backlit logo received the look of a neon sign, sometimes flickering rapidly, sometimes casting light rays through the rotating letters.

Ortmans's initial title sequence dates back to 1981 and the development started with the music. In motion graphics and TV branding sound and image enter a delicate marriage, and Ortmans (2023) 'respected the music as being more than half of the end result'. The producer in charge of *Top of the Pops* at the time had found a liking in the track 'Yellow Pearl' by Phil Lynott, and Ortmans recorded a short version of the track together with Lynott, however, with limited success. He shared the recording with Midge Ure from Ultravox, who had produced the original version of 'Yellow Pearl' (TOTP Titles 1981). Having heard Ortmans's newly recorded shortened track, Ure, who was honoured with an OBE in 2005 for his music and charity work including the co-organization of Band Aid, Live Aid and Live 8, instantly booked a recording studio to work with Ortmans on a re-edit. In the course of the following night, yet another version emerged, featuring a heavy set of drums as well as a piercing sound at the beginning. The latter was inspired by US-American sirens that Ortmans had heard on holiday in New York City. Adding this high-pitched sound and pushing the output close to the legal limits was designed to 'get people out of the kitchen' (Ortmans 2023) and make them associate the soundtrack with *Top of the Pops*.

Whilst the recording required little more than a day (and a night), the visual part of the title sequence took a good while longer. Ortmans was working very much as a one-man band (and the same applied to his successors), but he could draw on the feedback and ideas of many creatives from other disciplines. The BBC was such a large player that competent special effects experts, model makers, cinematographers and others were never far from reach. Ortmans and his successors enjoyed exceptional creative freedom and sizeable budgets. The 1981 sequence was significantly shorter than everything that was generated for *Top of the Pops* prior. Previous title sequences were not only thirty to forty seconds in length, their aesthetics often resembled the title sequences of feature films (Top of the Pops late 1970s Opening Titles). Ortmans's solution was a high-impact set of visuals cut sharply in sync with the soundtrack. Ortmans recollects that, being a purely analogue piece of work, there was 'more Sellotape than celluloid involved in the edit' (Marc Ortmans, 2023).

As pointed out earlier, Ortmans used an amended version of the existing logo, which featured the programme name in full with the words neatly arranged in a circle using italic letters with the vertical strokes appearing straight following a slight rotation of the logo type. As whilst complex and difficult to decipher as it was, it was certainly the most advanced logo that *Top of the Pops* had used to date. Ortmans recorded the logo both as a still image showing the mark in its entirety and as individual components of it that were backlit and rotated in front of the camera so that revolving light rays cast through the lettering travelled across the screen much like the beacon of a light tower. The theme behind the *Top of the Pops* titles was traditionally the notion of a countdown, since the programme has always been built around the charts offering an ultimate newsfeed on the latest rankings. In Ortmans title sequence the numbers flashed up very briefly, and these snippets were interspersed in quick succession into the appearance of rotating logo fragments. The key idea behind this programme title was inspired by coloured vinyl, which were novelty at the time. Ortmans decided to show coloured vinyl records flying towards the camera (see Figure 3.1). The last record on display comes to a rest in front of the camera before shattering into pieces. To achieve this impression, Ortmans and a colleague threw vinyl discs away from the camera which recorded the flying discs in slow motion on 35mm film before they disappeared in a tank of dry ice that looked like a layer of

Figure 3.1 *Top of the Pops* (1983) Vinyl disc models. Courtesy Marc Ortmans.

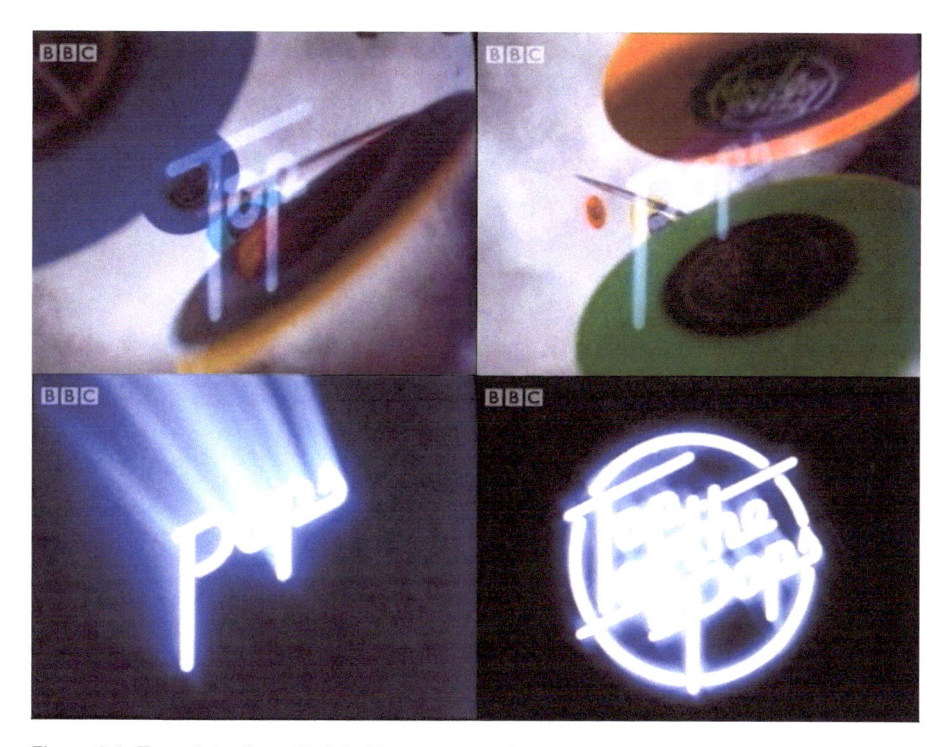

Figure 3.2 *Top of the Pops* (1981) title sequence. Courtesy BBC.

clouds. The film was then played in reverse so that the discs appeared to fly towards and past the camera, except the last one which was held in place in front of the camera with tiny wires. Following the flickering super-imposition of the logo, the record bursts into bits and pieces. This explosion effect was achieved through pushing an air-ram through a disc made of sugar-glass. While the music drove the frenetic fast cuts, much of the footage was actually used in slow motion. The sequence is as captivating as it is memorable, as much fun to watch as it must have been to develop. Ortmans's objective was not to drive revenue but to attract an audience. Although the two are obviously interlinked, the approach to creative work differs. The key motivation was to create something unprecedented, perhaps iconic even (see Figure 3.2).

Consistency or Change? 47

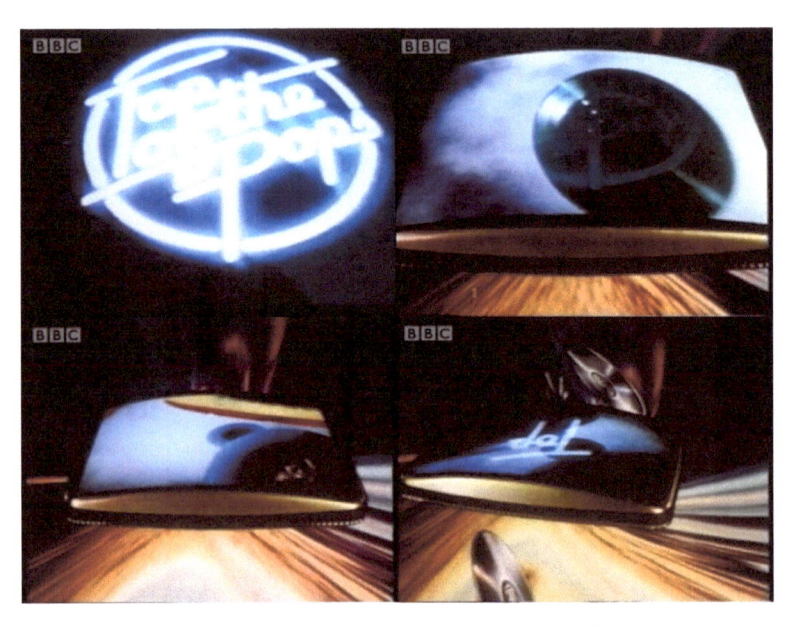

Figure 3.3 *Top of the Pops* (1983) title sequence. Courtesy BBC.

Designing the titles for *Top of the Pops* was a playground for talented designers, a comfortable safe zone for designers to explore, experiment and push the boundaries of existing standards in motion graphics and typographic animation. Having been awarded a Design & Art Direction Wood Pencil in 1982, Ortmans created a remake of his title sequence in the following year (see Figure 3.3). This featured the original version of the sequence on a TV screen that was floating in space towards concentric streams of colourful lights. Ortmans parted with the BBC in 1985 having been invited to head design Channel 4. He went on to start Ortmans Young International, an independent consultancy, with fellow BBC designer, Haydon Young.

Ortmans's departure made way for another sequence designed by Everol McKenzie in 1985. This sequence impressed through digital 3D wireframe renderings that virtually deconstructed objects ranging from cassette tapes and vinyl records to musical instruments and a newly designed logo. McKenzie's *Top of the Pops* logo used a set of wildly different fonts for the lettering, and the letters moved independently to each other before coming to a standstill and giving shape to the programme name. The transient nature of motion graphics can easily conceal typographic imperfections, and the devilish detail may escape designers every once in a while. Let us not forget that the late 1980s was also the point in time when digital computation gave rise to a rapidly expanding range of fonts, and not all of these were designed with the diligence Adrian Frutiger or Jan Tschichold would have applied. That aside, it is easy to get carried away if confronted with an unprecedented realm of technological possibilities, and, who knows, at times it may even be necessary to consider the most extreme options when exploring new territory.

Digital and analogue geometry

To reintroduce typographic consistency, Margaret Horrocks (Harvey), the next title designer in line, redesigned the *Top of the Pops* logo from scratch. Similar to Ortmans, Horrocks was blessed with this extraordinary yet challenging task at a very early stage in her career. Horrocks was working for the BBC as an assistant graphic designer at the time, often occupied with the weekly duty of inputting captions and credits into BBC's broadcast system to update the chart system. While her familiarity with the BBC's technical setup was clearly of benefit, it came as a surprise to her when the *Top of the Pops* producer called her into the canteen to inquire if she wanted to work in the new title for the programme. Fortune favours the bold, and Horrocks did not hesitate to accept and grasp the opportunity.

Although digital graphic design technologies were still fairly rudimentary and by no means wide-spread, Horrocks was already in the process of learning Paintbox, an early computer graphics kit by Quantel, designed for film and TV broadcasting needs. Her access to this technology paved the way towards an approach that was quite different to that which Ortmans had employed. Horrocks (Harvey) (2023) describes the late 1980s as 'a crossover period between digital and analogue production'. While she made extensive use of her drawing skills when sketching out the sequence, she developed her new *Top of the Pops* logo entirely within the digital environment. Geometric forms came to dominate the lettering, and the level of abstraction was taken to new heights (The BBC 2014). Perhaps not the most legible of all wordmarks, the general aesthetics are as striking as they are memorable. If it were not for the slightly discomforting squishing of the letter 'o' in Tops, one could imagine even the likes of Why Not Associates might have viewed Horrocks's work with a degree of envy.

As opposed to some other digitally rendered design solutions of the time, Horrocks's sequence was by no means devoid of conceptual depth. The underlying ambition was to develop a visual narrative that illustrated the journey of a song that is racing up the charts. Like Ortmans, Horrocks's love for music was not limited to pop. Exposed to the arts and classical music from an early age, she describes herself as 'a collager' and 'an assembler' (Horrocks (Harvey), 2023), and she tends to combine digital work processes with visual explorations within the physical world. Much like all other designers discussed in this chapter, Horrocks was acutely aware of the multidisciplinary capabilities that surrounded her at the BBC. She credits both John Swinnerton from the Moving Picture Company and the special effects company ARTEM for their inspiring contribution to the concept as well as the outcome.

In response to Horrocks's evocative story board (see Figure 3.4), ARTEM built a rather extraordinary special effects model in preparation of a camera fly-through recording that illustrated the aforementioned race up the charts.

This sci-fi-styled steel structure, the dimensions of which were visually extended seemingly infinitely through the clever use of mirroring surfaces, might have made Ellen Ripley (or at least her alien adversaries) feel at home. Having started with reds and greens, Horrocks decided to switch to a colour palette consisting of purples, reds and blues to intensify the 'techy' feel. The pace of the camera's twists and turns marked a neat progression from earlier titles. Paintbox graphics depicting soundwaves, flying satellites and flickering versions of Horrocks's new logo were mapped in by the Moving Picture Company (MPC), a third contributor. The concept behind this award-winning sequence – like Ortmans, Horrocks received a prestigious D&AD Wood Pencil for her extraordinary title design – revolved not only around conversations with 'phenomenally talented' experts from other creative disciplines (Horrocks [Harvey], 2023), but was also inspired by visits to CD factories. Of course, CDs had entered the music market a few years earlier, but 1988 was the year when the sales of CDs surpassed those of vinyl albums – timely for *Top of the Pops* to celebrate the new front-runner technology. Watching the production steps in the factory gave rise to the notion of music tracks racing through the charts in pursuit of the top spot (see Figure 3.5).

Given the kudos it received, it may seem surprising that Horrocks's title sequence had a comparatively short lifespan. But having spent several years enjoying 'the ever changing challenges of different types of programmes' along with the extraordinary creative freedom the BBC offered in those pre-marketing years,

Figure 3.4 *Top of the Pops* (1998) Storyboard from title sequence. Courtesy Margaret Horrocks.

50   Designing the BBC

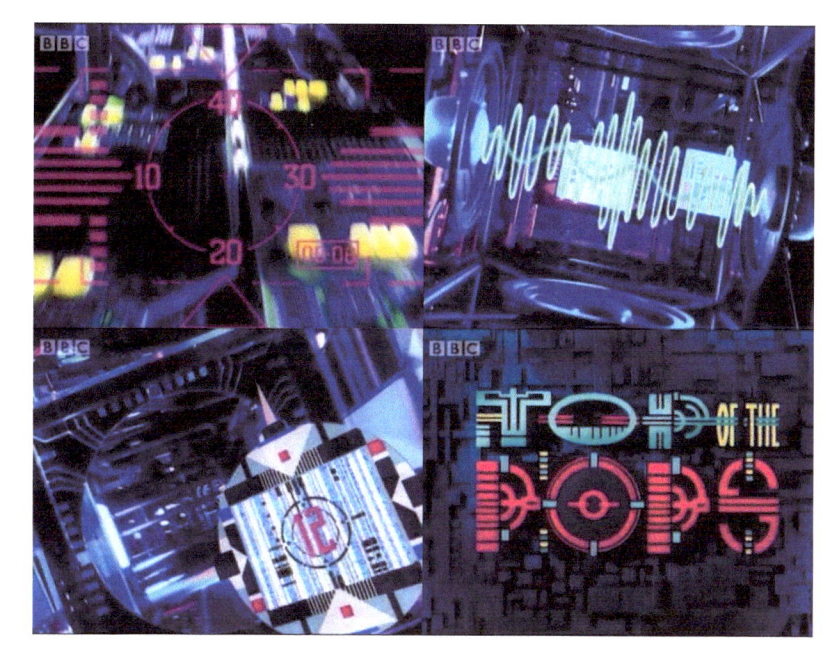

Figure 3.5 *Top of the Pops* (1988) title sequence. Courtesy BBC.

Horrocks was soon invited to join Ortmans Young International. Talent, passion and curiosity for what can be found off the beaten tracks can be like a magnet and bring people together.

Following Horrocks's *Top of the Pops* award-winning title sequence, other remakes of the programme's identity followed, sometimes taking the squishing of letters to extremes. Bernard Heyes's take on the title featured a computer-generated, three-dimensional assembly of distorted letters that moved in close range in front of the viewers' eyes, with dancers moving on a dimly lit, industrial stage in the background. This twenty-second sequence was longer than its earlier counterparts, and the lettering remained fairly difficult to depict even in the finishing frame, where all letters were in view and had come to a halt. In 1993 another title made its appearance featuring a retro-look. Symmetric depictions of classic music-recording devices – vinyl records, microphones and headphones – were grouped together with Victorian depictions of heavenly creatures to prepare viewers for the ornamental looks of the word DJ heaven.

Flexible coherence

Back on earth the fact that 'the show was suffering from poor ratings' (Ric Blaxill 2023) had become an undeniable reality a year later, and a new producer was brought into the BBC: Ric Blaxill. Although the *Top of the Pops* had evolved into 'a flagship programme' (Williams 2023), it was now at risk of being moved from BBC1 to BBC2, a prospect which, according to Blaxill (2023), had 'caused a degree of angst amongst the record companies' whose sales were thought to have benefitted from the programme considerably throughout recent years. Although the record companies' reliance on *Top of the Pops* was a sign of the programme's significance to the United Kingdom's music industry, simply tweaking the identity a little further was unlikely to entice more viewers to tune in. Now the programme itself needed redesigning.

Blaxill reviewed the rigid rules surrounding the programme as well as its presentation. The number one song remained a key item on the schedule, and this was celebrated next to the highest new entry. Those two key features aside, the programme became significantly more flexible. Blaxill focused on songs 'beyond the top 40, and put things on that were interesting or people would react to' (Blaxill 2023). From 1994 to 1996, during the golden mic phase, celebrity guests ranging from sports personalities to comedians and musicians were invited to present the show. Blaxill took it upon himself to handle the challenging logistics and communications necessary to attract headline acts as guest presenters. As a result Blaxill developed a new culture around the programme. *Top of the Pops* had existed for thirty years and entertained several generations. Blaxill's new format allowed different generations of musicians – aging rock stars, boy bands and spicy girls, to name but a few – to meet and mingle in the studio, and it also encouraged several generations of audience members to debate what was good music and what was not. Old and new came to meet, to establish a sense of progress (or perhaps the lack thereof). To add to the diversity, new camera crews, vision mixers as well as a 'fresh attitude on lights' (Blaxill 2023) were introduced. There was also a return to shorter title sequences, not for the sake of a more immediate aesthetic impact but to make more air time for music.

Paula Williams, who was part of the BBC Presentation Design team at the time and accustomed to storytelling within short ident time durations, was put in charge of the *Top of the Pops* new visual identity. Her title sequence from 1995 tied modern music Olympians together in a heated race to the top of the charts. Statuesque models were shot on 16mm in a green-screen studio clasping music-related objects – speakers, mics, headphones and so on – while on a turntable. The dramatic lighting contrasting a vibrant combination of blues and oranges with a touch of solarization effects on the shadowy blues, and flames applied to the orange-coloured highlights, made a strong impact before the logo emerges embossed on a bespoke-made metal disc held triumphantly above the head by one of the figures. The logo then explodes off the medal amidst an expanding set of concentric circles. The lighting and metal textures were inspired by the industrial language of nightclub design that was prevalent at the time and that Williams had seen at the Ministry of Sound, one of London's most iconic nightclubs during that period. Williams introduced a simpler 'dual' logo design that could work in the studio, on location and in print, meeting the needs of the time and audience touchpoints, more flexibly. An abbreviated version of the logo, which foreshadowed today's responsive logos, helped to facilitate the shortening of the title sequence to ten seconds. Despite the intentional use of a condensed and rather imperfect font, Template Gothic, which was designed by Barry Deck in defiance of modernist perfectionism and released by Émigré Fonts in the early 1990s, the typographic letterforms meant that that *Top of the Pops* logo type was more legible and useable than ever (see Figure 3.6).

Next to a new *Top of the Pops* magazine, *Top of the Pops 2* was introduced, a complementary programme format that consisted of archival footage from recent performances, or an exclusive performance recorded in the main 'TOTP' studio for *TOTP2*. It was designed to meet the interests of an increasingly diverse audience comprising several generations of music fans and to make best use of the BBC's rich library of archival footage. The logo for this used the abbreviated TOTP logo with an incorporated number 2.

The sister program's title sequence used a 'rewind' theme to represent the show's rewound content and was no less atmospheric than that of the main programme. Colourfully lit abstract objects were shot on 16mm and composited using flame in a seemingly endless flow, before the logo spins into view. Although Ric Blaxill had a very clear idea of how the programme design and delivery needed to change, he left Paula Williams free rein with regard to the design of the visual identity. As ever, briefs for the titles of *Top of the Pops* focused more on the pragmatic aspects such as format and timings than the concept and aesthetic

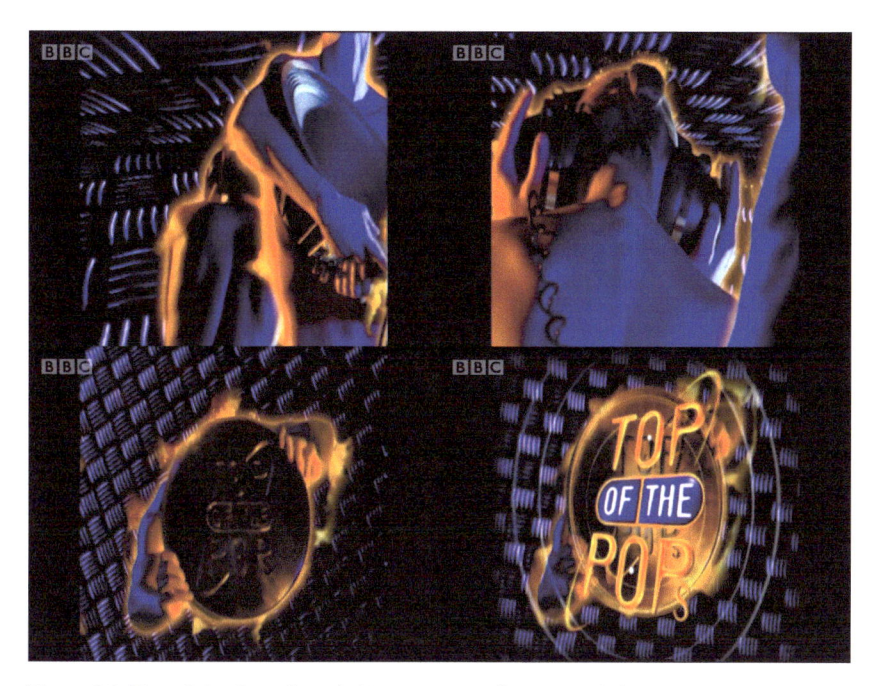

Figure 3.6 *Top of the Pops* (1995) title sequence. Courtesy BBC.

needs. For the title sequence music, Blaxill had approached Vince Clarke, who had been on *Top of the Pops* with Depeche Mode and Erasure, and Clarke happily agreed to contribute. As opposed to Midge Ure's track that drove the cuts of the visuals like a pace-maker, Clarke's music accompanied and intensified the visuals that had a rotational movement that echoed the nature of time shifts in the archival performances being shown.

Back to basics

Top of the Pops had evolved from a party-style show in the 1980s to a cleverly programmed event in the 1990s, the decade in which complementary assets such as *Top of the Pops 2* and a *Top of the Pops* magazine were introduced to support the main show. Moving the latter from Thursday to Friday evening in June 1996 proved to be unsurprisingly compromising. The *Guardian* was correct in assuming that 'self-respecting young people are out dancing . . . rather than watching television' on a Friday evening. Sadly the Brit Pop era had helped *Top of the Pops* viewership little. When Chris Cowey got involved in 1997 the *Top of the Pops* viewership had already dropped below 2 million for the first time. Cowey had made his mark as the director of 'The Girl from Nutbush', a highly acclaimed documentary on Tina Turner in 1992, and as the producer of three 1995 episodes of *The White Room*, a Channel 4 pop show, by the time BBC asked him to become executive producer of *Top of the Pops*. Not dissimilar to Blaxill, Cowey saw the need to 'rejuvenate' the show. To further reduce the amount of time used for transitions and stings, Cowey roped in Chris Jennings, who had been involved in the graphics used for *The White Room* to develop a new logo. The simpler the logo, the less time required for deciphering it. Cowey's approach was a call back to basics, and indeed, the logo that was introduced under his wing was one of the simplest and probably the most memorable. Cowey drew on a number of influences including Warhol's work with Brillo boxes, colourful Italian-style graphics and the inverted exclamation marks as used in the Spanish language.

When animating the logo, Cowey started with the end frame and worked his way backwards. As simple as it may sound, this can be a good way to ensure that a title sequence has a lasting impact on the viewer. One cannot always be certain that the more mesmerizing a logo animation is, the more memorable it will be. Where the aesthetic qualities are so compelling that people's minds are overwhelmed, viewers can be captivated to a degree that they may end up merely gazing at the information that unfolds in front of their eyes. As pleasant as such an immersive visual experience can be, it can make it a little harder for the 'penny to drop', and for the information to be remembered. During Cowey's reign, a number of variations of the logo animation were used, but the letter shapes always moved in simple ways and the end frame was always the same. Potentially distracting illustrative elements were avoided (see Figure 3.7). Cowey's idea to shorten the title sequences was born out of the ambition to make more time for music on the programme. The simplicity of the new logo also introduced a greater universality that was conducive to Cowey's ambitions to continue to introduce *Top of the Pops* in other countries including Italy, various German-speaking countries, the United States and even some Middle Eastern countries. The brand was communicated consistently, and recordings could be shared across the borders where needed. Cowey's agenda was different to some of his predecessors. With the show undeniably under threat, Cowey intensified the enterprising approach with a clear focus on viability and market capture.

Consistency was now key. The *Top of the Pops* magazine carried a version of the logo as the masthead, and the logo was also prominently featured on every stage, often multiple times. Product placement was pushed to the max. The idea here was that 'If someone was to turn on the TV in the middle of a show, you would instantly recognize that this was from *Top of the Pops*' (Cowey 2023).

Figure 3.7 *Top of the Pops* (1998) title sequence. Courtesy BBC.

Cowey's commitment to *Top of the Pops* was quite uncompromising. He was involved not only as producer and designer but also directed the majority of episodes. Celebrity presenters became a thing of the past, so all eyes were on the music. Cowey also reviewed the theme song for the *Top of the Pops* title sequence. In the 1970s *Top of the Pops* had used an instrumental version of *Whole Lotta Love*, a worldwide hit that Led Zeppelin had written in 1968 based on an old blues song. During his tenure Chris Cowey asked a friend of his, DJ/Producer Ben Chapman, to record a drum 'n' bass remix of Led Zeppelins's original riff. The record company who owned the rights to the song was initially hesitant, but Led Zeppelin liked the new version so much that the licence came to pass. For *Top of the Pops 2*, Cowey reintroduced the instrumental cover version from the 1970s, which had been recorded by a band called CCS, an abbreviation for Collective Consciousness Society.

Cowey was involved in *Top of the Pops* for over half a decade. It seems to me that he had spared no effort trying to make the programme survive well into the twenty-first century. Although domestic viewer numbers went back up to 5.5 million during Cowey's stint (Cowey 2023), rumours resurfaced that *Top of the Pops* could be moved from BBC1 to BBC2 and potentially aired on Sundays. Cowey (2023) prophesied: 'If you do the things you're proposing, you're going to be looking for a new show within six months.' BBC did some of these things, Cowey left and *Top of the Pops* held up for another three years before it was pulled in 2006. The viewing figures of the final show were reportedly less than 4 million. *Top of the Pops 2* continued to run, and the *Top of the Pops* magazine also survived (although some generations of *Top of the Pops* fans may find the latter rather difficult to recognize).

The end of an era

I don't want to write a song as good as, I want to write a song better than, more interesting than. Sometimes it's successful, sometimes it's not. . . . If you keep striving, you will never be disappointed with what you have come up with, because you haven't stood still or gone backwards.

(Ure 2018)

In 2016 Metro News (Westbrook, 2016) reported that Kim Wilde had spotted Boy George wandering amongst the audience during one of her *Top of the Pops* performances in 1981. This was only shortly before Boy George himself rose to fame after performing 'Do You Really Want to Hurt Me' on the *Top of the Pops* stage. While *Top of the Pops* was clearly centre stage for the British pop music scene at some point, it is difficult not to think that the programme was already fatally wounded, by the time Cowey was called to the rescue. With its identity almost constantly in the making, the chameleon named *Top of the Pops* never quite found its karma. But lost souls are often the most lovable, and *Top of the Pops* has not only made history, but the show will always have a place in our hearts.

The advent of MTV and music videos in the 1980s had confronted *Top of the Pops* with tough competition. Strategic branding was still in its infant stages throughout much of *Top of the Pops* lifespan. Blaxill, and even more so Cowey, had realized that a culture shift was needed. From the 1990s onwards *Top of the Pops* required not only a distinct value proposition but also competitive differentiation and consistency in communications. Effective brand solutions can be difficult to ascertain when a product is subjected to ongoing identity diffusion. While branding and market positioning are important facets in the context of innovation, long-term success depends also on various other factors such as product-market-fit. Redeveloping and pivoting products in response to market-environmental changes can be essential. In the bigger scheme of things, there was barely a chance for *Top of the Pops* to survive the shift in consumer behaviours brought about by online streaming, social media and smart phone technologies.

> It [The *Top of the Pops*] did try to keep up with each era, as it went along, graphically, visually, sonically. . . . It was a flagship programme, but it was losing its audience. So they just kept reinventing it, but perhaps the shakeup should have been behind the scenes, rather than on the screen. (Ure 2023)

Theoretically, *Top of the Pops* could perhaps have become a Spotify as suggested by Cowey (2023). However, such a radical transformation was unlikely to find the blessings of BBC's senior management. The BBC is a classic heavyweight; it is about longevity and lasting legacies. The BBC's liberal ways of working, in particular during the 1880s and 1880s, allowed the *Top of the Pops*' visual identity to travel and thrive alongside the music scene like a chameleon who used its changing colours not to hide, but to stand out. Sadly, a chameleon cannot change its shape, and no animal is immune to extinction. Eventually *Top of the Pops* succumbed to the changes in the music industry that social media and file sharing brought about. The icon came to rest in 2006 after more than four decades of pop music broadcast prominence (Kale, S. 2021), and wild identity transitions. Its evolution is not only a testimony to the diversity of the music industry but also a reflection of ever-expanding technological possibilities and an exemplary storyline of how extraordinarily talented designers periodically set new benchmarks for visual communication.

4 *Blue Peter*

'Here's one I made earlier'

IAIN MACDONALD AND KEVIN HILL

Introduction

Blue Peter is the longest-running children's TV series in the history of television, having survived and adapted to transcend multiple generations. It has been broadcast every year since its launch in 1958 and is still going strong. Since Biddy Baxter, founding producer and longest-serving editor (1962–88), there have been many who have occupied the editor's chair, and each has made their mark on the programme and its branding in an ever-changing broadcast environment. The programme has also celebrated many landmark birthdays: it's fortieth in 1998, fiftieth and sixtieth, each have established a new era in the programme's lifespan. In 2013 *Blue Peter* even celebrated Baxter's eightieth birthday as an embodiment of the programme's ethos and longevity. This chapter looks at the last quarter century, exploring how the programme captured media attention with its radical new branding in 1999, and how it successfully navigated the geographical move from London to Manchester in 2011, as well as the competition from online media and changing viewer habits were overcome.

'He who is tired of *Blue Peter* is tired of television' (Baxter and Barnes 1989: 100), to paraphrase Dr Johnson, was often used by Biddy Baxter. *Blue Peter* was launched in 1958, soon after the advent of commercial television in the United Kingdom and a subsequent dramatic decline in audience rating that had led to a 'thoroughgoing process of soul-searching. Those responsible for children's programmes were dismayed by their loss of the child audience, and increasingly came to doubt the somewhat middle-class, paternalistic approach they had been adopting' (Buckingham 2005: 478). The programme became 'the most universally loved of all children's programmes with an audience fanatical in its loyalty and devotion to the presenters, the animals and the whole *Blue Peter* ethos' (Baxter and Barnes 1989: 38). The original opening title was a piece of live-action film, the only such clip in the programme, showing a three-masted schooner running up the *Blue Peter* flag (Baxter and Barnes 1989: 13). In 1963, the producers Biddy Baxter, Edward Barnes and Rosemary Gill realized that they wanted to engage their audience and encourage them to write. Every letter deserved a reply, and so stationery with a programme letterhead was essential.

> We decided that it was essential for the programme to have a symbol. A logo that would not only be seen in the studio each week, but would be printed on every sheet of *Blue Peter* writing paper, every envelope and every photo of the presenters. The extended use of the logo would give *Blue Peter* its identity. Above all, the logo would be on the programme's badges. What should it be? We turned to Tony Hart, the young, up-and-coming artist who had appeared in some of the very early *Blue Peters*. He designed a symbol wholly appropriate for *Blue Peter's* nautical overtones, the galleon that was to become the most famous vessel never to sail the high seas. He received the standard graphics fee of a few pounds, for which he was immensely grateful. Later when *Blue Peter* was a household name…we

all bemoaned the fact that he hadn't been on an artist's equivalent of the composer's Performing Rights contract. With literally millions of *Blue Peter* galleons bobbing about in homes all over the British Isles and beyond, he would have been the first of the TV millionaires! (Baxter and Barnes 1989: 33–4)

'*Barnacle Bill*, the signature tune, has been rearranged and brought up to date (several times) but it remains the same tune' (Baxter and Barnes 1989: 13).

A radical statement

Following the fortieth anniversary of *Blue Peter* in 1998, designer Kevin Hill was given the brief by Editor Steve Hocking for redesigning the titles to make the show feel more contemporary. The producers knew that the programme was incredibly popular, but also that not many kids would admit to saying that they watched it, so the designer's challenge was to create something that felt of the time. Another important element of the brief was that the original *Blue Peter* ship emblem, designed by Tony Hart, was not to be altered. Motion designer Kevin Hill recalls:

> I was probably about 26 at the time, so I wasn't watching it, and I suppose I didn't have that reverence for it that I might have looking back now. Blue Peter was iconic . . . but it just felt part of everyday life, and that it was fun to be working on a programme I'd watched as a child. . . . I think I'd even entered a few design competitions as a youngster, so it was a nice full circle moment in a way. (Kevin Hill 2023)

Hill had received a call directly from the *Blue Peter* production office inviting him to pitch, having received a recommendation from another children's programme he'd worked on. This approach circumvented the formalized work allocation procedure in graphics, which might have offered the pitch to someone more experienced.

> I went to meet the team to take the brief and I just really remember it stressing, 'you can't change the ship, our ship is iconic. That is a given, that is not going to change.'
> . . . the brief was definitely to be very much alongside the audience, to celebrate the presenters and to be much more energetic and contemporary. . . . Part of what they wanted to do with the new look was to age it up in the best way possible, to absolutely honour the younger audience but also to make it a bit more sophisticated, and give those early and mid-teens who are still interested, who still love reading, love crafting and adventures something to enjoy and able to feel part of too. (Kevin Hill 2023)

On his way to lunch at the BBC Canteen, Hill concluded, instinctively rather than informed by strategic theory, that in order to signal to the audience that the parental institution of *Blue Peter* was refreshed and dynamic, then the answer lay in changing the ship, counter to what the brief explicitly stipulated.

> At that point in time I wouldn't necessarily have framed it as such, but it was a strategic decision . . . the thing that you need to consider is the icon at the heart of things and what that actually looks like or is saying about you. That's probably going to be the thing that signals the greatest change and creates the biggest cut through to the audience. (Kevin Hill 2023)

At that time the BBC's internal market revolution was well advanced, and with Producer Choice many programme makers would commission work externally. Hill had come through as a trainee in news and

Figure 4.1 *Blue Peter* (1999) sketch. Courtesy Kevin Hill.

Figure 4.2 *Blue Peter* (1999) original 3D CGI render. Courtesy Kevin Hill.

had worked with excellent internal talent that he felt particularly loyal to, so rather than go to Soho for specialist computer animation, he approached Andy McNamara, an in-house BBC computer 3D animator. 'I literally had a white paper serviette in hand and drew this ship and I just said to Andy, "can you do me a ship like that for my storyboard?"' (Hill 2023). McNamara and Hill were peers, equally creatively ambitious and eager to try new things, and so they created what they affectionately called the 'smarty ship' (see Figures 4.1 and 4.2).

> When we came to animate it, we thought maybe they can spin around, as if they're powering the ship. We tried some alternative versions where we experimented with different shapes and angles for the sails and body, more for completeness than thinking we hadn't got it right in the first go. (Hill 2023).

If it were easy enough to draw on a serviette, then it would be equally accessible and easier for younger audiences to draw, as well as streamlining it in a radical way to signal to older children watching that it's more contemporary.

> I was definitely somebody who would want to try and wow them with passion and creative firepower. . . . So I went in with a few options using the traditional ship and really recall presenting the ideas to Steve (Hocking) in his office on a sunny afternoon, feeling slightly nervous and taking a deep breath as I got to my last idea, turning the page and saying 'I know you said not to change the ship . . . but if I *really* think about what you're also asking for, which is to bring about a reappraisal, then that is going to be the key. So I'd love to show you what that might look like.'
>
> I didn't know he'd like it until the moment he saw it. It definitely had that thrill to it, where there was a pause, and everyone sat forward. You could tell that Steve was interested . . . you could tell he was thinking 'I'd like to have a bit of that, that's exciting.' I didn't walk out of there thinking 'I've nailed it', but I could see that he was surprised, a bit shocked and taken aback even, but in a really positive good way, so I thought I might be in with a chance.
>
> The next day they rang me, 'We love this new ship, you've totally done the thing that we told you not to do, . . . but we want to go with it because actually, yes, it's the right thing to do. But we need the original ship, it's our heritage and we do need to have it in there somewhere.' I immediately thought 'Well let's put it on there as a crest and let's have that as an endorsement, we'll celebrate and elevate it in that way.' That's how it then got integrated onto the body or hull of the new ship, as a final seal of approval. (Hill 2023)

Despite the brief explicitly stipulating that the original Tony Hart ship icon was not to be changed, Hill took a different tack. This was the first, and ultimately only, time that the *Blue Peter* ship was significantly redesigned.

Every generation that watched *Blue Peter* remembers the presenters of their time. Taking reference from contemporary pop culture, Hill gave the presenters a 'hero' role in travelling and adventuring through the seascape, guided along by the *Blue Peter* ships. This adventuring spirit was what the early Head of Children's, Owen Reed, had in mind in 1958: 'what *Blue Peter* offered that was entirely new was taking its young viewers on imaginative and informative journeys *out* of the studio' (Hendy 2022: 328).

> In the title sequence design it's all about saying let's hero the presenters, they're the real conduit to the audience. . . . The narrative was about all the things that make *Blue Peter* great; they're always adventuring or discovering in some shape or form, they're always encouraging the viewer to join-in, make or do. *Blue Peter* opens a door or a window onto different worlds, different lives and different experiences, either at home or away.
>
> It's like an older brother or sister for the audience . . . a peer or a friend who is saying 'let's go and do this, let's try this,' so I thought let's allow the presenters to fulfil that role within the title sequence. And let's go back to the sea, go back to sails and let's create this world where they're all travelling through this amazing seascape with a sense of camaraderie between one another, racing, seeing who can get to the horizon. But then also bringing the audience along with them as they do in the programme. . . . They were on their own little mini discs and ships with the new ship racing along between them, just layering in that relationship between each of the presenters with the ship itself now not being a static icon but being a proactive catalyst within this world we'd created of never-ending new horizons and the conduit for the programme itself. (Hill 2023)

The whole production was an in-house affair, with the sequence filmed in the *Blue Peter* studio at Television Centre and Ian Simpson and Dave Jervis from BBC post production also bringing their expertise to the visual effects and eventual composite of the titles.

Hill was given a soundtrack for the edit by contemporary composer David Arnold, performed by the BBC Philharmonic Orchestra. The production designer for the new studio set was Allison Jeffrey, with Ross Dempster on weekly production design duties.

> She fully embraced the whole new ship and she reinterpreted it for the set, I think brilliantly. . . . That simplified icon just worked really well as a gobo, works really well as a background icon, the crest really pops. So that really all came together, she designed the perfect set, in response to the new titles. (Hill 2023)

The adult reception to the new *Blue Peter* identity was very mixed. Hill recalls with some latter-day pride the tabloid coverage:

> After the first week of launch it got totally ripped apart in *The News of the World*, in *The Mirror,* and they called it 'Blob Peter'. 'Blob Peter kids show axe classic ship for high tech image.' It's kind of funny now, I was really mortified at the time. (Hill 2023)

According to Hill, Editor Steve Hocking was more reassuring and supportive:

> I recall Steve calling me to say not to worry. My impression was that they obviously had more experience in dealing with the tabloids and really just thought it was brilliant that the establishment thought we were being so radical with the ship and everything. It proved a point in a way, that part of what we wanted to do was to bring the programme closer to the actual audience, rather than grown-up memories of it, and so he was really on board with it all. I've lots of respect and admiration for him, because he did take a leap. They even made a new badge with the new ship on, which I still have. (Hill 2023)

Internationally, the radical new branding also won its plaudits and was the winner of Best Logo in the New York Festivals and a Promax Sliver Award for best original logo. Today, some on *Blue Peter* view that logo as 'like a paw' from a 'wacky place' in the programme's history. Comments online are gratifying and sentimental:

> There are some comments where people say, 'this was bonkers', which actually I think is great, and there are other lots of comments saying, 'Oh yeah these were my team, and I love these guys.' Ultimately that's what we wanted the titles to do, to create that sense of camaraderie, solidarity and connection. (Hill 2023)

Change of tack

In 2004 a new title sequence was commissioned, which Emma Lidgey designed with the support of Kevin Hill as creative director (see Figure 4.3). This sequence had an affinity with Hill's 1999 version of the titles, in terms of colouring, the use of CGI and the apparent participation of the current presenters in the action, but was otherwise centred around the activities of the crew of children, filmed in silhouette, as they went about the work of hauling on the ropes to hoist the sails of the good ship *Blue Peter* that was about to sail. There was a revision in the use of the *Blue Peter* logo, which had been redesigned as a CGI sailing ship floating within bubbles in Kevin Hill's original sequence. This had been a radical departure from tradition, as it had relegated Tony Hart's sacrosanct original *Blue Peter* ship logo to a relatively minor position on the hull of the new CGI ship in a bubble. In this remake, Tony Hart's original logo was restored to its former prominence in the sequence. The *Blue Peter* pets were also given a role in the titles, watching the rope action.

Figure 4.3 *Blue Peter* (2004) silhouettes of crew in title sequence. Courtesy BBC.

The rigging on the ship was removed and the marque simplified to remain intact and maintain its integrity across a range of sizes and media. The music was refreshed as well. A version by composer Murray Gold was never used; instead, David Arnold produced an orchestral version that brought a more cinematic majesty rather than a voguish pop beat that would quickly date.

Editor Richard Marson had to contend with a fall of viewing audience from 5 million down to 1 million as *Blue Peter* migrated from mainstream channel BBC1 that caught early evening adult audiences to the dedicated children's channel CBBC. Recognizing the increasing use of digital technology in the home amongst its audience, Marson introduced the Blue Peter Cyber Café to increase the interconnectivity between audiences and the production. The aim was to make the programme more inclusive and avoid being seen to be too worthy. The programme took the lead in the BBC to improve its representation of multi-ethnic Britain, and Diane-Louise Jordan (presenter 1990–1996) paved the way for Konnie Huq (presenter 1997–2008), Ayo Akinwolere (presenter 2006–11), Radzi Chinyangagya (presenter 2013–19) and Mwaksi Mudenda (presenter 2020–). In 2023 Abby Cook, from Scotland, became the first wheelchair user and the forty-second presenter of *Blue Peter*.

> So after having gone through such big radical redesign, the move back to something that felt sort of more traditional, or more closely aligned with the heritage of a programme, was I think, in part to do with a change in the team and just them wanting to bring their own vision to bear . . . in the same way that when Steve Hocking took over the programme he wanted to revolutionise it . . . shake it up, disrupt, and get people to pay attention, so the team now had a clear idea of where they felt it all needed to go next. (Hill 2023)

As is often the case, but never guaranteed, when a designer builds up a trusting working relationship with the production team through reliable weekly servicing, it begets more work. Lidgey and Hill created designs for programme spin-offs and were then invited to evolve the 'bubble ship' into a new form that was more akin to the original Tony Hart shape (see Figure 4.4), but more importantly, to represent the audience as part of the crew.

Figure 4.4 *Blue Peter* (2004) refreshed ship based on Tony Hart original. Courtesy BBC.

> We came up with the idea in the title sequence of a narrative that shows, much like the audience, kids coming together to participate in the programme. They're hoisting the sails. They are the people that make it happen. . . . we what we were really saying is 'you guys are the people that give us the power to set sail, to do what we do.' (Hill 2023)

Silhouettes of children were preferred as they avoided any issues of audiences 'categorizing' who they see on screen and disassociating themselves from representations of other children. They were generic enough to allow the audience to project themselves into that silhouette.

> When I look back at both title sequences that I was lucky enough to be involved with, at the heart of it is wanting to do something which connects with the audience, with young people, that honours them and doesn't talk down to them. But equally, in the best of worlds, isn't necessarily desperately trying to be their mate, because how can you, rather it's being able to walk with them, to lead the way and also able to be led at times, to show and guide the way whilst always having their back, and I think *Blue Peter* does that. (Hill 2023)

Sometimes radical times require radical changes of approach. In 1999 broadcasting and the BBC were being convulsed in a changing paradigm of commercial realism and global multichannel broadcasting competition. Design and branding practices were also changing.

> We weren't designing for programme brands in the way that you would do now, in which you would absolutely want to demonstrate your idea across every touch point. Life was still very much focused around on-screen presentation for TV and how that would come to life on set. But I think within that there's something which is quite serendipitous that lent itself to the brand being able to just go anywhere. Perhaps it's because the idea came from the desire for change or was born from breaking the rules. . . . And although it wasn't necessarily front of mind when I first sketched the new ship on a napkin, I definitely believe it was somehow bound up in the DNA of the idea to be able to do that, because it was ultimately born out of a desire to be more agile, to be more connected and to represent the world as it was at that time . . . it could now actually travel anywhere and on anything. (Hill 2023)

New rigging and trimming the sails

In 2007 Tim Levell was made editor, and it was seen as a transitional year with a change of presenters leading to the programme's fiftieth anniversary and a brand-new era to face a multichannel challenge for audiences. As such the end credits were cut adrift completely. In 2011 as part of the BBC's decentralization policy and the repurposing and selling off of the Television Centre in Shepherds Bush, London, the programme team were moved to a new harbour in Salford's MediaCity beside the newly regenerated canals. *Blue Peter* looked to its unique audience engagement and established an online presence as a conduit to the traditional broadcast. Taking a local approach, Manchester-based design company Mighty Giant was commissioned with the task of refreshing the titles and brand.

In 2013, Ewan Vinnicombe took over as editor in what he described as 'more evolution than revolution'. As series producer he took the radical approach in the fiftieth year, 2008, to remove all the end credits, except for times when someone left the show. There was an audience vote to change the presenter, and the titles were refreshed to remind the audience of the amazing activities and places they do. Shots of the episode's highlights were intercut each week:

We don't want a generic title sequence. We're going to really put our presenters front and centre because they we want to establish ourselves in the North. . . . Barney Harwood playing the piano . . . Helena doing sporting activities and things like that. So it's kind of like playing on what they love doing. And it was meant to signify as well, like the technology age at that point. It was kind of when apps were starting off. (Vinnicombe 2023)

Inevitably, a year into the role, Vinnicombe sought to establish his visual mark on *Blue Peter*. In 2014 he looked to redesign the look and feel of the set as a way to inform the on-screen titles that Liquid TV was commissioned to redesign. At a time when virtual sets and green-screens were taking over in news to provide cost-cutting measures, but also greater graphic and dynamic visual possibilities, *Blue Peter* clung to its physical rigging. The programme knew its audience and knew that if a child guest was to come on set, the sensation would be far less impactful if it was green screen and not real.

He also wanted to focus on the famous *Blue Peter* badges, and their colours were represented in a wave that went through the set, inspired by the screensaver they had at the time in the production office. This wave was then part of the brief for the title graphics. Vinnicombe also insisted that the flags be better spaced on the ship logo so it would be easier to draw. Sometimes it's the small things that make a difference. For Biddy Baxter's eightieth birthday in 2013 Vinnicombe recalls, 'I got her a birthday card that was just the Blue Peter of ships that all the kids had been sending in, because I said to her, like her choice of a ship and that logo was pertinent in 2013, just as it was when she first did it' (Vinnicombe 2023). For the sixtieth birthday he commissioned fashion designer Henry Holland to create a diamond badge. 'He did quite a few different designs and different batches made, and we got a group of kids to decide. And then Henry did the final rubber stamp, but it was great because he used the one that the kids loved' (Vinnicombe 2023).

Alongside the visual of the rigged sailing ship, the theme tune remained *Blue Peter's* brand signifier. The sixtieth birthday offered justifiable motivation to prompt a special remix of every theme tune there had ever been and a new version to keep up with the times. Enter a new decade. A new editor, Ellen Evans, wanted to warm up the appearance and brand of the programme 'to signify a new era' (Evans 2023). For her the titles were like 'ice blocks': dominated by blues, silver, chrome and white. Working with set designer Emma Dibb as a conceptual starting point, the titles were put out to tender to six companies across the Manchester region and London. After much thought and consideration of what *Blue Peter* means to its audience of children ranging from infant school to early teens, Evans's brief stipulated a requirement for the titles to reflect the importance of the Blue Peter Badge and that 'everything begins with a letter', irrespective of whether it's on paper, email or text (Evans 2023). Many of the production team, including Ewan Vinnicombe, still have the letters that they received as children, signed personally by Biddy Baxter and the presenters of their era, and the cycle continues with more mail bags every week.

Evans is proud to claim that the *Blue Peter* set designed by Emma Dibb is the most environmentally friendly and sustainable in broadcasting, as she utilized recycled and up-cycled materials and props to construct a sensory environment and a modular system that is adaptable to different-sized studios. Once again, the synergy and collaboration of the set designer and motion graphics team were successful in creating an integrated look where the set's colourful wave used colours that symbolized what each of the eight badges represented, such as sport, interesting letter, fan club and environment. Some of the most memorable *Blue Peter* moments in its sixty-plus years have been in the studio, and Evans introduced a regular studio audience to participate and witness the studio presenters and guests. 'When the kids come in the studio, there's like a little gasp when they come, . . . it's quite a sort of sensory environment. Like there's moving lights. It's colourful, it's friendly, you know it's a happy place' (Evans 2023). Children get a rare opportunity to see behind the scenes of how television is made and the different jobs people have, as well as meet the presenters, ask them questions live on air or play Spin the Badge.

The logotype was changed as well, and through a range of experiments and ideas with Salford-based company Tracks and Layers a new logotype was chosen: Cocogoose, a clean modern sans serif with some quirks. Changing the typeface had practical considerations and financial ramifications, as it necessitated a refreshing of iconography across all media, including printed letterheads, banners and merchandise. The previous typeface from 2013 never read clearly enough on-screen captions, 'so there wasn't a lot of love for that font' (Evans 2023).

Ellen Evans, the editor was rightly proud to receive Biddy Baxter's approval for the new titles and compliments for recognizing the unique value of the Blue Peter Badge, setting it within the logo, and that everything starts with a letter. In the last ten years Evans estimates that three-quarters of a million children received a Blue Peter Badge. Liquid TV's titles brought colour and a lively hand-drawn animation to the slick, badge-shaped windows that incorporated rapid-cutting clips of the presenters on their adventures. This was a long way from the smoothness and perfection of CGI animation over twenty years ago, and more of an echo of pre-digital photomontage rostrum animation. At twenty seconds, the title sequence moves at pace to include as much variety and footage from the programme as possible and rapid moving devices interlink and break up the frames. Yet even now, they are seen to be too long and may well be edited in the future into new forms of pre-titles and chapter elements at the start of the programme.

Conclusion

Blue Peter demonstrates a brand that has unique longevity in television broadcasting, and because of its audience, it has had immeasurable impact on the cultural upbringing of a particularly dynamic and changing society in the United Kingdom. Both the designers and the programme editors have been able to tap into their own childhood memories of *Blue Peter*, and many of the most successful editors have come up through the ranks imbued with the original ethos devised by its founding producer, Biddy Baxter. This longevity is also partly due to different programme editors who have seized the moment to read what their audience will identify with. Some risks have been taken to mark a point when broadcasting was in flux, resulting in changing programming schedules and channels.

Despite the changes in technology, today's titles are produced in a manner that was available decades before. What marks them is the acknowledgement of the core DNA of the programme; everything starts with a letter, and the badge is the emblem of participation with the programme and their presenters. Tony Hart's original drawing of the sailing ship is as iconic as any world-leading brand, and like those blue-chip, international brands, they manage to hold their visual identity and yet evolve over generations, somehow looking sharper and cleaner, yet recognizably the same. *Blue Peter* does not need the budget of these global brands to commission global design agencies to undertake this work. It has been the ingenuity and craft of in-house BBC designers and small independent studios to carefully execute and deliver these brand enhancements. It is a versatile and much-loved emblem of BBC values, a badge that is worn with pride and has even appeared on a balloon over the Arctic and as massed ranks on Royal Navy aircraft carrier HMS *Queen Elizabeth*. Having reached a milestone sixtieth birthday during a period of continuous broadcasting revolution, we might confidently wonder what its centenary year will look like.

5 A play in themselves

Drama titles and graphics

IAIN MACDONALD AND IAIN GREENWAY

Introduction

It has been a long-held view that the American graphic designer Saul Bass was the first to define the opening title sequence as an artform and craft of its own merit (Laughton 1966). Although his most widely seen titles were for movies, his influence on television drama was significant, especially in the formative years of the BBC Graphic Design Department in the 1960s. Encapsulating the essence and mood of the drama about to be seen in order to prepare the audience as well as inform them with the leading credits was what the designer aspired to. BBC senior designer Alan Jeapes (1937–2010) took the same view as Saul Bass: 'a title sequence creates a mood and an atmosphere to enhance the programme. It makes you want to carry on watching' (Jeapes in Kemistry 2004). Bernard Lodge, one of the BBC's great original designers, added: 'this must be achieved while remaining faithful to the programme's contents and spirit' (in Merritt 1987: 10).

At its most basic level a title is like a luggage label; it informs you with a name, who made it and owns it, and perhaps where it has come from. Often, especially with single dramas, the graphic designer only has the creative freedom to choose the typeface, size and perhaps, with an amenable film editor and film director, also its position and duration. Drama serials and series required a stronger identity that audiences could remember to tune back for on weekly schedules and which could be used in on-screen promotions and print. These had bigger budgets and gave the motion designer greater creative opportunity. The record of accolades and awards by BBC Graphic Design for Drama titles is testament to the quality and creative genius that found expression in this genre. The reputations and careers of designers such as Bernard Lodge (*Dr Who*), Alan Jeapes (*Secret Army*), Dick Bailey (*I Claudius*), Liz Friedman (*Pride & Prejudice*), Ros Dallas (*Testament of Youth*), Doug Burd (*Hitch Hikers Guide to the Galaxy*) and Christine Buttner (*Underbelly*), to name but a few, were established in the drama title.

This chapter will examine some case studies of the production process and relationship between motion designer and film producer/director and explore the different approaches to single dramas, short-season serials and long-running series that have become household names. Like all programme genres, the making of titles and graphics for drama films and programmes has gone through the technical revolution of film, video and digital production. This has seen advances in film optics, computer-controlled cameras, high-definition video, digital compositing and Computer Graphic Imagery (CGI). It has also allowed the contribution and commercial success of smaller freelance design studios that have made a reputation for award-winning work for BBC Drama productions.

The commissioning process typically starts with meeting the producer and director and becoming a member of the production team. The graphic designer is asked to read the script or book. In most instances the brief is toplined without any specific requests. After spending a number of weeks on research and design, early initial ideas are presented in style and moodboard presentations. In most cases today these are highly visualized animation tests created digitally, which would have been prohibitively expensive before the 2010s. A good part of the reason for the strength of this large body of BBC Drama work is in many ways due to this process of allowing the graphic designer to become a part of the creative team and having their input be a part of the 'creative soup'.

Single dramas

The BBC has a long reputation for making single dramas, and under the umbrella of 'Screen One' and 'Screen Two' many have had theatrical releases in addition to being broadcast. Due to copyright issues none of the opening or closing titles of these are able to be included in the online BBC Motion Graphics Archive. One notable film that is fondly remembered is *Truly Madly Deeply*, the debut feature film written and directed by Anthony Minghella, who went on to win several BAFTAs and an Academy Award for *The English Patient* in 1996. He had been a script editor on BBC's *Grange Hill* before becoming a director. His first day on the set of *Truly Madly Deeply* was at BBC Ealing Studios with graphic designer Iain Macdonald, leading actor Alan Rickman and a professional cellist. The opening titles were conceived in the script, where Minghella's gift and understanding of music made a powerful and poignant seamless transition from cello to piano and voice:

> He plays and we see him full length, bent over his instrument, intent. Pull out and then freeze the image. Keep pulling out and find that the image is now a photograph inside a frame and that the photograph is in Nina's living room.
>
> As the image freezes to become this photograph, the cello line is replaced by a voice, humming and the credit sequence is over. (Minghella 1989: 4)

This sequence required several shots of Rickman playing a cello against a black background. The professional cellist was used for hand close-ups. The final shot of Rickman freezing and becoming a photograph situated in another location (it became Nina's bedroom, on set in a studio in Bristol) required a film optical to marry the 35mm footage of him playing, a 35mm stills shot (to provide the lower half of his body) and the Super 16mm footage from the Bristol studio. The film optical editing expertise of Dave Farley ensured a smooth visual transition for a shot that would be relatively simple and straightforward in today's digital age.

The title captions for *Truly Madly Deeply* were originally set and created for television, and with the original title 'Cello'. The process was the same for most films at that time; artwork with white text printed on black backgrounds was filmed on a rostrum camera and added into the film as a superimposed text on live-action footage. The end credits were printed white on black as a long roll of paper that was mechanically moved on the rostrum as the film camera shot it frame by frame. These could be as long as 5 metres and may have had motifs or decorative elements, spelling corrections, replacement names, stripped in and glued to the paper roll. Having seen the original credits projected in a cast-and-crew screening at BAFTA, Macdonald realized that for cinema audiences he could afford to make the credits smaller in scale. When the film was renamed, this offered the perfect opportunity to revise the credits and shoot them with a different field size that was better suited to theatrical projection while still legible for television broadcast. High-definition television broadcasting today has allowed credits to be much smaller in size and still legible. As Bernard Lodge said: **'**the difference between titles for television and cinema is scale' (Kemistry 2004).

Some single dramas required the graphic designer to design the posters for the film, and one such film by Macdonald was *Genghis Cohen* (1993), directed by Elijah Moshinsky. However, *Truly Madly Deeply* had several different logo designs for the title across different territories and even the DVD once it was promoted by an American distributor. It was Saul Bass who strove to unify both the title design and marketing materials from as early as the mid-1950s in order to build and maintain brand recognition for a film, most notably with *The Man with the Golden Arm* (1955), *Anatomy of a Murder* (1958) and *North by Northwest* (1959).

In the following case studies, we will see how graphic designers were also commissioned to design props and other graphic elements within dramas.

Drama series and serials

Some television programmes are remembered for the design and mood of their opening title sequence years after they are made.

> Drama director, Tim Aspinall, said 'titles are the overture and they should be a little play themselves. If the graphics generate enough impact viewers will stay with a show. We should never be parsimonious about the graphic design.' (Merritt 1987: 16)

One such title is for the long-running BBC multi-award-winning and popular series *EastEnders* (1985–) designed by Alan Jeapes (1937–2010), one of the great motion designers in British television history. The process began with a meeting with the producers and involved meetings with the composer Simon May, and arriving at the idea of the map and type of logo. It is a deceptively simple camera move that required Jeapes's trademark attention to detail, both in typography and in choreographing a move to strict time. The production required something akin to military planning, no doubt instilled from his National Service days in the British Paratroopers.

> The map is made up of over 1400 separate photographs shot by an aircraft at 2500 feet. The centre of each shot was cut out and mosaiced on its partner. This was only possible because of the pattern of roads. You can't see the joins. The final map was 11 x 9 feet, and shot on a motion control camera. The camera spins as it tracks away from the map.
>
> Although the map is pretty accurate I cannot guarantee that it would stand up to an Ordinance Survey scrutiny. The shots were taken in 1983 and we have added some buildings on the Isle of Dogs and also the Flood Barrier. The actual map took some weeks to make up (see Figure 5.1).
>
> (Jeapes 1985)

> We had these tried and tested camera methods to make what we now have. These techniques create many limitations. For example we have never used all the master mosaic scene because the camera could not handle it. In fact we had to cut the artwork down to get it passed the column of the taking camera. It is difficult to update without remaking artwork and shooting all over again.
>
> (Jeapes 1998)

Since its first transmission in 1985, Jeapes revised the titles twice: to incorporate a water texture and reflection using CGI in the Thames while adding the Millennium Dome at Greenwich, and later with full colour imagery and passing clouds. It was not until 1998 that computers were powerful enough to create the necessary high-resolution images for the animating map of London. Even in 1994 when the first update was considered, he found that even flight-simulator computers, 'these enormous number crunchers could not output to video let alone digital tape' (Jeapes 1998).

Figure 5.1 *EastEnders* (1985) aerial photograph prints of London collaged on board for shoot. Courtesy Rupert Jeapes.

In 1998 as London's Docklands were being redeveloped and construction of the Greenwich Millennium Experience was underway for January 2000, Jeapes wrote to *EastEnders* executive producer, Matthew Robinson, to explain how the titles could be updated:

Now we have the technology.

I think the sensible way we should go is as follows:

1. Scan into the computer the negative of our master mosaic. Not a print or a copy transparency but master neg for maximum quality. This reverses to positive at the flick of a switch. This will be our master background. We scan it twice, once at high resolution and once at low res.
2. Scan the negs of our new overfly of the Dome and Docklands at high res. We will see these in close up.
3. It is now possible to make a working database using our master shot and position our new close up shots onto it using 'PhotoShop'. The finished result will be immaculate.
4. Repaint the water on the screen closer to real colour we can do this on the system.
5. Using 'Ray Tracing' light the scenes to our best advantage. Ray tracing creates the fall of light as in reality. We position the sun where we want it to be and the water will gleam as real water. It's a physics thing. This will also allow the light to move subtly over the top of the Dome as we twist away.

6. Create animated water over our set river taking advantage of the real colour and Ray Traced light. This will apply to the main and two End credit backgrounds.
7. Adjust the end scenes to work as well as possible with a roller caption. (Jeapes 1998)

Contemporary motion designers will be amused at the reference to Photoshop and the accommodation of different transmission formats as the BBC transitions from analogue to digital and from 12×9 to 16×9 formats.

According to Saul Bass, the ideal title possesses 'a simplicity which also has a certain ambiguity and a certain metaphysical implication that makes that simplicity vital. If it's simple simple, it's boring' (Bass and Kirkham 2011: 107). Like his contemporaries in the 1960s, Jeapes was an admirer of Bass's work, and one afternoon in a Soho edit suite, he was surprised to overhear an American voice discussing a title sequence, 'And there I was working 8 feet away from Saul Bass and I didn't even know' (Kemistry 2004).

Previously, Jeapes had perfected a long tracking sequence using an alignment of photographs of perspective landscapes that used the centre of frame as a focal point for the title sequence and end credits for *Secret Army* (1978).

> The most dominant part of the television screen is right in the middle, which must seem obvious now. . . . When we became aware of that and wanted to get maximum attention, we would hit them there, right in the middle. (Jeapes in Kemistry 2004)

In an earlier interview Jeapes explained the significance and inspirational importance of the music soundtrack to his creative process.

> He did not formulate his theme until he had listened many times to the music composed by Robert Farnon. When his proposals were made he was pleased that the producer, Gerald Glaister, accepted such a simple and seemingly low-key solution to a dramatic subject. (Merritt 1987: 94)

Another form of drama programming that the BBC excelled at was the drama serial; these are short series of four or more episodes. In order to capture a returning audience over a period of consecutive weeks or sometimes days, there was usually a budget for a title sequence that prepared the audience for the content and subject. Other important stand-out title sequences for drama series in the 1970s were *I Claudius* (1976), designed by Dick Bailey, which had a snake writhing across a mosaic floor with images of Derek Jacobi as the Roman Emperor (see Figure 7.4). Another animal that was used as a metaphor was Stephan Pstrowski's animated moth fluttering across a live-action Fin de Ciecle table lamp in *Madame Bovary* (1975). The moth was symbolic of the fate of Emma in Flaubert's tragic story. It had to be hand-drawn as an animation as there were no moths available in the season it was created. 'All visual art has at its base some aspect of illusion. In graphic design for television this element is very prominent' (Merritt 1993: viii).

A Sense of Guilt

Iain Greenway met producer Simon Passmore in late 1989/1990 along with director Tim Fywell. They were working with a powerful cast, with Trevor Eve in the leading role of the central character writer Felix Cramer in Andrea Newman's *A Sense of Guilt*. Talking with Tim Fywell, Greenway was inspired by his vision of using a technique where the camera seamlessly moves through the walls of the set, artfully implying the multifaceted nature of Felix's relationships. This inspiration led to research the graphic works of M.C. Escher and the surreal nature of the seamless environments he created in his drawings and paintings (see Figure 5.2).

Figure 5.2 *A Sense of Guilt* (1990) inspired by M.C. Escher storyboard frame by Peter Parr. Courtesy Peter Parr/Iain Greenway.

Greenway commissioned model maker Alan Kemp to build a scaled Escher-esque environment that was filmed with multiple main and matte passes using a prime lens mounted on a snorkel (an extension allowing the lens to get into tight spaces) with a ceiling-mounted motion control rig. A further pass using the same camera move was shot, allowing Trevor Eve to be composited into the title. However, as a precaution a scaled-lifelike model of the actor was positioned into the model set as a guide for the final result. Due to some technical difficulties that arose, leading to a mismatch of the matte passes, it ended up being the life-like stand-in that made it to air in the titles. Often then, when combining computer and traditional film techniques, there presented a certain amount of trial and error. When pushing these boundaries, designers like Greenway took some risks along the way that were part of the creative development of what may be possible to achieve – offering an irresistible urge to create new visions.

Between the Lines

In 1992 Greenway got the opportunity to work with one of his heroes from British film making in the 1960s, Tony Garnett the producer and one of the writers along with director Ken Loach of the movie *Kes*. Tony Garnett was the executive producer of a new serial called *Between the Lines*, a police drama following the team at the Complaints Investigation Bureau – the unit that polices the police, starring Neil Pearson and Siobhan Redmond.

This was a powerful and gritty drama at the time and featured realistic and hard-hitting depictions of sexual relations and violence. Greenway's design approach was to use a simple see-and-say letterboxing typography animation to showcase a powerfully edited sequence of highlights from the action. He also filmed Neil Pearson against a high-contrast, keyable black background to give more artistic freedom with the dramatic lighting. These live-action components were then edited together by Greenway and digital effects artist Mike McGee in a complex digital optical that included travelling matte passes that were invisible and seamless in the final edited spot.

Greenway remembers that there was a detailed discussion in the edit suite when he presented the opening edit to Tony Garnett, who felt that it may have been too graphic for the pre-watershed slot that it had been allocated. He also loved it!, so it stayed – testament to the man's strength of character and general 'Coolness' – he was a rock star! What a privilege.

Figure 5.3 *The Loves and Lives of a She-Devil* (1986) Mary Fisher book jacket prop roughs. Courtesy Christine Buttner.

The Loves and Lives of a She-Devil

On *The Loves and Lives of a She-Devil* (1986), Michael Graham-Smith worked, with assistant at the time, Christine Buttner, on a drama serial directed by Philip Saville and produced by Sally Head. The four parts of this unusual serial demanded a large number of props requiring graphic design: book covers, letterheads, posters and all the paraphernalia of a successful romantic novelist (see Figure 5.3). Christine Buttner recalls:

> My job was to design, create and oversee the production of all the books that the character (played by Patricia Hodge) was supposed to have written. . . . it was great fun. I remember being absolutely amazed at how detailed and authentic these things had to be. I created a strong cohesive look for the books: white backgrounds with a stylised gold foil blocked signature that overlapped the main title design.
>
> We took photographs of Patricia Hodge in different outfits with different hairstyles, because these books were supposed to have been written over a period of time. These portraits were then dropped onto the back of my book jacket designs. They were printed to a high quality because they had to look bona fide, even down to the logo of the publishing house (Cynara Publishing) that I designed which appeared on the spine and back of the book jackets. This logo was given to the set designers so that it could be incorporated as signage on sets of the publishing house when the character went to visit her editor.
>
> I also had to design a range of stationery for the publishers featuring the 'CP' logo, so when she got letters from the publishers you could see the logo in closeup and it had to look authentic.

> I call these invisible graphics, because nobody ever, ever notices them and thinks that somebody had to design them, but this attention to detail is what makes productions real. This sort of graphic design is going on all the time in productions and crosses over into props. (Buttner 2023)

While his assistant was working on the props, lead designer Michael Graham-Smith was immersing himself in the mood of the story and using the BBC Library to research suitable imagery. The internet had yet to be invented.

> It was a satire and as such there was 'a licence to parody the style of romantic fiction': white satin, flamboyant gold lettering and pastel shades. 'By the time it came to discuss ideas for the opening titles . . . I was already immersed in the mood of the series.' Graham-Smith used a CGI 'devil's eye' as a 'leitmotiv' which came from researching 'cabalistic symbolism and discovered the frequent use of two potent images – the triangle and the eye – both of which clearly offered interesting possibilities for our theme. The triangle echoed the nature of the relationship of the main characters. The eye corresponded to the idea of the all-seeing eye of the She-Devil.' (Merritt 1987: 27)

Digital compositing and computer-controlled rostrum filming of photographs were done in-house with the BBC Video Rostrum operators Peter Willis and Malcolm Dalton.

A few years later Christine Buttner was winning awards for her own opening title designs. She recalls the making of the title sequence for *Underbelly* (1992), a four-part political thriller by Peter Ransley starring David Hayman, Tom Wilkinson and Ray Winstone.

> *Underbelly* was about politics and big business, and the corruption and underhand dealings that went on at a high level. The main character played by David Hayman was called Stephen Crowe and I took his name (despite having an 'e') as the starting point for the opening titles.
>
> Working in a small studio with Oxford Scientific Films for two days, I animated, by hand, the deterioration of a crow's head, froze a wing using dry ice and pulled feathers apart; visual metaphors for the collapse of Crowe's business empire. I also filmed a crow's skull and a claw (representing the character grasping for power). For the rich textural backgrounds I used different types of rotting leaves and broken stones, some with moving shadows and some with water. This footage was shot on 35mm film. I then watched the episodes picking out the clips of the main characters that were going to be incorporated into the sequence. These different elements were then transferred to a digital format, ready for editing on Quantel's Harry. I remember talking to the Visual Effects editor, Mike McGee at Framestore, tasked with bringing all these elements together . . . and saying, 'Have you got enough now?' And then he added his skills and ideas to the piece. I wanted the footage of the actors to be fragmented and the panels to have different grades adding to the theme of broken characters. Mike was able to create all those layers and textures digitally. The finished sequence has many layers of effects and took about four very long days and a couple of overnighters to complete. The technology back then, though brilliant in what it could achieve, sometimes crashed and lost work and its processing time was very slow, the more layers the slower the processing.
>
> Often, once a storyboard had been given the green light, I would take it to the facilities house I planned to use to edit the job and say, 'Okay, this is what I want it to look like, what do I need to bring to you?'
>
> One of the many things I loved about the job was that it was very much a group effort, and I always valued the specialist people who I worked with and the skills that they brought to my jobs. (Buttner 2023)

Casualty

In 1988 Iain Greenway went to a meeting at Centre House on Shepherds Bush Green, in the offices of the drama department, to talk about a new pilot series they were working on called *Casualty*. It was to be shot in the 'fly on the wall' journalistic hand-held style that was in the zeitgeist due to US productions such as *Hill Street Blues* (1981–7), a ground-breaking gritty and realistic cop show set in New York.

Right from the start the producer, writer and director were on board for an intensively realistic opening sequence shot from the point of view (POV) of an accident and emergency victim strapped to a gurney in a life-or-death rush to the OR (operating room). To achieve this dash for life, Greenway directed the cameraman to lie down on the gurney and shoot the scene looking up from the patient's POV in a single take from the ambulance to the OR room.

Although the series was filmed on set in Bristol, Greenway shot the actual scene in the local Emergency Rooms at Hammersmith Hospital using real doctors, nurses and ambulance drivers. Greenway's direction to the team was simply that you all have done this thousands of times for real so do the same for the cameraman. The result was authentic and mesmerizing, putting the viewer in an identifiable experience that everyone can relate too.

To add to the dramatic atmosphere, Greenway added a blurring effect that helped the sense of disorientation using a reticulated photographic effect in the overlapping blurred edges of the image – a little like blurred vision due to the patient having received a shot at the accident site. The final narrative involved an abstract visual personification of the patient's lifeline, stretching out in front of the patient's POV, tracing the journey across the ceiling and articulating the opening of doors, with subliminal glimpses of the traces of the patient's heartbeat monitor lifeline trace. This lifeline element was created as a layer of animation cels that were rotoscoped over the live-action images frame by frame. Once the animation was completed, it was added into the composite using Quantel's Henry digital effects suite.

> The one distinctive element for the television graphic designer, is the ability to plan and produce images with *sound* and *movement*. Combining words, music and sound effects and then timing them precisely to pictures, frame-by-frame, is the essence of the craft, and this combination has proved to be one of the most compulsive ways of gaining attention. (Merritt 1987: 11)

It is telling how trusted and embedded into the production team the designer Greenway was, because he made a recommendation for the composer Ken Freeman, who had been mentioned to him by a colleague, BBC Director Bob Blagden. Blagden, who had worked with Ken on *The Tripods* (1984), knew that Greenway was also a musician and thought that they might work well together. Ken was very open to feedback and worked collaboratively. This fruitful combination led to the exciting and dramatic opening music score to *Casualty*.

Play for Today

Senior designer Sid Sutton gave an account of a live-action shoot with models for the titles to a series of single weekly plays called *Play for Today*. In 1976 it was an established feature in the schedules, and Sutton wanted to give the brand a refreshed modern look but had to suffer for his art.

> My idea was that we would film the sunrise and it would come up and it was like come over the top of the lettering and light the lettering from the front . . . shooting time lapse over a period from 4:00am in the morning to 1:00pm in the afternoon.
>
> I'd driven all around London, up and down all the hills, but I couldn't find anywhere where I could get a completely dark sky because of all the orange sodium lamps.
>
> Eventually through a friend I found a house on the East Coast, looking out to sea and no lights apart from the odd ship, and I thought that's the answer. We managed to get hold of this house for this weekend. It was in the summer of 1976, the long, hot summer where it didn't rain.

We didn't see any clouds for about three months and we went to Southwold up to the top of the house and set up the model out of the window with the 35mm time-lapse gear. So we angled the camera, because we started shooting at 4am when it was pitch black and by about 6am it was pretty obvious the sun wasn't going to come up over there, it was going to come up over there. Not only that, the sky was full of clouds, by 8:30 it was pouring rain. So we had sheets thrown over the model . . . again it was cloudy the next day, no sunrise.

And so now, I'd run out of budget. I had kept in reserve a small amount of money to shoot a sunrise on a rostrum camera. . . . And I thought . . . I've got to do this. So I got in touch with the owners and they said, okay. . . . So we stayed that night and we got our sunrise. Fantastic. In the middle of it we had a fighter jet from the American Air Force Base fly through shot. And we had to jump in between each time-lapse shot and knock the ladybirds off, jump out of shot, click one frame and carry on like that for about two and a half hours. It was quite exhausting, I can tell you. (Sutton 2023)

In Chapter 11 Designer Liz Friedman gives an account of her ground-breaking work on drama titles, most notably *Dorothy L. Sayers Mysteries* (1987).

Conclusion

Drama titles are arguably the single most powerful genre of motion graphics that can make a long-lasting cultural impression on its audience. In combination with a memorable theme tune, the drama title has the power to prepare an audience with anticipation, excitement and emotion. HBO, the American-based cable network, have invested heavily in original television drama since the late 1990s and have arguably been responsible for a renaissance in drama opening titles. This has had an influence on many productions that the BBC has made with co-producers seeking to sell their shows abroad in the US market.

It is only in the age of digital streaming of 'box sets' where audiences can 'binge-watch' episode after episode that the titles are likely to be skipped over and avoided. Before then, in a period now seen as nostalgic of 'appointment viewing', their aim was to call the viewer to the television and prepare them for the story ahead. Long-running and high-value co-productions often offered the designer a budget to realize their wildest creative dreams, and for many brought accolades and established their creative careers. In some rare cases, the experience of working with actors on live-action shoots offered a gateway to directing long form, or advertising commercials. The caché and prestige of being part of a drama production were attractive and part of the glamour of television. But it could also cut an ambitious designer down to size on occasions when the director or producer wielded the ultimate editorial control in the cutting room, and one learnt quickly what battles to fight and others to diplomatically retreat from. At the end of the day, every motion designer could have their own 'director's cut' for their showreel and awards entry.

As in other chapters, the image processing power of the digital age has had a profound effect on the creative possibilities of a drama title with modest to little budget. Today, the same aims apply, but the limits are more a matter of taste and creative imagination. We are living in a golden renaissance of drama titles, and only time will tell what this generation will revere in decades to come.

6   *Doctor Who*
Motion graphics for a Time Lord
IAIN MACDONALD

Any history of the BBC would be remiss not to include *Doctor Who*, the longest-running sci-fi fantasy series in the world, which in 2000 was voted third in the British Film Institute's 100 Greatest British Television Programmes (BFI). It is hard to imagine the effect that the opening titles of the first series had on its audience, but one can imagine that it was as seminal as the celebrated radio broadcast on the eve of Halloween in 1938 by Orson Welles of HG Wells's *War of the Worlds*, or perhaps the infamous BBC drama *Ghostwatch* (1992), now a cult classic.

A new dimension

In 1963, Bernard Lodge broke away from every convention of television graphics and drama titles. This may sound more dramatic than was felt at the time, when no one thought the show would go beyond one season and they could afford to be more experimental. The account of the 'howlround' is celebrated by many design historians and designers (Laughton 1966; Merritt 1987; Yates and Price 2015), a documentary, *Radio Times* interview, numerous conventions and countless online fan forums. Up to that point, all of Lodge's experience had been with film, making this his first foray into electronic imaging. He remembers the result as: 'these shapes; magic, just magic'.

> Verity Lambert called me over to show me some video effects she had. They had been created by a technician Ben Palmer for a 1959 production Carlo Menotti's opera *Amahl and the Night Visitors*. So the footage (recorded on film because there was no videotape in 1963) was free, which was great because the production had a small budget.
>   I was looking forward to making the title sequence for a sci-fi series, a chance to do some experimental work, but when I saw the astonishing floating clouds I was convinced that we had to work somehow with these effects. The title had to be created or affected by this process.
>   So I suggested that we try to set up a session and see what we could do. This was not what Verity had planned, because my job was to design an animated logo that would use this free footage. But Verity agreed to my suggestion. In fact it was an expensive session. It would require a tv studio for half a day. Verity had to plead with the drama head for extra money.
>   So about two weeks later we took over Studio TK4. There was a team of technical people, led by Ben Palmer. He explained the process which came to be called Howlround. In basic terms an image orthicon camera was pointed at a monitor to which it was linked, so the image was sent around in a loop. The cables went all the way around the studio. It could start with a point of light. The adjustment of the camera : tilt or pan, change of light level etc. would affect the image. The alterations would go around and it set up a sort of momentum and you got these shapes. (Lodge 2023)

Figure 6.1 *Doctor Who* (1963) titles created with howlround. Courtesy Bernard Lodge.

And eventually we had loads, and loads, and loads of wasted 35mm film, but we got these pieces. When the lettering came in and did this effect, it was magic. I mean, you may not see it as magic now, but it was to us incredible. It couldn't do it any other way. And we got that. And then Verity Lambert said, 'well, if you can, go away and edit it'. So I took all the film, went over to Ealing Studios with an editor and put it all together. (Lodge 2019)

The black-and-white images were like nothing ever seen before in people's living rooms (see Figure 6.1). The Rorschach-like patterns of white on black emanated from the centre of the screen like a psychological ink-blot test, the viewer could project their own meaning onto the rippling patterns. In Lodge's later versions, the face of the actor playing Dr Who was included, but in the first series, a face was deemed by the producer to be too scary for the young audience, and the only element they had to work with was a little 12×9 inch caption card with the title 'Doctor Who' set in a bold sans serif, centred, white on black.

Composers Ron Grainer and Delia Derbyshire were responsible for creating the audio atmosphere of the early series. Grainer wrote the basic melody of the *Doctor Who* theme, and Derbyshire, with the BBC Radiophonic Workshop, transformed it into a pioneering piece of electronica music.

Ron Grainer, who was a great musician, did the music for it and I had a meeting with him and . . . I had to explain what was happening, I couldn't show it to him. I was still editing it. And I said 'about 20 seconds, the title appears.' And he said, 'I'll bear that in mind.' So a week later, we had the music and I took it to the editor and we put them together. And it is magic and every frame affected by the music. But it's all accidental. You know, people think, how do you get these things? They just go together sometimes, you know? So that was it. (Lodge 2019)

There have been several arrangements used of the theme, but the basic melody has remained unchanged throughout the show's history. No new piece of music has ever been commissioned as a theme, making it one of the longest-serving signature tunes in television history (Art-of-the-Title 2013).

'The combination of television technology and conveying the storyline of space fiction and time warps, he encapsulated images which have endured as long as "Dr Who" himself [*sic*] and pioneered design via the medium of video' (Merritt 1987: 54). According to Jeremy Myerson and Graham Vickers, the 'animated Rorschach blots' of the title sequence, combined with the futuristic electronic score, together gave 'a long-running TV series its most unforgettable identity' (Myerson and Vickers 2002: 66).

New Doctor, new versions

In 1967, a year after Patrick Troughton had replaced William Hartnell as the Doctor, Lodge reworked the title to include the ghostly face of Troughton and replace the sans serif bold title with Times Roman. Delia Derbyshire remixed her music to make the opening bars more spine-chilling with 'spangle' sound effects.

> On the second one where we had a face, I knew you had to control the highlights because this effect came from the white, you know, this is the stuff that generates. We took a photograph of Patrick Troughton with white side, backlit and that gave it the effect, what you get electronically was a little bit unprepared. And that was a bit of luck, you know, because this was a good thing, it all sort of peeled away the face. And I used a wipe effect, which I control, which wasn't anything electronic. When we had done the edit, and electronically recorded it, I then used a tearing sequence which was done with a sheet of white polyester, which is against the light, and then it's all black, and then as it turns around, it goes all white. And that was used as a negative and positive wipe to get rid of his face. But otherwise, I think, you know, we had control of the techniques we used. (Lodge 2019)

In 1970, Series 7 was the first to be made in colour. Jon Pertwee's face replaced Troughton's in the titles, re-designing 'howlround' with red and green swirling flames and climaxing with another new logo design. Delia Derbyshire's theme arrangement was given a third new edit, retaining the spangles but shortening the opening bars, and for Series 7–9 adding a 'stutter start'. Closing music changed too, standardized at 52" and 1'12", starting with the now-famous radiophonic scream (Art-of-the-Title 2013).

> When we tried going to *Doctor Who* colour, they used a colour camera and it didn't produce anything. So we use the old image of black on black and white camera and I added the colour filmicly afterwards. And I think this is some of the most beautiful electronic images that we got. . . . It holds together quite well.
>
> On the third time . . . the producer said, 'can we do something else?' And I spoke to Ben Palmer about other electronic techniques. And he came up with a with another system where they were able to distort the image in perspective. And we set up a day, we got the Doctor Who, John Pertwee in the studio and took some film and electronic recording, and then it didn't work, it didn't work at all.
>
> (Lodge 2019)

So in 1973, for Series 11 Lodge took another technically innovative approach, and instead of a video effect, he used a computer-controlled rostrum camera to shoot on 35mm film, exploiting a new effect called 'slit-scan' that had impressed him on Stanley Kubrick's *2001: A Space Odyssey* (1968), originated by Douglas Trumbull, the Special Photographic Effects Supervisor for the 'stargate' sequence.

> We all admired it, but didn't know how the hell he did it. We got a copy of *American Cinematographer* magazine and we read it and we couldn't work it out, because Doug Trumbull, who did that sequence,

he wrote with great technical detail, and you read it and read it, didn't know how he did it. I mean, what is it? It's not film. It is film, but what sort of film? . . . And then it suddenly occurred to me it was on one frame of film, on one frame. He moves the camera, moves to make a frame. I thought, wow. (Lodge 2019)

After a lot of trial and error, using a film rostrum with a motorized camera and bench that could move east-west, Lodge worked with the operator to painstakingly synchronize the movements repeatedly, one frame at a time. Multiple long camera exposures of light refracting in plastic were filmed through slots in black masking card to create a tunnel effect. The *Doctor Who* logo was now a defined brand contained in a diamond, more easily applied for greater recognition in other media, such as print.

In 1974, with Tom Baker as the new Doctor, a further refreshing of the title sequence was applied. The police callbox-shaped TARDIS was introduced as a supporting motif through the tunnel vortex, as the slit-scan technique was taken to new heights to create a greater spectrum of subtle colours and range of movements (see Figure 6.2).

Later in 1980, with Tom Baker's last series, Senior Designer Sid Sutton took on the task. The new producer of Series 18, John Nathan Turner, thought the titles were now looking like 'a view through a vacuum cleaner tube', so Sutton approached the titles as a journey through space, rather than time. With specular starburst effects shot on 35mm film on the rostrum, a constellation of stars came together to form Tom Baker's updated photo and resolve the sequence with a new trapezoid-shaped logo formed of one continuous line, like a neon sign.

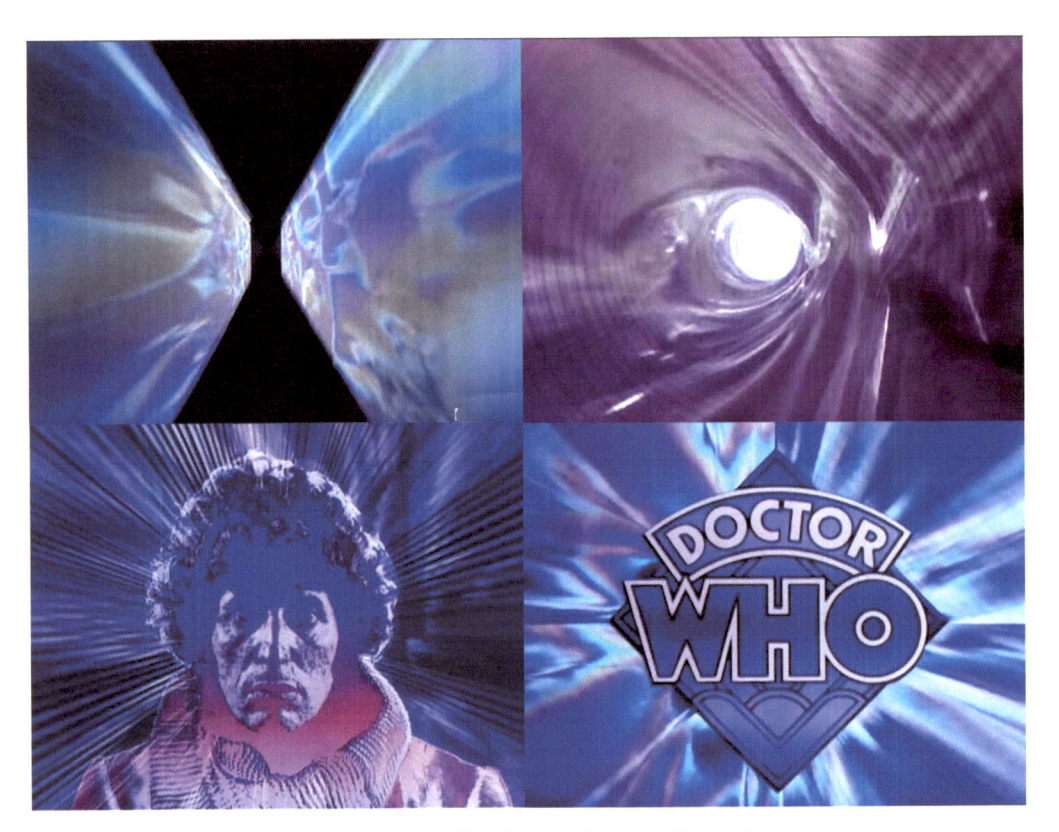

Figure 6.2 *Doctor Who* (1974) titles created with slit-scan. Courtesy Bernard Lodge.

That was a hell of a challenge because, you know, following Bernard Lodge, who was our guru, everybody looked up to Bernard, the tops, as it were. But I was given the job to do the titles for The New Era by John Nathan Turner when he took over as producer. And it was pretty tricky, really. You know, it was kind of a double edged sword, I suppose.

. . . I love Bernard's original. The very first one he did was fantastic and all the other adaptations of it. I loved them all. But the only thing I wanted to do, I wanted to give it a more expansive feeling. And we'd been through things like *Star Wars* at the time and seen these vast bits of space. Doctor Who, I know is a time traveller, but you travel through time and space. I wanted to reinforce the space side of it, as well as the time, and try and open the screen up. And so I thought I would start with the Galaxy. He's an alien, he comes from out there. You know, he's not one of us, really, although we tend to think he's an Englishman. He's not. He's an alien, and he comes from the stars.

And so I thought, well, you know, we've got the stars, we're traveling through the galaxy and the stars are coming towards us. And some of them stop and they build up the head of the Doctor. I thought that was an idea. And it kind of added a slightly new dimension, I think, to the to the titles. And I got a lot of praise for it and it was great, I mean, for the producers and people who were knocked out. (Sutton 2023)

Sutton continued to refresh these titles for the Peter Davison and Colin Baker Doctors. But for Colin Baker, Sutton was asked if it were possible to make it more colourful.

When we were making the sequence and testing different components it seemed obvious the more we put in the better it looked, also by reinforcing the time tunnel aspect with the new animation. More importantly, there are no digital or electronic effects in all three title sequences. Everything was created under or in the rostrum camera.

The logo was shot with a normal back lit 'Kodalith', but we shot it through a prism. The prism was immediately in front of the lens . . . (either) we taped it to the lens or had it on a stand some inches away. The interesting thing is that for it to work, the artwork had to be not in front of the camera, but around 20 to 30 cm to one side. The result is the purply glow and slight distortion.

With the tunnelling animation I tried to re-introduce the time travel side of things without losing the idea of the stars, which had become well established. This was achieved again with two overlapping back lit 'Kodaliths' revolving one against the other and shot using the 'Cokin' star filters. One lith was straight concentric lines starting at a vanishing point and getting larger at the edges, the other a spiral of concentric lines revolving over it. If you revolve one way the animation goes away from you, the other way it come towards you. I believe we tried this through the prism but the star filters were more colourful and looked much better. Phew! (Sutton 2023)

In 1987, another BBC senior designer, Oliver Elmes, who had recently designed the first computer-generated BBC1 ident, took a similar approach for *Doctor Who* when Sylvester McCoy took the role. From a spinning asteroid belt of stars, the TARDIS spins within a bubble, and then from this magnetic centre spins out the flying logo in individual letters of metal. It was a trope of the day, a sign of modernity in the 1980s.

Reboot-respawn 2005

For fifteen years the television series remained dormant, and in that time the landscape of children's drama, the sci-fi entertainment industry and London's computer visual effects industry were all transformed. Children that had grown up watching *Doctor Who* were now writers, producers, designers, crew and cast. 'Critics scoffed that this revival of a "dead series" would never work, but the 2005 version lived up to Newman and Lambert's vision and single-handedly revived the fortunes of TV drama and Saturday night family viewing' (Art-of-the-Title 2013). The show spawned an enormously successful franchise across multiple media, including video games, books, comics, exhibitions and toys: learning lessons in merchandising from American and Asian children's cartoon and fantasy programming.

Lead writer Russell T. Davies and the team assembled at BBC Wales by producer Phil Collinson brought award-winning visual effects to television drama that would normally have only been possible in Hollywood blockbuster movies. In London's Soho, Academy Award-winning computer effects artists and designers at The Mill proudly took on the rebooted television series as a prestige, high-profile project. The Mill had, and continues to have, world-leading visual effects experience following work on Ridley Scott's *Gladiator* and numerous *Harry Potter* films.

The series' logo was redesigned in a lozenge but remained a flying metal logo, and both the music and time tunnel motifs and police-box TARDIS were retained as key signifiers of the brand. The Mill's motion designer used computer animation to emulate the 1974's classic slit-scan sequence that had been shot originally on film, but the pace was also much faster to suit the taste of modern audiences now regularly bombarded with fast-action video games.

The Doctor came back with a distinctly authentic regional accent – Mancunian with Christopher Eccleston – and, after one season, was followed by Scottish actor David Tennant, making the Doctor more of a man of the people.

New titles in 2009 were designed by creatives at Red Bee using the 'DW' TARDIS, and again in 2012, this time by Peter Anderson Studio, all of whom paid homage to Bernard Lodge's original imagery and visual conception of time travel. The recognition and use of Lodge's signature 'howlround' and time tunnel, albeit in a digitally synthesized version, was no different from other design trends we see in the new millennia that hark back to the past, such as in automobile design, where a fragment of the brand DNA is manifest in an otherwise generic design solution.

When designing a trailer to celebrate the fiftieth anniversary of the series, designer and director Matthew Losasso was compelled to reflect on his own experience as a viewer in his youth, and also as a BBC designer who walked past the scenery stores every day where the TARDIS was docked.

> In 2013, I was approached to direct the BBC's flagship trailer for the 50th anniversary of *Doctor Who* and I knew instantly what my reference point would be: those dreamlike corridors of TV centre in the 90s, lined with the props and sets from my childhood. I wanted to capture that strange sense of these fragments from the BBC's history, jumbled together and frozen in time. But it wasn't only the aesthetic that I drew on: true to the roots of my career, the *Doctor Who* 50th trailer is largely created in-camera and is full of experimental tricks and techniques, like the painstaking re-colouring of a grainy black and white photograph of the first Doctor. The technology may have improved since the days of the HAL, but the creative legacy of the BBC's Motion Graphics is very much alive and kicking. (Losasso 2023)

That same reverence for the iconic heritage of *Doctor Who* has inspired many budding enthusiasts, eager to create their own vision to share amongst a growing online fanbase. In 2014, as Peter Capaldi (another Scotsman) took on the role of Doctor, a new motion designer came into the spotlight: a fan working from a laptop in his bedroom. A modest independent motion graphic designer working from a small studio at home in Leeds made international news. *The Huffington Post*, BBC America, the *Guardian* and local television and press picked up the fairytale story of Billy Hanshaw, whose homemade title sequence for *Dr Who* became a YouTube hit (60,000 hits in the first weekend) and was picked up by BBC Series showrunner Steven Moffat, who thought it was the most original title design since 1963. Hanshaw, like many fans, regarded the Doctor as a time traveller, and so took a visually literal approach to time by using images of cogs and coiling Escher-like clock faces. These were not within any brand guidelines; he was designing for pleasure and for other fans like himself.

At the age of forty-six, Hanshaw was delightedly thrust into the limelight, picking up a Royal Television Society nomination along the way. In a 2015 Radio Times poll of Top *Dr Who* Titles, Hanshaw's opening sequence for Series 8 was only beaten to the number one place by the 1963 original (Macdonald 2015).

The design process for creating and producing a title sequence is very similar today as it was in 1963 when Bernard Lodge took on the job. While the technology has changed, the process remains much the same: researching the project, reading a script, meeting the producer and director, visualizing ideas as drawn storyboards (rarely on the back of a napkin), signing off on budgets, presenting work in progress as rough edits and renders, responding to client feedback and presenting finished work (and the invoice). Even though Hanshaw's work was picked up as a complete 'finished' work on YouTube, it had gone through a process of idea generation on paper, test renders and a series of iterations. Once Moffat had secured Hanshaw's involvement, the title design then went through a series of client changes, losing the fobwatch and seal of the Rassilon motif. Unlike Lodge, who shot on 35mm film and had to wait for overnight lab rushes to return to Film Despatch at Television Centre, Hanshaw, using a MacBook Pro and Adobe After Effects, could render and review in real time from the comfort of his home.

Such has been the democratization of technology, now that the hardware and software revolution that came in the 1990s has enabled greater access to what was once the hegemony of television stations and high-end post-production companies. This has had a profound effect on the delivery of design education, in particular, because it has been equally liberating for motion design students. Technical skills are available to anyone with internet access and a computer. There is a 'cottage' industry of digital makers and designers that keeps the cogs of the creative industries moving.

Further revolutions continue, most notably the first female Doctor, played by Jodie Whittaker, in their thirteenth regeneration between 2018 and 2022. She was but one of three female leads in BBC dramas that year, which were met with regulatory approval as evidence of (some) movement towards greater equality (Ofcom 2019). Other female actors had previously been considered at various times after Tom Baker, nearly forty years earlier, notably Frances de la Tour, Joanna Lumley, Dawn French and Judy Dench. Time moves slowly in some corners of the galaxy.

With the latest incarnation of the titles, there was a fairy-tale ending. In 2018, as four years before, a young unknown was propelled into the spotlight (Radio Times 2017). Ben Pickles was already lauded by Whovians (as *Doctor Who* fans are known) for his own versions of the titles that he had posted on YouTube when he was noticed by programme director Rachel Talalay. Already emboldened by casting a woman in the title role and recognizing the positive energy of the fanbase, the decision to use Pickles was probably a relatively easy one for writer and series producer Chris Chibnall and producer Matt Strevens. Ben Pickles, aka John Smith VFX, posted on social media:

> Way back in 2010, I was sixteen years old and had just started learning how to use After Effects. I had no idea what I was doing, but was so excited for Matt Smith's first series that I decided to try what every Whovian-turned-VFX-Artist does at some point . . . making my own title sequence for the show! . . . it's got a whole 200 likes! So I figured that maybe this whole VFX thing might just be worth pursuing. . . .
>
> Until 8 years later, I somehow found myself another title sequence for a whole new Doctor. Except this time, I wasn't making my own fan-made test. . . . I was making the real one.
>
> I'm so privileged to be allowed to add to the history of one of the most iconic opening sequences in television. And of course even more terrified of what the response to it is going to be (I know how

passionate fans can get!!) But for now, I just couldn't be more grateful to have been asked to be involved at all.

It's been, in every possible way, a dream come true! (John Smith VFX 2018)

Pickles' titles were 3D computer animated and employed a 3D liquid shape that emulated the original 1963 'howlround' and then resolved in an accelerated time tunnel similar to the slit-scan effect of 1974. It was met with widespread applause from the fan-base who were particularly excited that one of their own had succeeded in realizing their ultimate dream.

It is worth reflecting on how much and how little has changed down the years. In a heritage show like *Doctor Who* that can only feel the burden of its own responsibility, it is reassuring to know that technology can make it possible to spurn conservatism and find the special courage to go out on a limb (Macdonald 2015).

Conclusion

The iconic status of *Doctor Who* has also been recognized by the British Establishment, when in 2009 the Royal Mint released a limited-edition range of *Doctor Who* medals, designed by the head of the Royal Mint's in-house engraving team, Matthew Bonaccorsi. This was the first time that television characters had appeared on a Royal Mint medal.

Then, in 2013 the Royal Mail issued a set of commemorative postage stamps to celebrate fifty years of *Doctor Who*. The set of eleven stamps featured each actor that played the Time Lord set against graphics taken from opening titles and the relevant logo for the show. William Hartnell and Patrick Troughton, the first two Doctors, were pictured in black and white to reflect the broadcasting of the time.

In 2023, the BBC and Disney Branded Television announced that they had come together to transform *Doctor Who* into a global franchise for UK audiences and the rest of the world. Rather than promoting a featured actor, the brand was relaunched with a sharp new rendering of Lodge's 1974 diamond-shaped logo. This has now become the de facto brand marque, harmonizing the contemporary with its heritage recognition.

It is extraordinary to see how times have changed, with enthusiasts and fans have launched careers in motion graphics through their passion on social media. Meanwhile, those of us who worked at the Television Centre through the 1980s would have blithely walked past a rather scruffy old TARDIS in the scenic store underneath our offices every morning, and occasionally, after work, might have witnessed the surreal sight of *Dr Who* characters in costume ordering drinks at the BBC Bar during a break in recording.

7 Global circulations, national traditions
BBC Motion Graphics and Canadian television
ANDREW BURKE

This chapter explores the conjunction of cultural memory and modern design by analyzing the circulation of BBC Motion Graphics internationally in the 1960s and 1970s. Extensive overseas sales of BBC programming in these decades meant that BBC Motion Graphics travelled well beyond the United Kingdom, with viewers seeing them in distant places and different national television contexts. Thinking specifically about the Canadian situation – BBC programming aired regularly on the Canadian Broadcasting Corporation (CBC) since it began broadcast in 1952 – this chapter takes up three interconnected issues. First, it examines how the material collected in the BBC Motion Graphics Archive has significance for Canadian viewers, with programmes ranging from *Maigret* to *Monty Python's Flying Circus*, along with their iconic credit sequences, occupying a key place in national cultural memory. Second, it examines the role of motion graphics as a marker of both distinction and difference. The growing internationalism of graphic design in the 1960s and 1970s ensured some overlap in design styles amongst national broadcasters, yet there remained minor differences that marked programmes from elsewhere. Third, it compares the work in the BBC Motion Graphics Archive to the history of motion graphics in Canada, mobilizing Jan Hadlaw's concept of 'design nationalism' to argue that both Hubert Tison's 1967 redesign of the CBC's station identification and Burton Kramer's comprehensive 1974 redesign of the CBC's graphic identity were tied to the deliberate, state-led initiative to modernize that defined Canada in the 1960s and 1970s.

This analysis deliberately combines television studies and design studies, drawing on the BBC Motion Graphics Archive to argue that, in their global circulations, BBC Motion Graphics both influenced and intersected with other national television cultures. Canada serves as an ideal case study because of the nation's historic ties to Great Britain and the ways in which the BBC model of what a national broadcaster could or should be exerted an influence on the CBC. Additionally, Canada was in the throes of accelerated modernization in the 1960s and 1970s and wanted to distinguish itself as a modern, wholly independent nation. It not only sought to do this culturally, economically and politically but also understood that it had to be done on the visual level. Motion graphics animated and archives this process.

My arguments here are both personal and polemical. Discussions of cultural memory almost inevitably draw on the stuff of personal remembrance. Rather than seeing this as a problem or an obstacle, I want to embrace it, to harness the personal to think about the impact of motion graphics on viewers, but also on the workings of televisual memory that looks back to an era when broadcast was significantly, but not entirely, bounded by the borders of the nation-state. This method comes with all the usual caveats recognizing the immensity of Canada itself and the diversity of its spectators, so I do my best not to universalize my own reflections even as I use them to prompt my analysis. My work here is also deeply polemical. Television studies in Canada is an underdeveloped field, shaped by a lack of archival access and the CBC's seeming disinterest in its own history, viewing it primarily as a source of revenue through footage sales. As a result, my investigations here are scattered and speculative, relying heavily on the work of enthusiasts who have uploaded credit sequences and station identifications to YouTube, as well as graphic design historians whose work often provides an alternate pathway into understanding the history of motion graphics in Canada. In this context, the BBC Motion Graphic Archive functions as an inspiration and feels like something that would be an impossibility in Canada. It would deeply enrich the understanding of the history of television in Canada, yet the conditions of possibility for something like it to exist are not yet in place.

Television in Canada dates to 6 September 1952, with the predominantly French-language CBFT in Montreal beginning operations just two days before the launch of CBLT's English-language service in Toronto. Over the next several years, CBC stations opened in major centres across the country, and by 1 July 1958, CBC's television signal was extended from coast-to-coast. Many, including Mary Jane Miller and Paul Rutherford, have argued that the earliest days of CBC Television represent a golden age of broadcast in Canada, with the young network animated by a spirit of formal experimentation and a taste for technological innovation. Throughout the late 1950s and early 1960s, CBC personnel frequently left Canada for the United Kingdom. Most notable, perhaps, was Sydney Newman, who departed the CBC in 1958, first to take up the post of Drama Supervisor at ABC and then to become the Head of Television Drama at the BBC. Many Canadian directors, several of them invited by Newman himself, also decamped to London, including Alvin Rakoff, Ted Kotcheff, Silvio Narizzano, Ron Kelly and Paul Almond, amongst others. This largely one-way traffic points to a complex relationship between the BBC and CBC at that time. There was clearly prestige in working at the BBC, but it is also clear the CBC had young talent of a calibre worth poaching (Newman 2017: 15–17).

While the CBC imported BBC programming from the earliest days of broadcast in Canada, the number of imports increased dramatically in the early 1960s, coinciding with the pioneering work of Bernard Lodge and the BBC Graphics Department. One significant British import during this period was *Doctor Who*, the original series of which, co-created by Sydney Newman, made its North American debut on the CBC in 1965. Lodge's title sequence, with its array of swirling and rippling electronic clouds out of which the title of the programme slowly forms, would have been striking in any context at that time, but it would have especially stood out on the CBC on a winter weekend afternoon (see Figure 6.1).

The CBC did not pick up subsequent series of *Doctor Who* – the show would only return to the national broadcaster in 2005 – but Lodge's updates and revisions to the title sequence nevertheless reached many Canadian viewers via the American Public Broadcasting Service (PBS). Not only did such a large portion of Canadians live close enough to the American border that the signal from nearby PBS affiliates was within reach, but the advent of cable systems in the 1970s and 1980s meant that Lodge's work circulated in and through Canadian homes. The programme was also broadcast in this era on Television Ontario (TVO), a public educational service. This is all to say that Lodge's motion graphics for *Doctor Who* circulated extensively in Canada from the 1960s onwards and, as such, form part of spectatorial memory and the history of watching TV in Canada.

The business of export meant the BBC material that circulated internationally was limited: marquee series, prestige programmes, and science and educational documentaries tended to travel better than lifestyle series, news and current affairs programming, or dramatic or comedic works too grounded in the specifics of a regional or national culture. In the early 1960s, the newly formed private network CTV scooped the CBC in its presentation of *Maigret*, with its strikingly modern title and credit sequences designed by Geoffrey Martin (see Figure 7.1). Martin would later design new editions for several novels in Simenon's popular detective series, *Penguin Crime*. For these he integrated images from the television series into the iconic Marber Grid, designed by Romek Marber and used extensively by Penguin throughout the 1960s and 1970s. The stylized title for Maigret, evocative of the fountain pen and of hand-lettering, gives way to

Figure 7.1 *Maigret* (1961) title sequence logo. Courtesy BBC.

Figure 7.2 *The Forsythe Saga* (1967) title sequence logo. Courtesy BBC.

Figure 7.3 *Civilisation* (1969) title sequence logo. Courtesy BBC.

the more modern type used for the credits themselves, the Marber Grid's Akidenz-Grotesk (Poyner 2004: n.p.). Martin's design at once draws on movements in typography gaining hold internationally in that period, while at the same time setting a standard for how motion graphics would convey and condense the crime serial in a series of typographical choices, design conventions and stylistic tropes.

While CTV had *Maigret*, the CBC in this period drew extensively on three types of BBC programming that travelled well: prestige historical dramas, significant educational series and surreal sketch comedies. Broadcast on both CBC and PBS, *The Forsyte Saga* set the standard for minimal, sophisticated and typographically driven opening sequences characteristic of literary adaptations (see Figure 7.2). Kenneth Clark's *Civilisation*, broadcast on the CBC shortly after its transmission in the United Kingdom, likewise features a typographically minimal opening, yet, paired with an excerpt of William Walton's *Symphony No. 1*, it assumes a weight and gravity that has perhaps become standard for longform natural history, scientific and historical series (see Figure 7.3). Keeping with documentary series, James Burke's *Connections* was a staple on Canadian television in the early to mid-1980s, and its Dick Bailey-designed opening sequence, with the series title appearing in bolded black and all caps in the white-out of an electrical flash, powerfully evokes the series' theme of the possibilities inherent in social, cultural and scientific conjunctions and cross-pollinations. These are just a few examples of how certain BBC Motion Graphics travelled in the 1960s, 1970s and into the 1980s, but they establish how the work of BBC practitioners had a reach and influence, even impact, beyond broadcast on the BBC itself.

I want to move on now, though, to the trickier topic of what these circulations meant and how they might have been experienced. My starting point is that many BBC series, when they circulated outside the United Kingdom, and especially when they were broadcast in North America, arrived with an air of prestige and sophistication. This is perhaps most obvious with the extensive rebroadcast of BBC series such as *I, Claudius* (1976, titles by Dick Bailey) (see Figure 7.4) and *Barchester Chronicles* (1982, titles by Stewart Austin) (see Figure 7.5) on PBS's *Masterpiece Theatre* in the United States and readily available to Canadian viewers. The working title of the series before it was launched in 1971 was *The Best of*

Figure 7.4 *I Claudius* (1976) title sequence logo. Courtesy BBC.

Figure 7.5 *The Barchester Chronicles* (1982) title sequence logo. Courtesy BBC.

the BBC, which has all the overtones of these programmes being the crème de la crème, but perhaps more important is the framing of the BBC originals. The BBC Motion Graphics were usually included in the broadcast but nested within the series' own various title sequences down through the years. All of these, from the classic *Masterpiece Theatre* opening featuring Alistair Cooke in an armchair – satirized on *Sesame Street* as *Monsterpiece Theatre* with Cookie Monster taking the part of Alistair Cookie – to the more recent Edward Gorey animations of the *Mystery!* spin-off, play on an ornate and stylized retro-Victorian colonial Anglophilia. The CBC presentations of BBC material in the 1960s and 1970s did not feature this same level of Anglophilic kitsch, yet the credit sequences for the BBC programmes themselves strongly influenced period productions worldwide. Even as, by the mid-1980s, the CBC had committed to broadcasting almost exclusively Canadian content in primetime – a policy adopted under pressure from a conservative government – the influences of the BBC in domestically produced period drama were clear. The opening of the CBC's *Glory Enough for All* (Eric Till, 1988, CBC), a dramatization of the discovery of insulin by Banting and Best, with its stylized type over a series of black-and-white archival photographs, very much picks up on a quintessentially British model for the graphical introduction of serious and edifying historical drama.

But perhaps the genre that travelled most readily during this period was comedy, with programmes such as *The Goodies* (see Figure 7.6) and *The Two Ronnies* (see Figure 7.7) appearing regularly on the CBC. Both series, straight down to their opening sequences, would have stood out from domestic productions of the period. As much as I was baffled and bemused by the CBC's choice to air *The Two Ronnies* immediately before *Hockey Night in Canada* on Saturday nights in the late 1970s and early 1980s, it did make Steve Connelly's 1977 title sequence perhaps one of the most viewed in Canada amongst those in the BBC Motion Graphics Archive. But I want to focus more here on *The Goodies*, since it points to the ways in which motion graphics can come with all kinds of expectations, associations and significations when they circulate internationally.

The Goodies was broadcast throughout the 1970s on the CBC. The title sequence for its first series consisted of a rapid-fire montage of clips from the show itself that featured stop-frame animation and speeded-up live action drawn from Richard Lester's toolkit of devices used in the Beatles films. These techniques bring with them inextricable associations of a playful, modern Englishness that are amplified by the typeface used for the title itself. Though Mania was an American invention, appearing in the *Psychedelitypes* catalogue published by New York's Photo-Lettering foundry in 1968, its rerouting in the

Figure 7.6 *The Goodies* (1970) title sequence logo. Courtesy BBC.

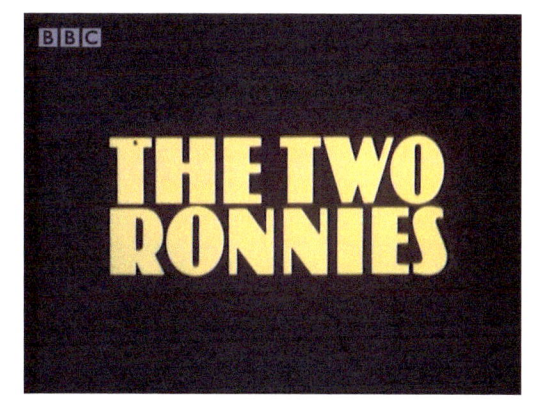

Figure 7.7 *The Two Ronnies* (1977) title sequence logo. Courtesy BBC.

motion graphics for *The Goodies* resignifies it in a way that makes it representative of a specifically English conjunction of comedy and psychedelia. Circulating through Canadian broadcast space, the title sequence for *The Goodies* is a prime example of how motion graphics came with a variety of significations tied to ideas of national identity and culture and how the foreignness of a programme was visible in its component parts, the elements that would have looked and felt immediately different from a domestic tradition even before the action started or the narrative began.

The most celebrated BBC comedy import was *Monty Python's Flying Circus*, which debuted on the CBC in September 1970 and garnered enough acclaim that the network picked up subsequent series and the troupe toured Canada to sold-out crowds in 1973. I do not want to focus on Terry Gilliam's animated opening sequence here, but on the way the series integrated BBC Motion Graphics into the show itself, satirizing television directly by thinking about the role these productions played in the flow, to use Raymond Williams's influential term, of the programme day (Williams 1974: 86). Perhaps most notably, throughout the second series, there were a number of sketches that featured a continuity announcer providing programming notices over the Sid Sutton-designed BBC 1 Mirrored Globe. These sketches satirized the formal conventions of television itself, rendering absurd the markers meant to guide viewers through the experience of watching television.

In a sequence from Episode 6 of Series 2, first broadcast in the United Kingdom on 3 November 1970, Michael Palin provides the voice of a continuity announcer who initially seems to be signalling the start of a new programme – 'it is five past nine and nearly time for' – but instead of delivering the name of a programme title, continues with the absurdity of these time markers:

> six past nine. On BBC2 now it'll shortly be six and a half minutes past nine. Later on this evening it'll be ten o'clock and at 10.30 we'll be joining BBC2 in time for 10.33, and don't forget tomorrow when it'll be 9.20. Those of you who missed 8.45 on Friday will be able to see it again this Friday at a quarter to nine. Now here is a time check. It's six and a half minutes to the big green thing.

The sketch exposes how routine and formalized the conventions of broadcasting had become. It mobilizes official BBC imagery – the Mirrored Globe ident (see Figure 1.14) – and juxtaposes it with the satiric continuity announcement itself, demonstrating the way television works by revealing the mechanics of its operations. The satire transforms the continuity announcement and the station ident from something that is normal, simply part of the contemporary televisual experience, to something that is weird and somewhat strange, a kind of defamiliarizing of the ordinary that reveals television as a construct rather than something that has a natural form.

This plays out slightly differently for viewers elsewhere, for whom the BBC Mirrored Globe ident would not have been as familiar and not part of the everyday televisual experience the satire targets and defamiliarizes. The joke still works because viewers in Canada and other territories would recognize the juxtaposition of unofficial speech and official image that fuels the joke and perhaps think of it in terms of an analogical juxtaposition within their own national context. Yet what is especially important here, thinking in terms of the circulation of programmes internationally in the 1960s and 1970s, is how embedding the station identification into the programme itself allows for the circulation of a category of motion graphics that does not usually circulate beyond national borders. It would have been a rare instance for international viewers to experience something like the everyday experience of watching the BBC, complete with continuity announcements and station identifications and even, in other episodes of *Monty Python's Flying Circus*, programme announcements and bumpers and closedown sequences.[1] In an era when television was largely a domestic enterprise, with borders producing a nation-specific set of signs of that national broadcast space, this would have been relatively rare. Cross-border signals allowed for the domestication of the American visual vocabulary of television to become ordinary for some Canadian viewers – those living near the American border – yet these elements of the BBC broadcast experience transmitted via *Monty Python's Flying Circus* are not as simple as transnational, terrestrial signals. The defamiliarization it makes possible is one that radically estranges the nation-contained experience of television, producing the effect of 'this is what television looks like there; the way it looks here is contingent and a product rather than necessary or natural'.

This brings me to the CBC's efforts in the 1960s and 1970s to produce a comprehensive visual identity for the network. The essential context here is Canada's Centennial celebrations. 1967 marked the hundredth anniversary of Canada's founding as a nation, and the government took this opportunity to promote Canada on the world stage. One motivation for this was to distinguish Canada as a modern nation, even a hip one, and both graphic design and motion graphics would play an important role in this process. But there was also the desire to project Canada as a nation unto itself rather than just a former colony. This perhaps began in earnest with the adoption of a new national flag, with the iconic red maple leaf at its centre, on 15 February 1965. But the flag was only a single element in what was basically a complete overhaul of the nation's visual identity, an effort that was not centrally coordinated yet saw government agencies, crown corporations and private businesses all refresh their logos over the course of the 1960s and 1970s, adopting the visual language of international modernism to project an image of Canada as a modern nation.[2] Allan Fleming's redesign of the Canadian National Railways, or CN, logo in 1960 marks a key early moment in this process, but in the years that followed, many organizations followed suit, hiring young graphic designers to update or create their visual identity. A partial list would necessarily include Air Canada (Hans Kleefeld, 1963), Expo 67 (Jacques Hébert, 1964), the Centennial Symbol (Stuart Ash, 1965), the Bank of Montreal (Hans Kleefeld, 1966), the National Film Board of Canada (Georges Beaupré, 1968) and the Montreal Olympic Games (Georges Huel, 1972). Such a list is by no means exhaustive but provides a sense of how radically the visual landscape of Canada changed in the period, and the CBC, not to be outdone, changed its logo twice in these years.

From the 1940s to the 1960s, the CBC used two different logos, both of which featured a map of Canada. By 1965, the network needed to signal the arrival of colour television in Canada and launched a contest for employees to propose an appropriate symbol for the transition. The winner was Hubert Tison, newly hired as an animation specialist in the Graphics Department at Radio-Canada in Montreal. Tison proposed a butterfly to represent the network's colour service. Born in 1937, Tison studied graphic arts and animation at the School of Applied Arts in Zurich before moving to London in the early 1960s and attending the Central School of Arts and Crafts. There he studied under Colin Cheesman, who would, of course, later go on to be the Head of Graphic Design at the BBC and who Tison's profile at the Société des designers graphique du Québec (SDGQ) describes as the 'grand pionnier du design graphique pour la télévision en Angleterre' (SDGQ n.d.: n.p.). Tison moved to Paris in 1963 for an internship at ORTF (Office de la radiodiffusion-télévision française) before returning to Montreal for the position at Radio-Canada.

Interviewed by *Ici Radio-Canada: Culture Information* magazine in 1966, Tison explained his choice of the butterfly: 'I chose the butterfly because it, in itself, symbolizes colour. Man has always admired the butterfly for its multitude of colours. Within the electronic frame of the small screen, the butterfly brings grace, lightness, poetry, freshness, finesse, and colour (Treyvauld 1966: 7). Tison's animation features a butterfly unfurling its wings, transforming from a single strip of colour in the centre of the screen to a full image of a butterfly. The design is clearly influenced by, and in dialogue with, John J. Graham's peacock, designed in 1957 for the National Broadcasting Corporation (NBC) in the United States, yet it is far more simplified and abstract. While perhaps unintentional, there is something slightly psychedelic about Tison's butterfly. The butterfly itself would come to be a symbol of the hippie era that would follow, leading to the

Figure 7.8 BBC 2 (1967) Ident. Courtesy BBC.

quip by popular CBC comedians Wayne and Shuster, Canada's equivalent of Morecambe and Wise, that the CBC stood for the 'Cosmic Butterfly Corporation'.[3] While Tison's *papillon* (the rhyme feels deliberate) feels most closely connected to the NBC peacock, it also shares with Sid Sutton and Alan Jeapes' 1967 BBC2 Cube colour ident a fascination with movement, the desire to capture the shift to colour and represent the component colours of RGB technology (see Figure 7.8).

Tison's butterfly was only ever meant to be a temporary identification, and with the advent of full colour service by 1974, the CBC sought a new visual identity. The commission for this went to Burton Kramer, already celebrated for his work on Expo 67 and with the Ontario Educational Communications Authority.[4] One of the central demands of the commission was to develop an integrated visual identity that could be used by both the CBC and by Société Radio-Canada (SRC), as well as Radio Canada International (RCI) and the Northern Service. It needed to be a design that would, adhering to the requirements of the *Official Languages Act* (1970), present English and French on equal footing. Kramer's solution to this was visual: the development of a logo and a graphic identity that had Canada, represented by a 'C', at its centre, but was minimal and geometric beyond that. The CBC logo Kramer designed, as well as the animated station identification that derived from it, consists of a red central C surrounded by a series of radiating orange and yellow half and quarter circles that represent the broadcast signal. As Kramer writes in the network's *Graphic Standards Manual*, 'With this profusion, not to say confusion, of names and initials, it is essential that we have a graphic system that identifies us clearly as one corporation' (CBC 1975, n.p.). For all the seriousness of this pronouncement, and despite the fact that it was referred to at the CBC as 'the gem', Kramer's logo affectionately became known as 'the exploding pizza'. If this irreverent name signals anything, it is the success of Kramer's design, the way in which it so quickly became part of Canadian popular culture. As with Tison's butterfly, there is something quite psychedelic about the five-second-long motion graphic station identification that Kramer developed. Emerging from the very centre of the screen against a blue background, the component quarter, semi and full circles kaleidoscopically expand outward until the logo reaches its full diameter. A horizontal line cuts across its right side forming the central C and a voice-over announces, 'This is CBC' or 'Ici Radio-Canada'. This station identification has come to represent a whole period of Canadian culture, from 1974 to 1985, when a redesign jettisoned everything but the basic shape of Kramer's original.

Rather than delving more deeply into this more recent history of motion graphics at the CBC, I want to return briefly to the heyday of Kramer's design to think further about the connections between motion graphics and national identity. As I hope to have already made clear, there is a way in which graphic design has been central to the formation of modern Canada, however complex and heterogenous the nation may be, in the postwar period. But I think there is a special place motion graphics occupied and occupies in this process, both in terms of when it was unfolding, in real time, in the 1960s and 1970s, and now retrospectively, from the vantage point of a present that, perhaps somewhat nostalgically, looks back on these motion graphics as key symbols of the period. Indeed, retro-nostalgic affection for Kramer's CBC exploding pizza logo is rife, with the CBC offering official licence for it to be reproduced on a wide variety of items, from socks to sweatshirts, tote bags to coffee mugs.

In order to explain how Kramer's CBC ident can bear such symbolic weight, I want to draw briefly on Jan Hadlaw's work on the Contempra telephone. The Contempra was launched in 1967 by Northern Electric, a Canadian-based company that sought to design a stylish and modern telephone. As Hadlaw argues, the sleek horizontality of the Contempra 'was a conspicuous departure from prevailing conventions of North American telephone styling in both its conception and design' and has gone on to become an icon of 'Canadian modern design and . . . a symbol of Canada's identity as a modern nation' (Hadlaw 2019: 240). Although Hadlaw's focus is industrial design and the production of market commodities such as the Contempra, there is certainly a way in which 'design nationalism' and 'the idea that designed objects express national identities and values' (Hadlaw 2019: 241) applies to graphic design and the production of visual objects and identifications as well. Kramer's gem ident for the CBC forms part of a widespread, but not legislatively mandated or centrally controlled, initiative that defined the Canadian 1960s and 1970s and now shapes our visual record of that period. Its kaleidoscopic permutations weirdly offer a visual representation of the process of modern Canada coalescing into shape.[5]

To conclude, I want to return to the central question that has animated my inquiries here: How does the BBC Motion Graphics Archive resonate for viewers outside the United Kingdom? The simple answer is that, due to the export of BBC programming, some of the material in the archive forms a key part of televisual memory for spectators in Canada and other territories where these programmes were broadcast. But the BBC Motion Graphics Archive also serves as an invitation to think about the role that motion graphics have played domestically. I hope to have started the preliminary work for the study of motion graphics in the Canadian context, looking at both how motion graphics at the CBC were influenced by the BBC and how they form part of a wider vibrant graphic design culture in Canada in the 1960s and 1970s. Innovations in motion graphics are perhaps always fuelled by the desire to experiment visually and to harness new technologies, but in Canada at least, these things are shaped and inflected by a wider cultural and political context. As such, the history of motion graphics in Canada is inextricably tied up with the accelerated cultural and economic modernization of the postwar period and the centrality of visual identity to those processes.

Notes

1. In *Hinterland Remixed*, I argue that satire facilitates a different kind of productive estrangement in the Canadian sketch comedy show *SCTV* (1976–84). With *SCTV*, the parody of a small-town television station, complete with station identifications, continuity announcements, programme promos and other televisual elements, both catalogues and itemizes these components and, in a Canadian situation where precious little of this material has been saved, also preserves and archives them as well, even in only satiric form. For more on satire, television and estrangement, see Burke, *Hinterland Remixed*, 88–92.
2. Greg Durrell's 2018 film *Design Canada* details this transformation in detail and includes extended interviews with many of the key figures involved. The Canada Modern website, designed and maintained by Blair Thomson, is a physical and digital archive of Canadian graphic design and has become the key resource for its study. It is available at canadamodern.org.

3. There are extensive references to this joke online, from Wikipedia entries to YouTube comments, but none pin it down to a specific *Wayne and Shuster* episode, many of which have been preserved but which, sadly, remain relatively inaccessible at Library and Archives Canada.
4. For an extensive overview of Kramer's work, see Durrell (2008).
5. Also essential for any understanding of the relationship between graphic design and national identity is Fallan and Lees-Maffei's introduction to *Designing Worlds*.

8 The Old School Cool: Youth Culture and Multiculturalism in Pre-2000s Britain

O HARUNA

Introduction

What does it mean to be British? And how on earth might thirty second, oft-abstract, title sequences tell us? This chapter sets out to explore the BBC's value in terrestrial television channels, and even in contemporary streaming contexts, as a public service provider projecting a vision of nationhood (Malik 2002: 9–10). 'For listeners and viewers at home, the BBC is not just one broadcaster among many: it is the national broadcaster, possessing a quasi-mystical place in the national psyche' (Hendy 2022: xii). Yet, in only two of its nine charters (occurring after 2007; BBC n.d.) in the BBC's 100-year charter history there is an explicit commitment to capture the diversity of its audience. So, what might be inferred about the type of Britain that was being constructed and broadcasted in the years prior?

An analysis of the BBC and Britain's past requires a sensitivity towards the differences in norms and challenges that typified the British socio-landscape. John Twitchin describes the late 1970s being a time of tensions between fears of immigration and difficulties of integration (1978: 5). Change, however contested it was, was nevertheless still desired by a dominant voice, and on the horizon. *The Black and White Minstrel Show*, produced by the BBC, revolved around white men, whose faces were painted with burnt cork, performing African American songs, using, what would be described today as, racial slurs. Isolated from America's Civil Rights movement, the programme enjoyed twenty years of broadcasting in the United Kingdom until it was discontinued in 1978 a few years after the 1976 Race Relations Act formally stood against racial discrimination. Despite being popular in the late 1970s with a viewership of 6–7 million people, '[t]he once top-rated show was banned from the small screen' over concerns for racist undertones (*Timeshift: Black and White Minstrels Revisited* 2005). Though Britain was waking up to the quickly shifting sociopolitical landscape, the degrees of tolerance demanded and expected by the differentiated audiences were by no means equal.

By the 1980s the colour bar was waning, though the exclusionary practices it brought had already forced racialized minorities into their own autonomous spaces. These black and Asian leisure centres, Back suggests, were more inclusive than their counterparts, enabling white adolescents to proactively support a redefining of Britishness (Back 1996: 185). Driven by increasingly popular reggae, soul and then rap music, the dancefloor movement became a melting point for all ethnicities in their youths (Back 1996: 216), often finding a voice outside mainstream parameters in pirate broadcasts (Back 1996). With youths sharing culture in various ways their elders did not, youth politics was unsurprisingly more progressive, standing against social injustice boldly through the infamous 1981 and 1985 riots of Brixton and Broadwater Farm. As a likely result, British television channels seemed to invest more of their energies in race relations programming such as the BBC TV Continuing Education and Training Initiative's five-year Mosaic project launched in 1989, which resulted in the anti-racist shows of *Black and White Media Shows* (I and II, 1984/5), *Living Islam* (1993) and *Racism and*

Comedy (Malik 2002: 52). Though documentaries of the era often leaned into the unconscious and biased narrative that fixed an association of racialized minorities with problem contexts (Malik 2002: 67), good intent was clear and notable, offering promise of a better future. In any account the 1980s were a 'critical decade' (Bailey & Hall in Malik 2002: 17) for alleviating racial tensions and discrimination.

Beginning with title sequences of *The Lenny Henry Show* (1984, 1985 & 1988) as one of the loci of (overt) multiculturalism, the other is *DEF II*'s (1988 & 1990) youth programming, covertly normalizing black & Asian culture within popular-culture contexts. These motion graphic title sequences, available to view on the BBC Motion Graphics Archive, will demonstrate how visual representations of multiculturalism were mediated through ideas of urban youth culture to forecast a harmonious and inclusive future. Following this is a brief outlining of the strategies and reflections of ex-BBC Motion Designers in relation to diversity within their title sequence work at the BBC in the pre-2000s. In each case, key works of the early career designers are spotlighted as symbols of the different philosophies that guided them to award-winning success. Overall, this chapter will demonstrate that although pre-2000s BBC had yet to develop a consolidated stance on progressive representation, the young designers who did ought to be praised, remembered and celebrated.

On-screen representation – Motion design

Standing out of this backdrop of youth culture and diversity is 1984's *The Lenny Henry Show* (1984), following in 1985 (see Figure 8.1), as a narrative-based situational comedy centred on Delbert Wilkins (played by Lenny Henry). Differing from the anecdotes of Henry's life, the 1985 and 1987 iterations of the

Figure 8.1 *The Lenny Henry Show* (1985) title sequence. Courtesy BBC.

programme explored Wilkins's escapades of maintaining a cool edge and balancing family dynamics while connecting itself to the pirate radio zeitgeist, dodging both the law and legitimacy in the process. Written by Stan Hey and Andrew Nickolds, two white Cambridge University graduates, the show is described by the duo as a preoccupation with the working class rather than race (Medhurst 1989: 55), from which Hey, Nickolds and Henry all have experience. Nevertheless, Henry feels 'a lot of material is generated by him' (Medhurst 1989: 55; Pines 1992: 213) using his lived experiences to modify plots, behaviours and deploy slang (Pines 1992). Any notion of multiculturalism here is caught between the heritage of the writers, Henry's West Indian roots and *The Lenny Henry Show*'s London setting. What better site could there be to home these inextricable struggles between voices, ideals and locales than the ironic and irresolute world of comedy?

Humour provides a polarizing and deceptive ground where any claims of offence can be dispelled with the absence of overt aggression and laughter might erupt from the confrontation of the absurdity of one's own politics (Carroll 2014: 9). But it also has its risks, holding the potential to further alienate those it seeks to liberate (Carroll 2014: 32; 77). This uncertainty of laughing at or laughing with Henry's performances of race (Hall 2003; Da Costa 2007: 53; Hall 2013: 264) is exactly what makes readings of the clown as a social delinquent stereotype (Hall 2003: 91; Da Costa 2007: 53; Malik 2002: 67; Back 1996: 45–7) interestingly ambivalent, resisting negative ascriptions as much as it supports them. Regardless of one's stance on what was being signified through race in the various series of *The Lenny Henry Show*, the programme stood out for its award-winning stylistic bravura and positive cultural references.

Designed by Paul D'Auria, the final title sequence, aired in 1987 (see Figure 8.2), found a middle ground between its 1984's live-action-driven approach and 1985's highly illustrated style predecessors. The forty-seven-second opening reuses 1985's hip-hop backing track with Henry-as-Wilkins rapping. The first shot

Figure 8.2 *The Lenny Henry Show* (1988) title sequence. Courtesy BBC.

is a radio tuning out of different stations until it finds Wilkins's pirate frequency, along with visualizations of what sights might accompany the sounds. This title sequence thus places the audience in the position of a devoted Wilkins fan, seeking out the secret station, and letting their imagination run free once the session has started. Motion graphics sit on the periphery, literally creating a decorative frame from which snippets of Delbert, dressed in a bright-coloured zoot suit, as he travels through Brixton. Here, Hip-hop supersedes jazz to become the anthem of cool youth and urban identities, and of course, blackness itself. It never shakes off its proximity to Wilkins's pirate station, and so recycles myths of criminality (Malik 2002: 16; 78–9) in a comedic ambivalence of a Robin Hood persona. Constructed and illustrative motion graphics are also overlaid against live-action sequences and are generally confined to literalizing Delbert's rap lyrics, reinforcing basic hip-hop imagery more generally. For example, bouncing words metamorphosize into music notes, equalizers rhythmically move up and down and photographic images are collaged together with sketch-like filters, always maintaining a choreographic flow that seems to be innate to everything Wilkins performs or produces.

The technical mastery of motion graphics offered in the title sequences as a whole mixed with hip-hop's, as a genre, relative newness, tie youth, the city and blackness into symbols of future thinking and burgeoning society. So impressive was its execution that the title sequence won a Design and Art Direction Wood Pencil for Television Graphics in 1988. While Delbert Wilkins and his show only offer a single instance and identity of racialized territories, the limited representation of/interactions with racialized minorities might have led audiences of its time to inflate such visions to generalizations. Nevertheless, *The Lenny Henry Show*'s place on the BBC may have assured the nation that diversity is indeed a part of British fabric. Not only that, but Henry, feeling it was his own programme (Pines 1992: 213), held a candlelight that diverse representation might be more greatly owned by those it captured.

The late 1980s, when *The Lenny Henry Show* came to its end, saw an evolution of familiar fast-paced motion graphics, dynamic filming and multicultural motifs; this time, these elements were more pronounced but cryptically frenzied in the rise of youth television. As commissioning editor for Youth Programmes at Channel 4, Janet Street-Porter had begun to recognize young adults as a distinct market different to children and their parents. Reportedly believing the young adult market was characterized by an openness to new ideas, and a hunger for unconventional television (Lury 2001: 29–30), she produced *Network 7* (1987–8). This magazine-format programme, aimed at sixteen to twenty-four-year-olds (*Network 7* 1987, Episode 1), pioneered British Youth Television, ensuring 'youth' would become replaced with the *yoof* symbolizing urban customs (such as slang) centrality to youth coolness (Lury 2001). So, when Janet Street-Porter moved to the BBC and became the Editor of Youth and Entertainment at BBC, her visionary approach to programming was described as more progressive than her peers in off-screen and on-screen contexts, placing a celebratory emphasis on designers' differences and diversity alongside using female-led teams (Almeida 2023). Consequently, *DEF II* (1988–94) championed ideals of fast-paced, cosmopolitan lifestyles, building on the popularity of the *Network 7*.

DEF II was a magazine-format television programme offering reports on popular culture (music and fashion), narrative-based content (animation) and trending consumerist lifestyles responding to a newfound importance of exchanging knowledge of consumerist artefacts rather than personal thoughts and feelings (Lury 2001: 33) amongst youth circles. In a post-modern sense, identity was evolving away from individual practices of producing products and towards collective practices of consuming them. This, combined with the overlapping sensibilities (dance, fashion and music) of working-class children who had grown up together, irrespective of race (Back 1996: 186), resulted in a collage of ideas and symbols that reflected various cultures that take place across *DEF II*'s episodes and it's 1988 and 1990 title sequences.

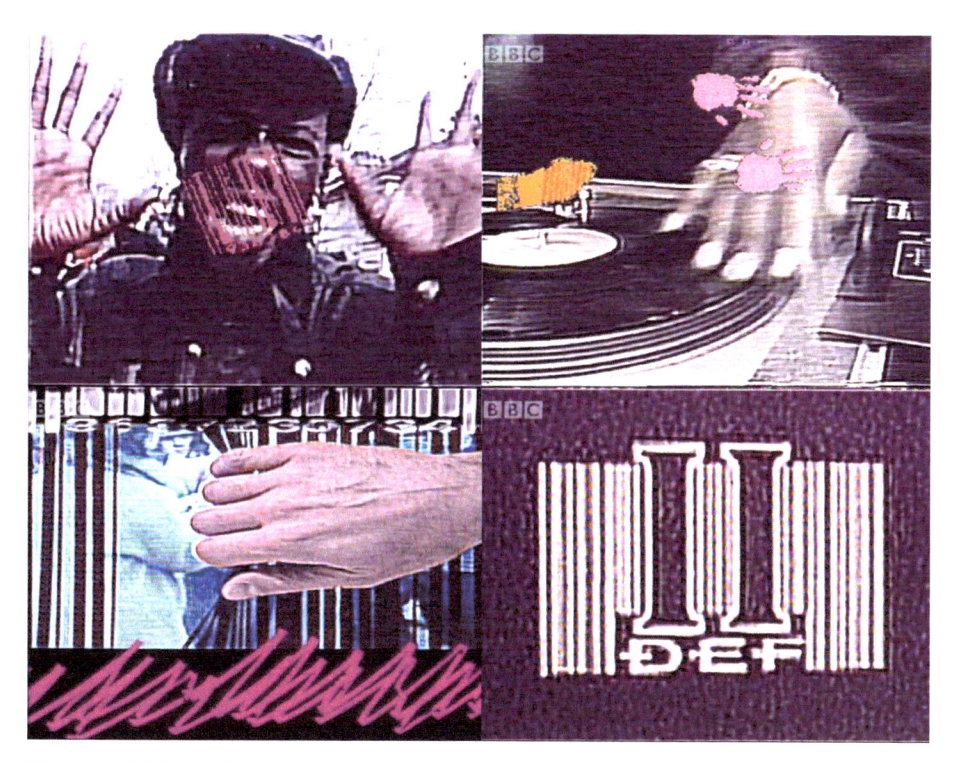

Figure 8.3 *DEF II* (1988) title sequence. Courtesy BBC.

DEF II's 1988 title sequence, designed by Lucy Blakstad and Harry Dorrington (see Figure 8.3), features an assemblage of heavily edited and filtered live-action footage of male and female models wearing stylized clothes, snipped recreations of horror film tropes, musicians (almost all of whom appear to be racialized minorities) and highly abstracted, brightly coloured illustrations. *DEF II*'s signature crosshairs are animated, appearing throughout. Jane Wyatt-Brooks's 1990's iteration creates a sense of direction and focus in their version (see Figure 8.4). This time, a cross-hair-head stick man runs through a corridor of large screens towards, and eventually out of, a DEF II doorway. The television screens all play the same imagery, an extreme close-up of lips, hands and eyes, appearing one after another, and likely a subtle way of suggesting sexualized femininity (through lipstick and long painted nails) in line with current and *youthful* trends. A variety of brightly coloured patterns and drawings overlay all of the screens, constantly changing after a few brief moments. In both cases of the title sequences, *DEF II*'s iconic barcode-infused logo appears at their close, fixing ideas of the consumerist commodities, not only as the heart of the programme but also as the heart of youth culture.

Defining both of *DEF II*'s title sequences is an overload of information, a distinctive characteristic rooted in *Network 7* (Lury 2001), consequently enabling readings of the two programmes to be shared. Though the dynamism from *The Lenny Henry Show* feels evident here, *editing* is not working towards clarifying a narrative, but rather, reinforcing the busyness of popular magazines and their corresponding television format. 'In relation to Generation X, the busy screen and information overload implied . . . that they, as an audience, were self-consciously media literate' (Lury 2001: 32). The frenzied visual spectacle of the *DEF II* title sequences also reflected the irreverent attitudes the wider programme, itself, held as well as the varied tones of each of its reports and imported content it housed. In a different vein, these title sequences tacitly recognized that television-watching (for young adults) was forming a hydra head of activities, such as talking

Figure 8.4 *DEF II* (1990) title sequence. Courtesy BBC.

Figure 8.5 *Dance Energy Lift Off* (1993) title sequence. Courtesy BBC.

on the phone, doing homework and playing games (Lury 2001: 32). Thus, demanding more attention through more complex layering of imagery might ensure youths' imaginations were arrested. Clear readings of multiculturalism here are deceptive. Arguments for it rest between the musical underbelly of youth culture and the (black) musical icons that appear for brief moments in *DEF II*'s title sequences (especially in *Dance Energy Lift Off* [1993] (see Figure 8.5). Furthermore, suggestions of its meaning are equally in tension, with exoticist perceptions of a black spectacle on one side, and the sincere celebration of a trending British sub-cultures on the other.

Off-screen representation – Motion designers

While *The Lenny Henry Show* exemplifies how fictional narratives could create spaces for title sequences to explore the themes of race and sub-culture, and *DEF II* pitched itself towards non-fictive reporting, these were not the only spaces. The accounts of ex-BBC Designers describe how their heritage played a role in the politics of design, strategies of representation and the weight of responsibility in giving a voice to the underrepresented. Extracts from interviews of five black, and Asian designers from BBC's broadcasting departments of the 1980s and 1990s demonstrate how rich creative outputs manifest from teams' collective identities and the unique backgrounds of the individuals who make them.

Ruhi Hamid, originally from Tanzania in East Africa, came to the United Kingdom in her childhood with a passion for the creative arts. After graduating from the Royal College of Art, Hamid designed for a couple of studios, including the renowned Studio Dunbar. After, she joined the BBC News Graphics Department, attracted by legends of quality training, as one of its few female racialized minorities in 1985. Driven by a concern that people like herself could 'be seen as odd, as others, as something weird, or something to be ridiculed, or something to be laughed at, or something to be dismissed' (Hamed 2023).

> I think everything you do can have a political or a social edge to it and because that's how I was always guided by my political principles; I couldn't divorce that from my creative work. . . . So that's what my graphics was all about in the graphic design department at the BBC. (Hamed 2023)

1993's *Gardeners' World* (see Figure 8.6) and 1995's *QED* (Quad Et Demonstrandum; what was to be shown) (see Figure 8.7) are two examples of Hamid's title sequences that deploy her principles. In either example, the featured actors include racialized minorities alongside white people despite the programmes revolving around gardening and science education, rather than race relations. Hoping to increase the visibility of underrepresented groups outside of niches and stereotypes, Hamid still considers how graphics, filmmaking and storytelling can shed light on overlooked groups of people. As a result of these experiences, Hamid became an award-winning independent documentary filmmaker, working with Channel 4, Al Jazeera and the BBC.

One of the ex-BBC designers, Hamid, spoke highly of working with Morgan Almeida. Born in Botswana and joining in the BBC in the mid-to-late 1980s, Almeida keenly remembers the difficulties he and other colleagues faced in overcoming stereotypes and suspicion pitted against racialized minorities in on-screen and off-screen contexts. Concluding direct challenges to more conservative representation would be discredited, Almeida, much like Hamid, adopted covert strategies in offering diverse representation.

> Most of the departments I worked in were open-minded, but some upper management members were less supportive of change. . . . At the time, there was no official strategy for representation but rather individual people seeking to do it themselves. . . . Essentially, we had to sneak in small degrees of change at the time. (Almeida 2023)

Figure 8.6 *Gardeners' World* (1993) title sequence. Courtesy BBC.

Figure 8.7 *QED* (1995) title sequence. Courtesy BBC.

Figure 8.8 *Sportsnight* (1990) title sequence. Courtesy BBC.

Contrasting with this general experience, BBC's 1990 flagship weekend show, *Sportsnight*, might have been one of the few cases where diversity could have been expected. Seeking to match the dynamism and excitement of the sports audiences expected, Almeida and Tim Platt broke the dominating mould of masculine sports and the impersonal 'monolithic 3D logos' that featured in sports title sequences prior (Almeida 2023) (see Figure 8.8). Including vibrant colours, a variety of races amongst men and women, and a broader catalogue of sports, the duo, along with post-production expert Linden Gall, delivered a warm exhilaration in their title sequence. After working on a number of BBC title sequences for programmes that explored culture, disability and ageism, Almeida worked for other famous news outlets including CNN and Al Jazeera.

Joining the BBC in 1988, after Almeida, was John Herbert, a black British Olympian who won gold in the 1986 Commonwealth Games and continued to compete in Olympic-level events throughout his time in the BBC. While freelancing at, the now defunct, London Weekend Television, Herbert was told that, despite being overqualified for long-term graphic design broadcasting roles, he was unlikely to get them. Spurred on by these suggestive remarks, Herbert pulled his sporting philosophy of pursuing world-class standards into his design work, finding permanent employment with the BBC. Recalling how support was offered in the fortunes of individual effort rather than by systematic defaults, Herbert highlights:

> I was lucky to meet a lady called Rosalind Dallas . . . as well as a guy called Roderick Ellis but Rosalind . . . helped me to hit the ground running. The first thing I worked on was Juke Box Jury. . . . Rosalind took me under her wing and showed me the way. (Herbert 2023)

Figure 8.9 *Juke Box Jury* (1990) title sequence. Courtesy BBC.

Much like Hamid's approaches, Herbert and Dallas worked on *Juke Box Jury* (1990) (see Figure 8.9), a programme centred around predicting the latest music's success or failure, offering a diverse range of young people dressed to symbolize different music trends. With greater confidence and experience, Herbert became responsible for the servicing of various programmes' titles, graphics and overlays, including *Match of the Day*, *Sportsnight*, the 1992 BBC Sport logo, and *Tomorrow's World*. After leaving the BBC, Herbert's gold standards led him to win awards (PromaxBDA & Monitor) at Meridian Broadcasting (now known as ITV), retiring from sport into coaching.

Forming 'part of a new wave of designers that came with the technology' (Mitchell 2023) in the 1990s, black British Paul Mitchell was hired by the BBC in 1994. At the end of his studies at Newham College of Art and Design, Mitchell, who was headhunted for a BBC internship, stayed on for a full-time job due to his familiarity with new software and Apple Macs. Though Mitchell was aware of the lack of non-white designers, editors and managers, he noticed a new wave of young and diverse workforce was being cultivated in the 1990s.

> But it wasn't really about colour, it was about culture. . . . We're excited to be here and create things, collectively hang out and have fun. It made a really great group of people socially, and work wise we started to really grow. (Mitchell 2023)

Upon contemplation, Mitchell mentioned that there were certain genres where audiences would be more receptive to seeing a greater diversity of people, or even expectant. Title sequences and programmes that involved sport and music are two major examples, both of which straddle the line between myths of musicality (i.e. primitivism) and athleticism (i.e. animality; Shohat and Stam 2014: 137–8) and adequate representation. In the case of BBC Sport – Mitchell's *Olympic Games* (2004) title sequences were executed with so much splendour that it earned a BAFTA nomination (see Plate 14.4). Mitchell's later work, Creative Directing and Directing in America won him numerous awards and nominations for PromaxBDA, BAFTAs and Emmys, resulting in membership of the prestigious Directors Guild of America.

One of the new staff Mitchell recalled joining shortly after him was black British Mark Walters, another student of the Newham College of Art and Design. Taking a different route, however, Walters worked in industry between trialling his own company and freelancing, specializing in interactive, digital content. After helping create the first Yellow Pages website and BT website, Walters's talent was discovered by Mitchell at an interactive kiosk showcase in London leading to his employment in 1996.

> I did the BBC HD live broadcast opening titles. . . which was the World Cup in 2006, and those World Cup titles won me the BAFTA. . . and that particular broadcast, as I say, was the first [of it's kind]. (Walters 2023)

In reflecting on his contribution and approach to the 2006 *World Cup* titles, Walters highlighted that his characteristic boldness and colours stemmed from street art and graffiti. In the world of title sequences, where content is often abstract, and highly symbolic, he wonders what form multiculturalism should take if any. In some cases, he asks, 'why should you know whether it's black or not, just it's just excellent' (Walters 2023). Described as having a career of firsts, Walters and his colleagues worked with/on the first versions of Adobe software, the first electronic programme guide (EPG), BBC's first HD broadcast and the first television-internet shopping service. Taking his insights from BBC, and later, Virgin Media, Mark reinvested his pursuits of youth creating his own design brand: Mark One Group winning BAFTAs and PromaxBDA awards along the way.

The experiences of BBC's multicultural talent are stories of resounding success. The BBC of the 1980s and 1990s, despite its fame for reporting news and politics, was generally considered an apolitical workplace without discussions of race, gender and surrounding tensions. In one view, the supposed overlooking of a designer's ethnicity enabled a spotlight to shine on their merit and nothing else. But in the other, colour-blind and genderless approaches to workplace dynamics only enabled discriminatory practices and inequalities to remain unchallenged and unexposed. As a result, this transitionary period, for some of the designers, was painful but necessary to birth a workplace more open to different people cultures and ideas. In the anonymized words of such designers, 'the older generation . . . were the first guard, and in any war, the first guard always gets shot down first' (Anonymized 2023), and their sacrifices should not be forgotten.

Conclusion

The world of broadcasting was undoubtedly different to what we can expect today. Explicit statements about anti-racist policies and targeted calls for diverse workforces and programming were nowhere to be found. Despite this, testimonials from the growing young, multicultural workforce of the 1980s and 1990s were, overall, positive. Unanimously, the motion designers I interviewed either recognized the opportunities the BBC afforded them or how individual staff offered nurturing mentorship beyond the demands of their role. Their individual mentalities ranged from a conscious self-awareness of their racial identities to the negotiations of how title sequences might support a more inclusive agenda. In rare cases, television programmes of the 1980s demanded minority representation in their title sequences to ensure they accurately conveyed the themes and characters of the programme. *The Lenny Henry Show* was one such example, exemplifying how multiculturalism could be engaged with outside of solemn, factual, television, using playful, technically exceptional motion graphics as a remedy. *DEF II* offered a counterpoint of how multiculturalism could feature indirectly in title sequences, only appreciated and observable with a certain socio-temporal knowledge.

By the 1990s, individuals within the BBC used covert strategies, both known and unbeknownst to themselves, to draw out their unique identities and graphical talents into a variety of title sequences. By the 2000s, the BBC's charter formally recognized the need to proactively seek multicultural and multiethnic representation on- and off-screen, forever changing its programme content, strategies and the opportunities their accompanying title sequences. Since then, other British companies and organizations have also grown more sensitive to problems surrounding diversity.

In 2018, the Design Council's research concluded: '[t]he design economy employs a slightly higher proportion of people from Black, Asian and Minority Ethnic (BAME) groups than are employed in the wider UK economy' (Design Council 2018: 17). UK Screen Alliance's 2019 report highlights that within the UK's Video Effects (VFX), post-production and animation industry meet or are above average in terms of workplace diversity against the national average of 14 per cent as well as within the wider Film and Television sector. Though these design, VFX, post-production and animation-related statistics, when cross-referenced against the 2021 census (Office for National Statistics 2022), suggest BAME designers are still underrepresented by 2 to 6 per cent. More problematically, UK Screen Alliance goes further to point out that the BAME members are particularly underrepresented in creative roles and senior management roles (2019). Though there is still work to be done in investigating the roots and incentives in fostering diverse workplaces, with the increasingly diverse workforces the BBC is continuing to recruit, visions of race and multiculturalism might fully extend from the surface of the screen to beyond it, pulling a reality from fabricated images of a Britain where no one is the same and everyone is equal.

Section II

9 Revolutionary practices
No width, no speed
GRAHAM MCCALLUM

Introduction

If there was a single moment of realization that a big change was coming, this was it. Sometime at the beginning of the 1980s, a memo went around the BBC's Graphic Design Department inviting designers to a demonstration of a new piece of technology. A 'Digital Drawing Machine' had been developed at Kingswood Warren, the BBC's research and development facility. It seemed the equipment was a by-product of a failed project to try to digitally patch out the ads that were appearing around the barriers at football grounds in breach of the BBC's strictly no-advertising policy. Footballers, it was discovered, had the annoying habit of running about in front of the ads, which proved to be an insoluble problem.

Nick Tanton was the brilliant young tech genius in charge of the project, and he was there to present the spin-off that had resulted from his research, a digital drawing machine which they had christened *Eric*. On the day, only a handful of designers turned up. Before them was *Eric*, which turned out to be a large ceramic tablet about the size of a small coffee table, so heavy it had taken two people to lift it into place. In a holder on the side of the tablet and attached by a wire was a sort of pen. On the floor beside this setup was a suitcase-sized computer with a port to carry a 6 inch floppy disc and beyond the tablet was a digital television.

What happened next was a genuinely astonishing moment. Tanton picked up the pen and proceeded to draw on the tablet, the result appearing on the screen two feet away. It was astonishing because nobody had ever remotely thought that anything like this could be possible. It seemed like magic. We felt like a remote tribe that had just been shown a mirror. I remember one of our number, to much laughter, saying, 'This is definitely flying in the face of nature.'

We all scrambled to have a go and it proved to be totally intuitive. We instinctively looked at the screen, not the tip of the pen; it felt completely natural. From a menu printed along the top of the tablet, a whole geometry set could be selected, and brushes of different sizes could be used to draw freehand with colours selected from a pop-up palette that appeared onscreen. Areas could be filled with graduated or plain colour fields, and things could be resized and moved at will. The brilliant thing was that there wasn't a keyboard in sight; we were operating a computer without even being aware that we were.

After the excitement died down, the inevitable question arose, what would we use it for? The edges of the lines were pixilated and appeared jaggy and crucially there was no type. It was almost as if we'd taken a step back to earlier days when we would prepare still graphics on cardboard to be placed on caption stands in the studio. This was just the electronic update.

Things were about to change rapidly, however, and there is no doubt after meeting *Eric* we sensed the tectonic plates for the BBC's Graphic Design Department were about to shift.

Production factory

I joined the BBC as a graphic design assistant in the mid-1960s. The Design Department was housed in the Scenery Block, which was stuck on the side of the famous Television Centre doughnut, the world's first purpose-built television facility. Consequently, the Design Department was the first group of designers specifically assembled to service the emerging industry. There were no courses in television design in the colleges and universities, and so graphic designers, in particular, found themselves creating the packaging and promotion of programmes and distinguishing the BBC through building an identity for the entire organization. In effect they were inventing the very grammar of television.

On the third floor of the Scenery Block were the production designers who were top dog in terms of hierarchy. They worked at large drawing desks surrounded by references and sketches stuck on the walls. Samples of all the various materials needed for the final construction were to be found in a special samples room. On the floor below were the Graphic Design Department, designers' offices, admin, a lab for developing photographs taken by the 'Toggies' the staff photographers, a print room and a rostrum camera unit. Everything needed to support the creative effort was in place.

Also in the Scenery Block was a library which, apart from books, had thousands of carefully indexed reference pictures. Images covering just about every subject could be found. There were also small props, an Aladdin's cave of both antique and more modern objects –a huge collection of packaging for example. There was also an armoury, full of guns and assorted weaponry, which was always locked. To borrow from there, it had to be done under the full supervision of the armourer.

Running the full height of the building was the scenic artist's studio. The walls were hung with huge canvases that slid up and down on pulleys, the bottom edge disappearing into a slot on the floor. This was to ensure that the artist could just stand and paint at floor level. This was always a great place to visit with amazing skills on display. Life-size street scenes, rooftop views, huge skies and forests would emerge with amazing speed. The scenic artists themselves, their overalls always covered in paint, worked on a floor that resembled a giant Jackson Pollock canvas, where they flicked their brushes. Their studio overlooked the construction workshop where the scenery was built – a world of noise. Whistling and shouting men, with their radios blaring, and the constant sound of banging, sawing and drilling round the clock. This was a twenty-four-hour operation, the eight studios having to be constantly fed with new sets while old sets were dismantled and stored.

In the main building the makeup and wardrobe departments were sited. This was in order to be close to the actors for fittings and dressing. Costume designers made exceptional costumes with a full staff of specialist seamstresses and tailors. The finished work was stored for reuse and conservation. The makeup department did not only the day-to-day studio makeup but specialist prosthetics and realistic wounds.

Off-site was the visual effects workshop, located in a building in nearby Acton. All sorts of specialist props and models were made there, as well as various pyrotechnic projects. the Television Centre was a well-organized factory where everything was on hand to make the programmes watched by millions. The architect Graham Dawburn had created a building that was not only iconic but also designed to link all the different disciplines together to make a single creative force. Being part of such an operation was an enormous privilege and incredibly exciting.

Forces of design

I initially shared an office with Alan Jeapes and a young Martin Lambie-Nairn (then just plain Martin Lambie), who, like me, was fresh out of Art College. There was no sign that he was going to become such a major force in changing the face of television. It was Lambie-Nairn who realized in the face of great opposition that TV was a brand just like any other product and could be sold as such. Those against him thought of themselves as auteurs and creative artists untainted by cheap commercialism. The success of Lambie-Nairn's insights became apparent as tens and then hundreds of TV channels came on air, each needing their own distinctive look.

Jeapes was a larger-than-life character. He was a big man, an ex-paratrooper and rugby player who had joined the BBC from advertising so was always immaculately suited, showing just the right amount of cuff. You could always hear him coming before he moved into view. He was one of the individuals who wanted to change the department from being a bunch of gifted amateurs to a more professional agency.

Both men have now sadly passed on, but their legacy remains. Jeapes's titles for *EastEnders* are probably the most famous on British television. Although they have passed through several versions, they remain essentially unchanged from the original concept, a perfect example of how a striking visual image supported by a memorable piece of music combines to provide something unique that can worm its way into the public consciousness. They also embody the great change in production techniques that have taken place.

Jeapes's idea was to start the sequence close-up on the River Thames near the fictional East End borough of Walford. The camera would then spiral out to encompass nearly the whole of the Greater London area. The only way to achieve this was by creating a giant piece of artwork, which he did. Ariel images taken by the RAF were patched together, and the seams were artfully blended. The whole thing must have been about 12 feet square and was filmed on a rotating rig. Just before I resigned from the BBC in 1985, I remember seeing this huge piece of work rather ignobly tossed into a skip behind the Scenery Block. What a sad end for a bit of TV history, but the new production techniques no longer needed this sort of solution. A new version of the titles was created in 2000 copying the old, but this time produced and edited entirely digitally. The newly built Millennium Dome was added and drifting clouds pass through the frame as the camera pulls out. As the architecture of London changes, new buildings such as the Shard and the Gherkin are added as the titles are regularly updated. More recently (BBC 2022) a one-off striking version of the familiar end credits was aired to promote the final episode of the critically acclaimed series *Frozen Planet II*, highlighting the warming climate and rising sea levels that could one day affect us.

There were only two channels when I started work as a graphic design assistant, BBC and Independent Television (ITV). By then, television was in nearly every home, and the programmes they produced had huge audiences. The shape of the picture, not quite square and not quite oblong with its rounded corners, was dictated by the need to create a vacuum in a glass tube, and this was the optimum shape. The picture itself was quite low resolution being transmitted on only 405 lines in black and white. On top of that many viewers put up with a pretty appalling reception. The commonest interference was 'Snow', the image speckled with white dots that we now know is the background radiation of the universe left by the Big Bang itself. Roll bars were another common problem, black bars slowly traversing down the screen. Sometimes pictures would just unaccountably just twitch. It was a common sight to see the side of the television set being given a hefty thump in the vain hope this would solve the problem. Interestingly, research showed that people developed a high tolerance for distorted pictures, but the slightest distortion of sound was unacceptable

Screen typographic craft

The fundamental task of the graphic designer was to put words on screen – What's it called, who is in it, what time is it on and so on. Legibility and readability were the keywords when specifying type. This meant size was crucial. Anything less than 24pt type on a 12"×9" caption, the standard format, was deemed unacceptable. The department had an interesting link with the past from the days before the Television Centre was built. Dan Ginger, Jack Harris and John McWatt, universally known as 'Mac', all shared a room. They were not graphic designers but lettering artists and sign painters. The three of them used to dress in artists' smocks and the tools of their trade were all around them. Brushes of every kind stood in glass jars, shelves held pots and tubes of paint and racks held cards. They all worked at easels, their wrists resting on mall sticks to steady their hands. As with the scenic artists, the floor was speckled with paint where they flicked their brushes. Their lettering skills were exceptional. One of their numbers, I think it was Ginger, had started his career in the silent film industry lettering dialogue cards. Another link with the past was 'The Maseeley Boys', housed in an adjacent room. They operated the Maseeley Press, a system for transferring type onto card by placing a thin plastic sheet of film onto the card, composing brass type on top, and then applying heat and pressure. The type selection was limited, but this was useful when large amounts of words were required such as for end credits. There was a certain tension between the old guard from Alexandra Palace and the new young Turks recruited from the top art schools which sometimes bubbled over. The main office across the corridor was run by Alf. He used to answer the phone at regular intervals in his loud voice with ''Ello, Graphics'. This used to drive Jeapes mad because he felt that this belittled the work we were doing and lacked professionalism. One day he stormed into Alf's office and said, 'For God's sake man, when you answer the phone could you say "Good morning, Graphic Design Department. How can I help you?"' Jeapes returned to our office rather flushed and sat down only to hear the phone ring in Alf's office to be answered with ''Ello, graphics'.

Forging ahead

The world was changing rapidly. In 1967 *Our World* was transmitted. It was the world's first satellite link-up transmitted across five continents and seen by millions. I remember watching it at home. Each country was given a five-minute slot to showcase their wares. Predictably a parade of national costumes and folk dancing followed together with a kind of tourist eye-view of the country in question. Then it came to Britain's turn, and there they were, the Beatles singing *All You Need is Love*. It seemed as if Britain was the coolest country on earth.

The creative mood of the 1960s was sweeping through the department. People were experimenting with all sorts of new techniques and forging a new ideas-based approach to design. The Holy Grail was of course the title sequence – thirty seconds of picture and music designed to sum up the spirit of a programme in a memorable way. For inspiration we looked across the Atlantic to the great Saul Bass. He had single-handedly invented titles for the feature film industry. On a visit to London, one of our most pioneering designers, Bernard Lodge, had acted as his host. Lodge had an extraordinary creative mind. For example, he had developed a technique by coating an animation cel with black ink and then scratching it back with a sharpened brush handle to create a convincing wood engraving look. He used this on titles for the BBC production of *A Tale of Two Cities* (1965). His masterpiece was the title for *Dr Who* (1963) (see Figure 6.1). The only artwork was a card with the programme title printed on it. He then used a 'Howl round' effect by pointing one TV camera at its own output. The resulting abstract pattern seemed to make it look as if we were passing through aeons of space and time. Combined with unearthly electronic music composed at the radiophonic workshop by Delia Derbyshire (1965), the titles were the signal for millions of children to dive behind the couch where they would peep out waiting for the Daleks to show up.

During the 1960s, the Graphic Design Department helped to establish the BBC as a progressive and creative force. In 1968 colour television was launched together with a new channel, BBC2, 625-lines replaced the old 405-lines system. The bold black-and-white designs were now replaced by more subtle and complex design solutions. By the 1970s work practices underwent a change. The Maseeley Press was gone, the signwriters had retired and phototypesetting had arrived. Photosetting companies like Face and Alphabet were highly lucrative enterprises and for the first time had a resource which the BBC didn't have. Now designers could fax the copy of the words to be set and select a typeface from the free catalogues supplied by the companies. These contained hundreds of typefaces in all weights, and new fonts were being added monthly. The competition was fierce, salesmen prowled the corridors and were always on hand to buy a round in the bar. It was no longer necessary to specify type by point size, type was specified on the phone, and within the hour, a bike messenger would arrive with the artwork ready.

Other external resources, which the BBC didn't have, were increasingly being employed both technical and human. Film compositing was now an essential element of many sequences. Companies like Roy Turk in Soho had Ariel image systems, which could combine multiple images. Animators, art workers and specialists of all kinds were being hired on a project-by-project basis. Change was in the air.

I remember chatting once with an engineer. He made a rather prophetic statement, which neither of us understood the implications of. Drawing a graph on a bit of paper he marked the width of videotape in descending order on the Y axis from 2-inch to 1-inch to ¾-inch down to . . . . On the X axis he marked the speed of the tape past the recording heads. This was getting slower. Extending the coordinates, the logic was the lines would eventually cross at no width and no speed. 'I can't see how that is possible,' he said and neither could I. Of course, it did happen and happen very quickly, which brings us back to 'Eric'.

The digital revolution

After further development, 'Eric' was sold under licence to Logica, the software development company. They renamed it 'Flair', which always sounded to me like the name of a suburban hairdressing saloon. They sold a couple, but the real story was happening elsewhere. Quantel had launched 'Paintbox' on the market, a much more advanced machine and one that could be directly plumbed in the suites in television studios. This became the standard graphic equipment and was a mixed blessing for graphic designers because it overnight effectively turned them from designers into operators. Producers and directors discovered the delights of back-seat driving. They had no idea how it worked so their instructions were often prefaced with 'Can it do that?' In frustration I heard one put-upon soul reply, 'Why don't you ask it?' The directors' natural instinct to direct everything in sight was given a new lease of life. 'Make that a bit bigger, can you make the lettering yellow? Can you move that a bit to the right?' It was depressing. The Paintbox was especially useful for news and current affairs. The Paintbox operators got caught up in the rush to get stories on air as soon as they broke. One monumental blunder occurred when the news of the Chernobyl disaster broke. One of the inventive Paintbox designers had found a picture of a Nuclear Power Station, turned it into a ruin and superimposed a mushroom cloud over it. This went out on air, and there was a furious enquiry into how this had happened. Newspapers were calling in to ask how the BBC had obtained the photograph. If I'm not mistaken, I think the incident was even raised in Parliament – an early example of fake news.

On another occasion, my friend Paul D'Auria was working on a story with the headline 'East German Spy Scandal'. As no picture of the spy was available, he took the usual solution of taking a picture from a newspaper, turning it into a silhouette and sticking a question mark on it. Unfortunately, when it went on air, it could be clearly seen that it was a picture of Robert Maxwell. Even more unfortunately, Robert Maxwell was watching the news. Paul had retired to the BBC Club and was nursing a pint when he saw the florid face of the Head of News weaving towards him through the crowd. He grabbed Paul by the lapels and shouted in his face, 'You call Robert Maxwell and tell him I don't like being called a C**t.' Happy days.

In the meantime, Quantel were expanding their footprint by launching 'Harry' the first nonlinear digital editing system. No width and no speed had arrived. These and other machines like Flame were being bought by a new breed of facility companies opening in the west end.

The effect on the graphic design industry and methods of production was swift and devastating. Within a matter of weeks, photosetting companies closed one by one. As a last flurry, the reps used to call up to say that they had got rid of their photosetting machines and had bought computers. They could set our type on these and send us a disc – a rather forlorn request as designers now had access to exactly the same computers they were using. Film optical houses also went out of business. Roy Turk, who once upon a time you would have to book literally months in advance, appeared with his showreel which suddenly looked terribly out of date. There was an air of desperation about him. It was sad to watch him have to close his company and get rid of people who had such incredible film knowledge.

What was once routine activity was now gone. Every morning at 6.00 am, vans used to arrive from various labs where the film had been processed overnight. Those days meant an early start as you searched for your can of 35mm film stacked on racks. There was always a moment of panic if the label on your can carried the dreaded message 'H in G', Hair in the Gate. You would sit in the viewing room, and there it would be a thin black fuzzy line flickering away in the corner of the picture. Deadline looming, reshoot required. Damn!

Now the vans no longer arrived, the shelves were empty and the projection booths were silent. Likewise the scenic art studio. A few remaining backcloths rolled up on the floor, the large space now used for storing scenery. The analogue world was going fast along with Letraset, scalpels, artwork, cell animation, 35mm photography and all the other tools of the graphic design studio. Along with these went the people, the art workers, the lettering artists, the typesetters, the paint and tracers, the lab technicians, the film editors and other specialist suppliers, all consigned to history.

Endings

A short time ago I visited the Television Centre on a whim. It was being converted into luxury flats. A person in a high-viz jacket came running towards me shouting, 'Private property'. I explained to him that I'd worked there for twenty years and just wanted to look around, but he was adamant, I had to leave. I waited until he'd gone back into his hut and then snuck in again. I wanted to see what they were doing to the Scenery Block. Rounding the corner it soon became clear what they had done, they'd pulled it down. Nothing remained. Visiting the TV Centre I felt a bit like Charles Ryder must have felt at the end of 'Brideshead Revisited' when he revisited Castle Howard. The life had completely gone out of the place.

The Design Department at the BBC grew up in the glory days of television. It brought together a group of creative people who were a major influence on design in television worldwide. It was a competitive environment, with people striving to be the best, a place where people experimented and tried new things always with good humour, a sense of pride and the comraderies forged by shared experience. Now it's gone, and perhaps that is the best ending after all.

10 A hybrid creator's tool

The introduction of Quantel Paintbox

MARGARET HARVEY

The introduction of the Quantel Paintbox was a very specific and exciting time of operational change for many graphic designers in BBC Television Centre, and in retrospect we can also see how significant its arrival was within the wider industry as media production began moving towards digital methods on many levels. This chapter illuminates the impact on the creative working practices and approach to creative thinking that this revolutionary equipment enabled when it was introduced to the general BBC Graphics Department after the original set-up in a large studio occupied by a team led by Senior Designer Charles McGhie in 1987.

It should be noted just how unique a situation it was and what a privilege to have twenty-four-hour access to this kind of tool so early in this niche of the digital revolution. We might have taken it for granted that we could, with some practice, combine seemingly endless combinations of imagery, typography and painted graphics at broadcast quality sitting alone on a tablet, but as Lev Manovich observes in *Software Takes Command* (2013), the cost of the Quantel hardware and supporting infrastructure setup could only be afforded by network television stations and a few production houses. It was not until the 1990s that the ability to integrate multiple media sources became more widely affordable.

At the time that Quantel Paintbox was introduced to the general television graphic design department at BBC Television Centre, those of us producing title and credit sequences, presentation material, idents and in-programme information graphics were called 'graphic designers', doing the job described now, as moving image design or motion graphics. At this moment in time the BBC Television Centre Graphic Design Department was a melting pot of hybrid creators who came predominantly, from educational backgrounds that had introduced them to a vast array of art, design and craft skills, but many had not designed on or used computers of any kind previously. By combining 'heritage' techniques with computer technology, designers could now harness the 'endless malleability of digital benefits with the individuality of the human mark and the haptic resistance of handmade materials' (Macdonald 2014: 150).

Art school training

The creative education of many who made up the department would have included some study in the areas of typography, commercial illustration and printmaking, fine art painting and drawing, photography, advertising, animation, film and more, including 3D design and textiles.

Quantel had built a system that allowed for a natural fusion of these influences at the tip of a stylus. The pen and tablet operation of Paintbox was an intuitive interface for the designer immersed in a grounding of haptic art-based skills and materials – scalpels, paper, glue and mark making with pencil, ink, paint and more.

The subtle sounds and smells of the tactile materials, along with the one-off nature of producing imagery by hand in combination with photographic and film processes, could now be augmented and integrated into the digital process – still guided by the hands of the designer. This 'designer-friendly' quality was a development that may have been augmented by some sessions organized by Quantel and the BBC to collaborate with designers who were 'invited to explain their patterns of work and asked what they would like the machine to provide and in what sequence' (Mina Martinez 2023). Mina Martinez encapsulates the moment in time when Paintbox arrived:

> That wonderful moment when it became possible to work directly in the medium in which your audience would receive your work. (Releasing the designer from) waiting until the next day to see if your rushes did actually deliver what you had planned!
>
> The very best thing about it was for me the freedom from the suspense inherent when taking work to a next stage without the very real possibility of 'spoiling' it. The facility to revert to a previous stage gave a magnificent creative freedom to experiment and try out ideas galore. (2023)

The Paintbox could be seen as having been the perfect introduction to computer use for the designer. A creator's tool, not a 'box of tricks' with pre-programmed effects. At this time new visual clichés were appearing onscreen including 'page turns, green grids, flying chrome letters, and pictures within pictures' (Macdonald 2014: 40). Art was meeting technology head-on and hands-on, and we taught ourselves, pixel by 'pushed' pixel. With the powerful focus on 'On Air' broadcast deadlines to meet, the process of change in method was swift, with the culture for BBC designers at all stages in their careers to have a flexible and open mindset towards embracing progress in technologies.

The way this generation used Paintbox truly embodied the era of hybrid analogue/digital design. This significant career development has influenced some in their methods and ideology in later years as educators, encouraging students to incorporate traditionally produced imagery with digital processes on current software, at least at the stage of idea generation.

Unofficial apprenticeship

The in-house environment provided a degree of mentoring and unofficial apprenticeship for designers in general. Those who were ahead in this process of self-training on the Paintbox shared knowledge as was the culture with many aspects of learning the ropes in the department.

We learnt from each other, technicians being as important as designers in the development of our moving image practice. The in-house availability of the Paintbox facility with this cross-fertilization of ideas and skill sharing encouraged creative uses of the setup.

Essentially, Paintbox enabled us to do easily for the first time, what is now commonplace in software programmes such as the Adobe Creative Suite and applications like Procreate; grab stills from different sources and combine them with typography and digital painting to produce richly layered colourful images. From tablet to television screen, these creations were of broadcast quality. We were now able to paint with light. Indeed, *Painting with Light* (1986) was a BBC series broadcast on BBC2. Six artists including David Hockney and Sidney Nolan were given the opportunity to have a session experimenting with creating work on the Paintbox.

These films observe artists, accomplished in other fine art mediums, using the pen and tablet for the first time. Their skill level was generally limited to the basic painting and simple cutting functions and arguably, as a 'painting' medium Paintbox was functioning as just another haptically operated tool. This intrigue sparked by the Paintbox amongst visual creators in fine art and photography, although significant and related, was a separate route to the one we were taking as broadcast designers.

When Quantel Paintbox arrived we became part of the very early stylistic shift and aesthetic logic that Manovich (2013) describes as 'a new hybrid visual language'. He is recognizing Adobe After Effects as the main instrument of this shift, but Quantel was undoubtedly a precursor to these systems with their digital layering capabilities.

Pre-digital storyboards – An evolving process of developing ideas through working with trusted teams

A hand-drawn storyboard can obviously communicate a designer's intention well when the idea is described, researched and referenced, but the digital Paintbox allowed for a few stages of that development process to be clarified upfront by a designer. It could also offer the skilled operator/designer the opportunity to depict ideas that were very close in appearance to a finished title sequence. For some clients whose main area of expertise was not primarily the visual arts, this could build confidence where relatively large budgets were being allocated.

On the flip side, it could also be argued that this may have contributed to the start of a new and possibly less creatively flexible era where some clients began to expect this level of 'finish' at the idea stage, becoming more risk averse. This particular period was pre-marketing in the sense that we recognize it today. There was still a general understanding and trust that the chosen or allocated designer would take the brief and produce a product that packaged or promoted the programme in a style and to a standard that suited the quality of the BBC output in general.

Sometimes a more impressionistic presentation at this stage could allow for an organic process of idea development through incidental discovery while filming and editing. Consultation and interaction throughout the planning and production of elements for a sequence, with craftspeople, lighting camera and technical crews would often enrich the finished job. The Paintbox as a tool for image creation did not exclude this creativity and innovation. For some designers it simply shifted the development of elements and ideas to a more autonomous stage at the start of the design process.

As designers and design directors our working styles might have been separated into different groups; some being 'detail controlling pre-planners', others preferring the 'set the scene and see what happens'. But even if we inhabited a happy medium, the Paintbox facility added another choice to our toolbox of individualistic methodologies.

The breadth of programme strands, the diversity of technical facilities available to us both in-house and within specialist companies outside the BBC (often ex-BBC staff themselves), as well as the openness and trust between production teams and the Graphic Design Department, nurtured this culture of individual styles and approaches.

Analogue to digital process using rostrum camera with real objects

There was an important aspect to the Paintbox setup in the Graphic Design Department at the time that provided the perfect theatre for the designer with eclectic tendencies, the collage makers, the haptically

Figure 10.1 *Reputations* (1998) by Tom Brookes, hybrid objects shot under rostrum and digitally composited. Courtesy BBC.

trained or those whose style was particularly filmic. The tablets and screens were in a contained darkened room with a rostrum camera adjacent to the tablet workstation (see Figure 16.3). This facility to input directly from a small studio-like setup played into a fascination for some with image-making using varied materials, textures and props, as well as the further visual explorations afforded by the application of directional lighting. The ability to arrange then digitally grab and save images of material shadows or solid-lit objects then edit and layer them digitally gave autonomy and immediacy to the process of making elements from which to build ideas and presentations.

It was a period when we began to create Paintbox images that combined analogue and digital processes in an experimental and iterative way (see Figure 10.1). Creative use of simple lighting setups was a natural progression from observing the skilled work of rostrum and camera crews over previous years while filming diverse studio shoots. These included Directors of Photography Doug Foster, John Swinnerton and Karl Watkins, who were involved in many BBC Motion Graphics shoots. After all, lighting for any filmed arrangement is key and can give endless opportunities for creating atmosphere and character.

This in-camera part of the workflow remains significant to those who were working across the period of change where analogue and digital processes overlapped. Combining of elements remains part of the DNA of many designers and still influences their current work and teaching, as they seek 'to embrace a pluralist approach that accommodates the sleek and perfected solutions but also the sublime accidents, the contaminated and the hybrid' (Macdonald 2014: 45). Jane Wyatt-Brooks describes the setup as allowing for 'happy accidents' with experimentation and real lit elements promoting individuality in design solutions, a skill that fellow Designer Tom Brooks excelled at. Matt Losasso was similarly engaged with the in-camera aspect of the workflow. The 'tactile' quality of real lighting effects and the 'controlled randomness' of being able to work iteratively between rostrum and digital tablet contrasts with following years, which saw a prolific use of pre-programmed effects, where design individuality was often replaced by generic software solutions.

Conclusion

It may be dependent on motion design educators, such as John Salisbury, to encourage students to create haptic elements and scan them in, rather than automatically choosing to produce completely digital projects. Funnelling design students from an increasingly earlier stage into specialisms and pathways may suit certain abilities and potential employment settings; however, remembering to encourage the cross-referencing of techniques where possible may prevent too much homogenization of style and reliance on generic software solutions.

The benefits, and indeed pleasure, of being able to browse digital asset libraries and choose the perfect bokeh effect to embed or an inking brush with just enough jitter or grain to almost, but not quite, recreate that look of a Lino-cut illustration offer an opportunity to mimic a trained craftsperson. But individually tailored elements will surely help to separate a designer onto another level of individuality, just as it always did.

It only takes a bit of resourceful creativity and realistically a small amount of extra time. With a camera phone in one hand and an improvised light source, in my world, I would be accessing swathes of fabric to the backlight, a tonne of printed ephemera to distort and macro focus upon, the odd rat's skull and maybe a box of rusty keys – and a door to infinite possibility is opened.

11 Drawn to Paintbox

MORGAN ALMEIDA

Introduction

Television always fascinated me. Growing up, TV became a tabernacle of reverence, and an incredible device that allowed us to share moments as a group and yet experience individual cinematic emotions. My wise mother often banned it, seeing it as a terrible influence; of course, this made it an irresistible box of forbidden curiosities and boundless fun. An influential memory was the film *The Man Who Fell to Earth*, where Bowie watches eight televisions simultaneously. How I envied that luxury, that was my dream, constantly curious about the other three channel choices, especially before the days of remote controls. When Channel 4 launched in 1982, the creativity of Martin Lambie-Nairn and Bob English sparked an obsession with television graphics, and everyone wanted to be part of it. Naturally, as an urban Londoner, it seemed an impossible dream to contemplate a career in TV.

Perhaps that obstinate dream, and a little luck, drew me into a career of boundless creativity, from pencil to Paintbox to titles and TV branding.

Thinking through drawing

Of our five neural senses – visual, auditory, kinaesthetic, gustatory and olfactory – we tend to have a primary preference. It defines our cerebral logic and communication style. Mine was visual, and I was luckily encouraged to draw at an early age. When you draw, even doodle, it communicates a thousand words in a second in a tiny picture. I believe that everyone can draw competently within a month, and within three months better than most. However, it requires daily one-hour practice. Sadly, the arts were not considered worthy within my grammar school, so I studied the sciences; drawing was just a hobby. Later, that innate ability really helped in art college and became invaluable at BBC TV.

Sketching changes your ability to think, express and create without being continually reliant on the internet. Further, it leaves an interesting paper trail of documented ideas and art. Drawing is a primary design language for all creatives, from architecture to fashion, product design, book design and even graffiti. Arguably, it should be compulsory creative training for all design students, at least one hour a week. This develops an extra tool that isn't reliant on the computer and holds them in good stead later on.

Drawing gives you an outlet and the rapid ability to instantly visualize an idea, allowing you to see if it works in concept and execution, in typography, in books or in actual construction. Sketchbooks tell visual stories; it's almost like toying with literary notions, but visually and quickly. By the side of my computer, I always have a pad of paper on which I write my to-do lists, but within that, there are always hundreds of drawings, doodles and sketches, designs or just abstractions, that I come back to look at again.

Currently, a significant artistic influence on my work is Cy Twombly (1928–2011), who essentially 'scribbled' blindly. The appeal lies in the unlearning, the dis-inhibition and abstraction, which is the opposite of pictorial representation; it's the absence of narrative, the refusal of a storyline and even the denial of beauty.

However, when I first joined the BBC, drawing skills afforded all designers the ability to easily conceptualize and experiment. Sketches often impressed the client and were a direct means of communication before the advent of easy internet access for reference visuals.

Early Paintbox

Easily bored, constantly distracted, with the 'scattered attention surplus' of ADHD – I coped by simultaneously working on multiple projects, unable to focus for long. So, the idea of creating graphics by traditional methods of TV design or typography, hand-lettering and painting cell-by-cell was mind-numbingly dull. Then along came the Quantel Paintbox, which combined the entire creative studio in one box, all at once, in real time. It included paint, graphics, effects, cutouts and a library, eliminating the need for cutting mats, drawing boards, Cow Gum, Letraset, loose materials or messy physical airbrush. What a dream, way beyond the expectations of the extant generation of graphic designers. Paintbox was a huge revolution for designers, a milestone for visual storytelling led by designers like Paul D'Auria, who created the multi-layered *The Lenny Henry Show* (1984, 1985, 1988) titles (see Plates 8.1 & 8.2). Paul and Saz Vora, both tough and talented teachers, trained me well on the Quantel systems. Fortunately, I was drawn to Paintbox easily, perhaps because of my strong visual sensibilities and drafting strengths.

My television career started in BBC News Graphics, later migrating to the Main Block Graphic design. News Graphics demands were brutally tiring, tedious and repetitive: location maps, information charts and lower thirds, but it developed resilient innovation muscles, preparing us for any creative challenge. The Paintbox created a tough gymnasium of daily creative practice, where the learning curve was steep, and solutions were required fast (see Figure 11.1). This daily practice of rapid design, all created within

Figure 11.1 News graphics from drawings to Paintbox. Courtesy Morgan Almeida.

extremely limited time and resource constraints, necessarily made designers more inventive with a technological edge. In news, we regularly had to swiftly respond to breaking stories within half an hour. For example, when the NASA Challenger Space Shuttle blew up while on air, we had to create instant Paintbox visuals for a panicked Newsroom. Often, ambitious journalists would come in for their graphics, simply to score points, to be mentioned in a dispatch the next day; the more beautiful the graphic, the better. Naturally, we would have to curtail their wilder indulgences. It was an interesting time of learning TV and managing editorial expectations. The Paintbox became an almost invisible design tool, especially for those who were able to use it as fluently as handwriting, giving some designers a slight advantage in that respect.

Further, we also had to integrate Paintbox with parallel digital systems ready for transmission: record it, take in information, add typography systems and set up automation. Andy Davy, the creative head, was astute in teaching us the methodology. He understood the overall structure of numerous bulletins and their repetitive nature, and therefore he was able to create repeatable, teachable, scalable processes into a day-to-day path for designers to follow. This methodology, looking back, couldn't have been achieved without that overview and holistic design architecture. While designers were obsessed with the actual execution, he understood the operational infrastructure and the integration from concept to sketch, to Paintbox, to Edit systems, to operations to editorial and transmission. This Quantel pipeline saved time with cost efficiency, real-time reviewing and tech integration.

In Main Block Programmes, Paintbox really came into its own. It was useful for program concept and logo design, storyboarding and quickly taking ideas to a more finished stage of production. Producers were convinced by hand drawings, especially sketching in front of them, but some wanted to see a finished design, which was facilitated by Paintbox. You could quickly take something under the camera, add colour or patch it in with different elements. Its versatility allowed for integrating found elements with drawing, text or video and creating mattes for successful post-production keying and background plates. Although this was sometimes limiting, it gave a final result that the client quickly judged.

Paintbox attributes

Importantly, this magic box of Quantel technology was co-developed with graphic designers and artists. The interface was brilliant, simple intuitive on/off swiping: left and right for the menu, up and down for the palette, which had never been seen before. It was only many years later that Mac adopted a similar swipe and pop-up menu. But back then, it was unique: to paint, to cut out an item, pick it up, all with a pen. It created a virtual dance and duel with the Paintbox. For the designer, it was not only about speed but also about infinite freedom in creativity.

The initial experience with Paintbox was a little weird, like driving a car. Using the tablet, the stylus pen and TV monitor required accurate hand-to-eye coordination. Rather than touching the screen itself, you touched an equivalent point on the Wacom tablet with the pen, similar to a PC mouse. The concept of 'double mapping' a position on your tablet to a coordinate on the screen was very clever. Suddenly, you could actually design directly onto the screen with the stylus. Initially, the tablet and pen were wired, so you continually flicked away the wire. When it became wireless, using Paintbox was like rapidly conducting a design array, instantly versatile in every way.

The menu broke down into five categories: paint, graphics, effects, cutting and library. Each one was manifold and flexible, offering everything from a digital paintbrush with airbrush quality to multi-layering animation to digital frame storage. You could mix up any colour or tap anywhere on an actual photo to pick up the exact shade and further blend hues. Adding type was no longer a headache. It was simple to choose a font, put it on screen, change it, twist it and even animate it.

The stencil was a superb masking tool. It could be made by digitally translating a black/white key or drawn to mask out specific areas. You could easily create faux 3D effects. For example, you could take a circle, airbrush a globe within it, then reverse the stencil to create a shadow outside, thus making it look like a 3D ball. For instance, the red ball in *280 Useful Ideas from Japan* (1990) title was simply a flat 2D circle that I airbrushed into a convincing sphere (see Plate 11). By flying it around, it didn't need to be an expensive CAD 3D ball because the light source remained constant. Paintbox allowed people who could draw to create realistic elements that could often fake 3D CAD renders.

A key attribute of Paintbox was its integration with a live copy camera to capture actual objects and reference material, to distort it and manipulate it into something new. Many happy accidents were created under the camera (see Chapter 10). Additionally, understanding lighting – adding a fill, a reflector, shadows, chiaroscuro – was essential in combining analogue and digital techniques.

Paintbox offered a new playground for ideas. Where it truly excelled was in its daily, and weekly, creation of program content graphics, which saved significant time and cost over laborious cardboard graphics. Combined with its sister Quantel products, Harry followed by Henry, it became invaluable in TV motion design, holding its own until Discrete Logic and the Apple Mac emerged.

Paintbox advantages and drawbacks

As a Paintbox artist, you had the advantage of being able to execute ideas quickly and impress clients with various concepts at the execution level. The previous generation of designers was caught up in a different were steeped in traditional methodologies that were valuable, relevant but painfully slow, while the newer generation took to digital tools more readily. Previously, we needed drawn storyboards, which were costly, time-consuming and visually limiting. Titles evolved from hand-drawn animations to integrating drawing, found materials, 3D animation, live action and typography, allowing for greater experimentation. Paintbox provided great flexibility to explore initial design ideas and prepare final graphic elements for logo design and branding across each programme's content.

However, programme graphics could become clouded, where good design ideas were replaced by generic, dazzling video effects. The packaging often overshadowed the content through the seduction of digital prowess. The simplicity and powerful elegance of ideas like *Arena* (1979) or *40 Minutes* (1985) or even *The Good Life* (1976) were replaced by graphic excess, with self-indulgent, glitzy 3D or Quantel effects from the television studio gallery, where lazy studio directors would fly images around for no good reason.

Paintbox often shattered the simple vision of one good idea into a thousand bits of nonsense, so the clarity of concept often suffered. For me, the purest title of all in the whole archive is *The Good Life*. It is simply a flower animating petal by petal. It's not multilayered with hundreds of forgettable elements, which was a drawback of the Paintbox era. Instead of an iconic image, you were left with digital overload.

Paintbox process

I preferred to sketch an idea first. The beauty of drawing allows you to quickly formulate the concept on paper and assess its possibilities, even while sitting on the bus or at home. Then you would begin to materialize it on the Paintbox. Back then, we had to book time on the Paintbox as it was a very expensive tool. I often stayed overnight because it was an opportunity to explore 'off the meter'.

Designers helped each other by sharing their processes and techniques, often asking, 'Oh, how do you do that?' We worked in a very collaborative, communal way, especially sitting together in news, sports or presentation graphics suites. Everyone shared the resources because the Paintbox was so expensive; we started with at most two machines. We had to collaborate because not everyone had digital expertise, while others were better at designing the concept. Hence, some designers operated the Paintbox for those less experienced, creating their storyboards, visualizing ideas and often just experimenting and having a laugh. That close collaboration changed as the following generation of Apple Mac users worked more solo and independently from start to finish, producing broadcast with online motion graphics.

Paintbox logo design

Paintbox was primarily dedicated to the creation of still graphics for servicing news, sports, presentation and programme content. It was also especially useful for the design and creation of programme logos, following the initial storyboarding and approval by the client. Experimentation, playing around and visualizing were possible, without the costly commissioning of an expert typographer for finished artwork. These are a few examples of that development process.

Sportsnight (1990)

Paintbox handily created preparatory elements for this thirty-second opening. Various action sports were filmed against green to 'chroma-key' onto vivid moving textures, to echo the vibrancy, diversity and spectacle of global sports. These were composed of billowing silks, digitally fused on Quantel Harry with thin TV lines prepared on Paintbox.

We also used its crude cell animation function to execute the *Sportsnight* logo. I noticed the eleven1-character title perfectly matched the multi-fraction digital clocks used for sports timings. Thus, the logo became a countdown to symbolize competitive precision. Each letter was a clocking number matching hours, minutes, seconds and milliseconds of all sports timers. Hence an animating transition from 00:00:00:00 into S P : R T : N I : H T . Finally, I split the logo into black and white to echo its night-time transmission.

The Paintbox animation process was very basic and limited by size. It involved subdividing the screen into a grid of cells and then painting each one differently. The Paintbox then played back a small 'flickbook' effect of the animating cells. *Sportsnight* involved the creation of a sequence of eighteen cells, each about 1/10th the size of the screen. Each cell was text paintboxed with different numbers and then replayed as a virtual 'flickbook'. This small virtual element of a number-spinning sports clock was then finally keyed onto the title background and resolved as the final logo. On reflection the logo could have been better executed, with more authentic number sequencing and an authentic digital clock font (see Figure 11.2).

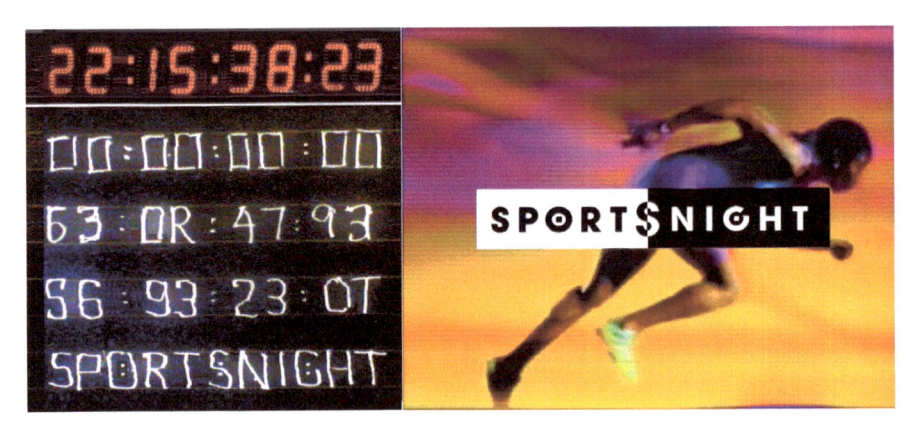

Figure 11.2 *Sportsnight* (1990) Paintbox rough. Courtesy Morgan Almeida.

Youth programmes aesthetics

I grew up in the punk generation, which embraced a more chaotic and iconoclastic approach to creativity. Hence, if trends were heading in one direction, by nature we did the opposite, despite others' frustrations. This maverick trait resonated while working for Janet Street-Porter, who echoed that same philosophy. This tall, imposing TV exec, whose fearless approach scared us all, would often say 'Fuck it up a bit more!' to engender more daring attitudes for her Youth Programmes Division.

280 *Useful Ideas from Japan* (1990)

280 Useful Ideas from Japan (1990) was inspired by a very simple line drawing book about hundreds of innovative Japanese ideas. Given this brief and a very small budget, I didn't know where to start. My initial idea was the Japanese juxtaposition of the traditional and modern. Hence, a sumo wrestler lurched forward to fight a machined robot; or a demure geisha, revealing as the camera zooms out, operating a complex electronic nerve centre; or a bald monk praying, as the camera pullback reveals, in the middle of terminals on the money markets. However, these ambitious concepts were too limited and expensive.

Then I conceived of a package arriving from Japan, exploding with all these ideas such as love hotels, complex toilets, gastronomy, money, bonsai, pornography and sumo wrestling, all the different aspects emerging out of the 'Japakage' (see Figure 11.3). Hence, I built a little balsa wood box and numerous drawings to visualize the sequence on Paintbox. It also allowed experimentation with the granularity of the background. My obsession with TV was always about the texture of the screen on the 1960s and 1970s televisions, with 625 lines scanning across the tube. That was how TV was in those days. Many of my titles featured TV screens, and because I admired both *Blade Runner* and Japan, I incorporated all of those inspirations and references into both drawings, models and the digital.

It was all cost-driven, achieved for £15,000, including model-making, execution, my time, filmmaking and post-production edit. The shoot came together in a fantastic machine built by model maker, Tom Palmer, and shot by lighting cameraman, Karl Watkins. Post-production was edited on Quantel Harry, to music by Anne Dudley from the Art of Noise. The title looked fascinating, with complex curiosities and even embedded pornographic images for sheer irreverence. However Janet Street-Porter said, 'It's too long' (it was thirty seconds), 'make it 15'. Sadly, we had to double speed the final title, which lost quality and depth of understanding because it was too fast to comprehend. I do wish I had said 'No'.

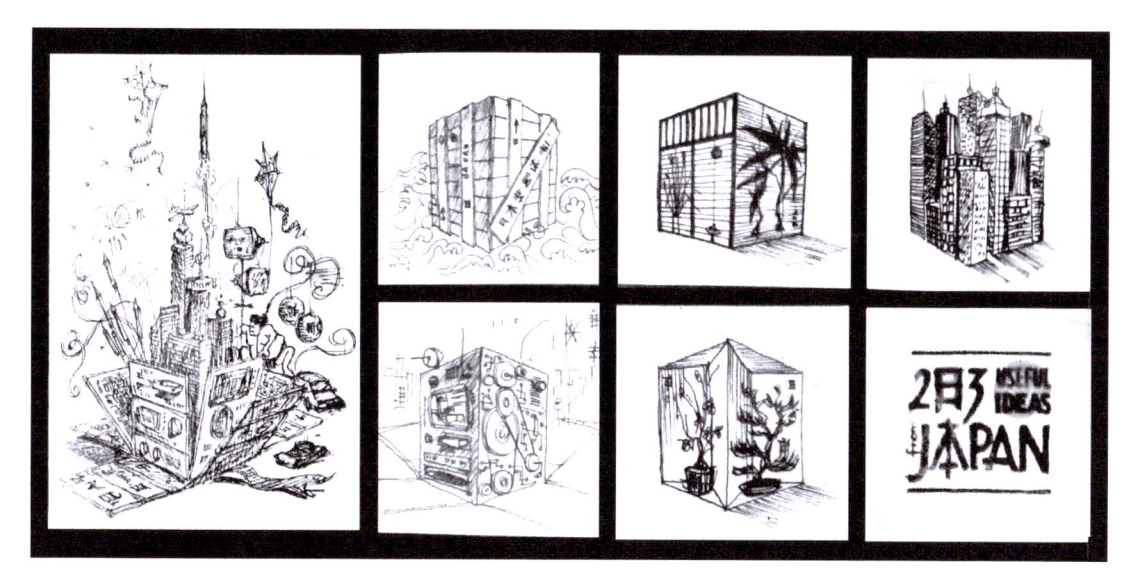

Figure 11.3 *280 Useful Ideas from Japan* (1990) Sketchbook roughs for concept board. Courtesy Morgan Almeida.

Figure 11.4 *280 Useful Ideas from Japan* (1990). Courtesy Morgan Almeida

Paintbox was essential in the careful composition of the logo. The calligraphy for Japan (Nippon) looks like an '8' on top of an 'A'. Cleverly combining the two languages, gave the 'A' of 'Japan' and the '8' of '283'. The red circle of the Japanese flag became a 3D ball flying through the sequence (see Figure 11.4.).

Apple Mac and beyond

When the Mac arrived, it received the same disdain from the Paintbox artists as the analogue traditionalists had viewed Paintbox. The first-generation Mac was a little slow, but later on, its incredible precision, accuracy and flexibility with Adobe software were acknowledged as another revolution. It brought an economic, direct relationship with a personal dedicated tool.

The Mac offered a sharper version and a closer personal relationship as an owner-occupied device. However, it was going online that was truly transformative and eye-opening, and this accelerated in the 2000s. Interactivity and internet access changed everything because you no longer had to go anywhere far for information. You could exchange ideas in real time with people in different locations. Not only could you share materials, but you could also access vast global libraries for sources, integrate it and send it to render farms abroad, completed and returned without ever leaving your chair.

Conclusion

Those of us at the dawn of digital graphics were very lucky, surrounded by genuine talent, pioneering technology and incredible opportunity. At times, working in BBC's Television Graphics Departments felt like being in Disney World or *Charlie and the Chocolate Factory*. The Paintbox and similar electronic design tools revolutionized the media industry with better, faster and cheaper realization of ideas. Those same complex digital tasks can now be achieved instantly and freely on our smartphones. Nonetheless, technological gimmickry will never easily substitute for strong concepts and authentic creative expression will remain paramount and prized.

The key lesson for designers is to truly understand 'the business', because not enough colleges teach students that design is primarily a promotional commercial tool. The BBC Motion Graphic Archive is a testament to that successful achievement for hundreds of BBC broadcasts. In the delight of creating, we must not forget our own worth and our fundamental contribution to business success. Multi-billion-dollar brands from Apple to Tesla, IKEA to Nike, BBC to Chanel know this and live by that creative/commercial relationship.

Notably, it has all slowly merged into simultaneous, ubiquitous 360-degree media on the TV, the PC and the phone. They each offer a different experience: the public, personal and private choices of 'on air', 'online' and 'on-hand' media. TV was designed for communal, shared viewing at 12 feet; the PC was made personal and exclusive at 12 inches; and the phone, a wholly private interaction at 12 centimetres. Now they even coexist – while watching TV, you refer to your laptop, or look at your phone.

We face a future of unimaginable abundance and opportunity with everything from Artificial Intelligence (AI), to blockchain, energy, space and genomics, computational power, robotics and even neural implants, where you electronically navigate computers with your thoughts. This is literally the merging of imagination and technology. Generative AI seems to be emerging as the ultimate digital tool, but perhaps we may all return to and value that innate human ability of creativity through drawing, painting and sculpting, and all the sensual arts. This is because we still need and appreciate genuine human endeavour.

12 The best technique for the job

Making the right choices for the right reasons

LIZ FRIEDMAN

Introduction

The dimension of movement allied to graphic design enriches the designer's vocabulary of images and forms. Successive inter-related patterns can be used to communicate an idea or message with much greater force than a static piece of print. (Laughton 1966: 11)

What may seem obvious and ubiquitous today, in its early development, a significant advancement in television graphic design offered an additional dimension compared to the print designer, which was motion. The art of communicating an original idea in ten to thirty seconds, which flowed and developed seamlessly and was also appropriate as well as having the right mood and pace for the subject matter, was something worth striving for.

Using examples of my own work, this chapter will examine how designers employed ever sophisticated and innovative ways of animation as we strove to create arresting motion graphics to communicate whatever the programme required. During the era when video was still developing, programme makers were shooting on 16mm film, and graphic designers were using the preferred high quality of 35mm film, which was the best medium for film optical work and the only way more complicated layering and visual effects could be achieved. The unique visual quality of 35mm film was its superior resolution to video tape (Merritt 1993). Not only was video not really an option, but computers had not yet arrived, and there was no laptop available containing every bit of software necessary to complete a project from beginning to end. The designer had to rely on his/her imagination and often their own ingenuity, as well as the indispensable help of others such as cameramen, editors, optical houses and model makers, in order to deliver their vision.

As designers at BBC Television, we were learning the trade of television graphic design 'on the job', often pushing boundaries, delivering something new, striving for an original idea or approach by experiment. The BBC was a 'fun factory' allowing its employees freedom to be original and experimental. As Roy Laughton, head of design, stated in 1966, 'Television technique can only be learnt by familiarity with the medium, an understanding of its limitations and constant exploitation of its possibilities' (1966: 23).

Cel animation

Before the advent of computers and digital media in the early days of television graphic design, the designer's toolkit, though basic, used to consist of a variety of possibilities. The choice of which way to go was usually determined by the 'big idea', but often by the budget and the time available to deliver.

Grange Hill (1977) was an early sequence, which didn't command a generous budget, but once again allowed total freedom in coming up with an idea. As a new series at that time, nobody knew how popular it would become, let alone imagine the cult status it would ultimately command. The drama series was aimed at children, and the brief was to reflect 'everyday' kids at a secondary modern or comprehensive school, and this would be the first time children would see a drama specifically created for them handling current and often controversial 'gritty' everyday issues. The title sequence was designed to give a feeling of what was to follow without telling any specific story. Having spent a lot of my childhood reading comics and from an inner London Comprehensive school myself, I felt I knew what the production wanted.

I decided early on that an illustrative comic style would be appropriate. Comics were widely available and read by children at that time, such as *The Beano*, *Dandy* and *Bunty*. The slight retro styling was chosen to be reminiscent of the comics of the 1950s, the heyday of the British comic, before the distraction of TV, which was in its heyday in the 1970s when this sequence was designed (see Figure 12.1). Fully animated, traditional animation was out of the question with the budget allocated, so using a series of still drawings instead was the only way around this. Having seen the work of Bob Cosford, I knew he was the best illustrator for this sequence. We both had a very good understanding of what was required and how to achieve it. Illustrations were created on a clear cel (short for celluloid, a transparent sheet on which objects are drawn or painted for traditional hand-drawn animation) in black outline using a chinagraph pencil (a soft crayon style pencil that could be used on glass), and the back was painted in colour using animation cel paint.

Due to financial constraints, the animations were created by using only three illustrations in each sequence. These were shot on a 35mm film rostrum camera (had there been a lot of footage, then it would have been significantly cheaper to shoot on 16mm and compromise on image quality) and were filmed either cutting or fading from one illustration to the next. This gave an impression of sequential movement. The sequence also had a 'feeling of animation' simply by the use of whip pans (twelve frame moves), cuts, mixes and zooms. The sausage on a fork was on a separate cel layer and panned in (single frame) over the main background illustration. The entire sequence was created in camera (no edits) and worked the first time (no retakes).

I remember marking up the sequence until about midnight the night before filming and leaving the work in the rostrum camera area for the morning booking. I stood on a chair with the main large artwork on my desk covered in an overlay piece of tracing paper ready to mark up for the cameraman. I used the transparent plastic field sizes as viewfinders to work out the zooms and pans counting out aloud and then marking on the trace overlay the moves and field sizes before writing the timings down on the dope sheet. It was not necessary to attend a rostrum shoot if everything was marked up properly for the cameraman, so designers would often just deliver the artwork together with a dope sheet and await to see the filmed rushes the following morning. The choreography and pace were worked out without music, but somehow, I managed to create a visual rhythm in my head. In fact, this was how most of my work was done. I rarely had audio before creating a sequence.

Music was commissioned afterwards by the series director and recorded to match the rostrum shoot. Even though the music fitted fine, the executive producer disliked the specially created audio and two days before the first transmission chose a piece of music from the BBC gramophone library to partner the sequence. You can imagine my shock when I saw the sequence transmitted. In hindsight, watching the sequence now comparing both audio tracks, I think she made the right decision, as the first piece does sound a bit dull compared to the 'off the shelf' one chosen. Of course, it was never envisaged that this series would have such a long and successful run.

Soldiers (1985), presented by the best-selling author Frederick Forsyth, was yet another early sequence where an illustrative style was used for a specific reason and thus dictated the filming technique. In this

Figure 12.1 *Grange Hill* (1977) comic-style illustration by Bob Cosford. Courtesy Liz Friedman.

The Best Technique for the Job   131

case money wasn't really a restricting factor. The brief was to create a vibrant sequence, which should be uplifting but not glamorize war. To be honest I found the brief so 'open' and a bit of an oxymoron. How could I create a sequence that wasn't dull, predictable, done before and be 'exciting', yet not make it look like I was depicting war as a glamorous and exciting subject? I thought about it and realized 'energizing' and 'full of action' even 'chaotic' might be more appropriate. I still hadn't solved the problem or come up with a solution on the day I was meant to 'sell' the idea.

I walked across Shepherd's Bush from the Television Centre to Kensington House, where the documentary producers worked, and as I entered the building, I had a 'vision' and knew straight away that it was right. I had no storyboard, no roughs, no mood boards, as I entered the office of John Gau, a big name in documentary filmmaking at the time. I explained that my idea involved rotoscoping (drawing from live action) in the style of a French impressionist painting, or even more like an abstract expressionist painting, with elements of Anthony Pollock, the American painter who threw paint onto canvas. I explained that if you were to stop one frame of the sequence, you might not even recognize the image, but when moving it would show the action. I also explained that the idea would give a feeling of chaos and action as one might see in a battle. He really liked the idea and gave me carte blanche to go ahead (as could happen in those early blissful days of television). My next problem was to find the action from which to rotoscope. I obviously couldn't film anything for this sequence, so needed to find existing footage, possibly from the BBC Archive, from documentaries, from newsreels, from the First World War and the Second World War and potentially from feature films. Copyright could have been a big issue, but in my ignorance and the hope that the footage would be unrecognizable once made into paintings, I went ahead. I cut the film clips together mute without a music track with Dave Farley, the graphic design in-house editor at the time. This obviously looked a real mess as the footage was from all sources, all eras, colour, black and white, good quality and bad quality, but this didn't matter. We transferred it to a VHS tape, and I took it to three different animation houses to get quotes and also to get a feeling of who I might want to work with.

One of the top animation houses at the time, Hibbert Ralph was chosen. Jerry Hibbert, the co-owner, really liked the idea and was willing to do it at a reduced rate. Their core business was commercials with very high budgets but sometimes would subsidize television work that interested them, which also helped to develop styles for their showreel. Years later and after several other jobs working together, Jerry told me that they made over a million pounds with *Soldiers* on their reel and that they incorporated the style into a video they created for the band Queen for the song called 'Innuendo' (1991). Jerry allocated this work to Dennis Sutton, one of his in-house animators, who was very much a fine artist. He drew and painted in his spare time, usually dogs and horses in a very clean and painterly style, not at all impressionistic, but the fact was he understood art and was not just a cartoonist. He did a rough using just one short scene of horses charging. This has remained my favourite clip.

The technique to create the animations was simply to play the VHS tape of the edited action on a monitor, that was lying on its back, so the screen became a lightbox. About every sixth frame was stopped to use as the image. A peg bar was sellotaped to the monitor and a background paper measuring 12×9 inches was pegged in position to draw onto. The master drawing of each scene was done on this paper, then clear cels were pegged over this on an animator's peg bar. These cels were used to add scribbles and roughness to the master scene using coloured chinagraphs (see Figure 12.2). I would go and visit frequently, and each time I asked for more cells to be added to rough up the sequence even more. At one point we added a cel and threw splats of cel paint to add even more chaos and vibrancy.

Once the entire sequence had been painted, the artwork was shot stop frame, just like a traditional animation on a 35mm film rostrum camera. Once again, the audio was created at the end, as was quite usual for me. Some people think it's difficult to create a rhythm with visuals alone, but I actually prefer it

Figure 12.2 *Soldiers* (1985) end caption with animation cels by Dennis Sutton on a peg bar.
Courtesy Liz Friedman.

that way, as a motion designer you are not limited to someone else's perception of what the atmosphere, style or pace should be. Rod Argent, a founding member of the rock band the Zombies in the 1960s, was commissioned to create the music for the sequence. I had to drive to his mansion for the recording, in the country where he had a recording studio in the basement. The sequence was played out many times on a screen, and he built up the audio while I was there. The music was quite unusual and not typical opening title theme music, which I think was right for the piece and therefore a good choice by the producer. The work was recognized with an 'in book' at the D&AD Awards.

Some years later I used a similar idea for *Storm from the East* (1993), depicting the marauding Mongols on horseback. However, this time it was in the digital era. Mattes were made from the live action, and textures could easily and quite quickly be dropped into these to give the impression of movement and vibrancy and changes and variations could be made instantly. However, the sense of satisfaction for me was not the same; though technically quite innovative, it lacked the fresh immediacy of an image never seen before.

Live action directing

Another project that relied on the rotoscoping technique was done for the drama series *Dorothy L. Sayers Mysteries* (1987). This, however, was approached in the complete opposite way to *Soldiers*. For a start, I directed the live action to be used in the sequence, rather than having to rely on existing material cut together in an edit. This was done in a very large studio with a Rolls Royce car. I had to choreograph a succinct sequence with the leading actors in the knowledge that all the shots would be used sequentially in a continuous narrative and that they would then be drawn by hand afterwards. This method still required costumes to be chosen, hair and makeup applied and lighting perfected for the shoot. It was almost like doing the sequence twice. In fact, it was!

The actors had to act at a certain pace and exaggerated style with the knowledge that their actions would be interacting with the typographic credits, which would be added later. I created a storyboard, which they found very useful. I was in awe of their total professionalism at the time of the shoot. It was a simple idea, but a deceptively difficult sequence to produce. A few years after creating the sequence, it would probably have been possible to create the images digitally from the live action, but this was created just before that digital era.

My idea for this late 1920s drama was based on those iconic Art Deco railway posters of that era. The clean lines, flat colour and sophisticated poses were so reminiscent of those images at that time and could only be achieved by using an illustrative approach. The difficulty I faced was finding an animator or illustrator who could copy each drawing so perfectly that it didn't shimmer or move from frame to frame. This was the complete opposite brief to *Soldiers*. Two years later in 1989, Pat Gavin used a similar period poster styling inspired by French designer Adolphe Cassandre (1901–68) for the series *Poirot*, but by then digital technology was more readily available, allowing him more flexibility in approach. The style required for the *Dorothy L. Sayers Mysteries* really warranted an illustrator rather than an animator who tended to paint on cel in a more cartoon way, which would have been totally wrong. However, illustrators were not necessarily used to working with moving image, so working with an animator who could deliver in a more painterly style was essential.

Again, I took my storyboard and mood boards around Soho to get quotes and a feeling of who might be right for the job. I also needed to find someone who was willing to spend the time it would take doing the job for a BBC budget! In the end I commissioned Richard Purdum Productions, who had been working for a while on the *Pink Panther* for Walt Disney. I think they felt that this was light relief from the more commercial world, and Richard wanted to take the challenge on himself. This company were a joy to work with, as they were so professional. A small section was done in order to agree on a style, and they completely understood what was needed.

For this drama series, I designed a typeface called Wimsey, to be used in the opening and end credits. This was drawn up for me by Ted Cload, an artworker frequently used by the in-house designers at Television Centre. The typeface was hand-drawn on whiteboards at about 2 inches (50mm) high. It was then made into a typeface by Dave Farey at Panache to be used for photosetting, a technique deployed at that time to produce type for print and for television. The subtitles for the drama were treated in the same way as the title sequence, except the live action came from the first few seconds of the drama, which 'came to life' from drawings, a device repeated in other movie credits since then. This was done to seamlessly transfer from the title sequence to the action of the drama itself. The work was rewarded with a Primetime Emmy Award, a first at that time, for the Graphic Design Department.

It is interesting looking back at pre-digital, to see how much digital and computer-generated imagery (CGI) would have been useful in some cases. It is almost as if there was a subconscious anticipation of CGI coming and certainly a need for it. This is so obvious in a few early sequences I created, where the ideas were executed by hand because there was no other way, and yet the use of CGI would have made them so much easier to produce and far more sophisticated, even far more acceptable!

Aping computer imagery

The idea for *De Bono's Thinking Course* (1982), from the Further Education Department, was to symbolize the scrambled brain, which then unscrambles and reveals the name of the programme. The artwork was produced by hand, as black-on-white drawings without the aid of a computer. These were pegged together in register to each other as done in traditional animation style. The difficulty in hand drawing was that the artwork was totally linear (made of lines), and it was essential that the lines were of consistent thickness and without any flaws (i.e. bits missing, glitches or blobs), otherwise the entire sequence would wobble and shimmer. A computer could have very easily worked out the transition from a jumble of lines animating into a logotype, but this had to be physically worked out on paper first by the artworker Freddy Shackle. Each drawing was copied photographically and reprinted as a clear on black Kodalith (i.e. the lines were clear and the background solid black on a large photographic plastic-like material) then re-pegged in register to each other. This allowed for the sequence to be shot backlit on a 35mm film rostrum camera with a coloured gel over to make the clear lines a colour. The glow effect was achieved by adding a filter to the lens of the camera.

Computer Graphic Imagery (CGI)

When CGI finally arrived, the wireframe, the linear artwork I had tried to implement suddenly became an easy solution to deliver. The entire department was sent in small groups to Middlesex University, where the developer of CGI in this country, Professor John Vince, was delivering workshops to teach designers about computer-generated imagery. We all had a go at creating a short, very basic animated sequence, which could be drawn out on paper. This was the very beginning of computer animation when perfect wireframe images could be produced in three dimensions, but when hidden line removal had still not been conquered. This was a time when the development of a sequence could be plotted, and the computer could miraculously work out the in-betweens. Imperial College London, a leader in science and technology, had a massive computer-generated 'machine' that allowed you to draw out on huge clear cels with a black rapidograph (an ink pen used by artworkers to draw very accurately using different nib widths). We experimented with abandonment, waiting for a job to come along to try out this potential new designer's tool. Initially, I dipped my toes in by using the technology to create just a few small elements of sequences trying both traditional toplit and backlit filming methods in *Ken Hom's Chinese Cookery* (1984) and *The Italians* (1984) for instance.

Computer graphics were fast developing. Hidden line removal was finally solved, and fully rendered, textured and coloured more lifelike images were being produced. In 1988 I was commissioned to create some maps for a programme called *The War in Korea*, written and presented by Max Hastings. Television graphic designers were requested to create maps hundreds of times for programmes, and it wasn't exactly considered to be the most creative or 'juiciest' of briefs. However, in this case I saw the potential of using the latest computer technology to deliver. Digital Facility Houses were often keen to get involved in potential TV innovative projects to further their capabilities and attract other projects from possibly more lucrative advertising clients. This was the case with Peter Florence at Digital Image.

The BBC production office managed to secure Ministry of Defence maps of Korea showing numerically the plan and elevation of the entire country, but with strategic military areas blanked out. With this data a CGI map of Korea was created so we could move around showing troop movements and areas of attack. We also created a three-dimensional sequence to travel through the snow laden Hungnam Valley, where software for snow and mist had to be specially written and developed. The sequences had a few issues, which needed more time and money to solve, as it was early days in the medium, but the work was still heralded an innovation and there were numerous press releases about it. In hindsight, the work would have been easier and without flaws done in a tried and tested traditional method, but the lure of trying to develop something new and original was at the time too great.

In comparison, a few years later, *Chronicle* (1989) could actually have been created in CGI. However, the sequence would have looked more like the starter for a game show than a documentary. I felt that a documentary series about real archaeological places required a certain realism, integrity and soul. At that time CGI wasn't as super realistic as it can be today; atmospherics and optical realism, which today are

Figure 12.3 *Chronicle* (1989) Liz Friedman on set with models made by Alan Kemp, and motion control rig. Courtesy Liz Friedman.

taken for granted, were still a long way from being developed. Computers did, however, play a significant part, as one was used to programme a 35mm film camera motion control rig suspended from the ceiling (see Figure 12.3). This allowed the move itself to be choreographed to the frame with registered precision. This sequence won the Prix Pixel at Imagina Monte Carlo 1991, Gold Award at BDA USA and Finalist RTS UK.

Conclusion

Examining the different animation techniques that I've employed over several decades for documentaries and drama series demonstrates how ideas for titles and content sequences have in many cases forced innovations and advances in animation practices that were cutting edge at the time. Sometimes a limited budget or other external constraints can be the mother of invention. As new digital technology became available in the animation studios, more options for achieving ever ambitious motion graphics became possible. Working at BBC Television Centre also meant that the Visual Effects (VFX) facilities companies in London's Soho were easily accessible. A BBC budget may have been considerably lower than an advertising one, but the *cache* associated with a primetime television programme and an opportunity to push creative boundaries made it a worthwhile investment for many commercial animation companies. Even better when they win industry accolades.

13 BBC Open University

Moving education design from analogue to digital

HAYDON YOUNG

Introduction

Alexandra Palace, an 1860s Victorian entertainment centre in North London, was chosen as the site of Britain's first television transmissions on 2 November 1936 for its vantage point 300 feet above sea level, to accept the Very High-Frequency band (VHS). To facilitate this, the building was topped by a 215-foot transmission mast. The black-and-white programming was transmitted analogue at 405-line resolution, being seen by around 400 receivers on 10×8 inch screens. After the war the BBC developed rapidly, and in the early 1950s 'Ally Pally' (as it was affectionately called) was becoming too small and run down for this burgeoning television industry. In 1960s the opening of BBC Television Centre in Shepherds Bush, West London, offered eight large studios rather than the two at 'Ally Pally', and when BBC News moved out of Alexandra Palace to Television Centre in 1969, it provided space and resources for the BBC and Open University (OU) educational partnership to evolve.

Prior to this, educational television in the United Kingdom was broadcast in closed circuit systems such as the Inner London Education Authority (ILEA) serving schools and colleges, while some universities also had audio-visual facilities–founded by the Labour Government in 1963 led by Prime Minister Harold Wilson's plans for higher education of ' A University of the Air'. Few people thought this was possible, but he was determined that this should go ahead.

OU broadcasts began in January 1971 on BBC2 at odd times in the schedule, so as not to compete with other programming. This television and radio service quickly proved it possible to teach university-level subjects, to unqualified students of all ages, at a distance. In the first year there were four foundation courses in mathematics, science, social science and arts. This later expanded to six faculties adding education and technology. By 1974, 40,000 students across the United Kingdom were watching BBC OU programming.

Housed only in the northeast wing of this huge decaying brick and glass structure, surrounded by parkland, Ally Pally was a mini-BBC with all the resources, facilities and skills to create its educational programming. In addition to video production it boasted in-house set design and construction, graphic design, a photographic studio, model and effects workshop, film editing and, importantly, its own BBC Club Bar. The course production directors were academics previously having had three months of BBC training in video studio directing and filmmaking. The programme presenters were also highly regarded academics, not broadcasters.

OU graphic design

In the early 1970s the graphic design studio at the BBC OU was an evolving group of around twelve designers and assistants led by its manager, John Aston. I came in as an assistant having previously worked as a senior print and book designer. They were a pioneering, dedicated team creating a huge body of work across the faculties. Designers were heavily involved in the programme making as the design interpretation was often crucial to the understanding of the subject matter. A designer with assistant was assigned to courses within each faculty. Coming from print design or audio-visual backgrounds, they were not employed for their academic qualifications but for their ability to translate and communicate educational material in a concise visual style. As a gauge production directors often treated them like students with a minimal knowledge of the topic. Briefing sessions were long and intense, in order for the designer to understand the main educational requirements of the programming. This rapport led to strong working relationships. From these briefing sessions the designer and assistant would create storyboards, plans and layouts of their graphic solutions, presenting them for correction or final approval.

This was a pioneering time for educational programme-making as there was no definitive blueprint. The academic programme presenters, who were used to giving ad hoc lectures to students, had to communicate their subjects via television, a totally different experience for them. Together with the production directors, they had to commission graphics six weeks in advance, so they needed to know exactly what they wanted to achieve for the studio recording. Typically there would be a one-day rehearsal and one-day recording. The same challenge could be said for the motion designer. There was no past design blueprint or template to work from. A general consistent type and image style would be set after a briefing without knowing what the full design implications of the subject course might reveal further down the line. Over time production processes and templates were created to eliminate such problems.

There was a definite Levi jeans, tank top dress code and facial hair style compared to the scholars' ties and crumpled suits. Also more, 'roll your own' *Old Holborn* cigarettes than the pipe-smoking academics. The enormous, allocated space for the BBC Club Bar was a focal point for downtime activities whether playing snooker, badminton, a game of darts or just hanging out. Here you could meet anybody in a truly egalitarian environment. Ally Pally was an extraordinary place to work with its huge open areas and intimate cubby holes. In one large area small wooden huts were built to house the film editors. Going to a classical concert in the grand hall, you could watch the house sparrows and pigeons swoop above your head, in time to the music, through the broken glass roof. It had spectacular entertainment in its past from horse racing, a skating rink and Victorian Theatre to music gigs such as the 14 Hour Technicolour Dream, 'the seminal psychedelic happening, in 1967'. It hosted the Rolling Stones, Led Zeppelin, Jay-Z and numerous classical and jazz concerts.

Every year the OU would hold summer schools at various universities in the United Kingdom. This was an opportunity for students to meet up with fellow students and their tutors for a few days to discuss their courses. I went to Stirling University one summer and was highly amused by what I saw graffitied on the concrete tunnel wall entering the refectory. It had been put there by the young full-time student(s) from the university and said, 'One day when you grow up you can become an Open University student too!'

In 1970 Peter Montagnon became the first head of the BBC OU Production Centre at Alexandra Palace. Before this appointment he had co-produced and directed the award-winning BBC landmark series *Civilisation*, hosted by the Art Historian Kenneth Clark.

Of educational television graphic design, Peter wrote,

From the point of view of the television producer, television graphics are perhaps one of the most potent tools that he has at his disposal. What then does he want, style, impact, wit? Yes, but above all, when he is making a documentary or educational programme, he wants clarity, economy and purposiveness. The truism that genius is 1% inspiration, and 99% perspiration holds good in this area, just as it does for the producer, director or writer. Before you can deploy the essential 1% inspiration you have to do the spade work, you have to know not only what the techniques are but how to use them. Above all you as a graphic designer must understand why the programme is being made, what it sets out to convey. Graphics work for television is not just the icing on the cake – it is part of the cake. (Clarke 1974: 7)

In the main Ally Pally, motion designers could not produce in-house the volume of artwork themselves, so over time a cottage industry grew around north London. They were given the responsibility to manage their schedule, budget and workload. Work was commissioned with professional animators, animation and special effects film studios, hand-lettering artists, artworkers as well as hot metal printers and small companies creating studio display boards and pull captions. This required a close working relationship between talented people. Supplying accurate storyboards and layouts, work was contracted out on an ad hoc basis, often with short schedules and small budgets.

Tools of the trade: Video

In those formative days of video motion graphics tools ranged from basic for video to sophisticated for film. Black and white, 405-line definition, 4×3 aspect ratio was not kind to large amounts of textural information. Reproducing mathematical equations and formulae was a challenge, as tests by the BBC suggested thirty-six characters being the maximum line length for legibility. Also, television receivers were not accurately set up, so a 'cut off' area was designated to safeguard information. Up to 20 per cent of the TV perimeter area was considered not suitable for essential graphic material. A set of plastic graticules was designed, which showed this cut off from a 1-inch to a 20-inch field size (4×3 aspect ratio) enabling the designer to accurately plot the safe area. Also, these graticules would be used to plot sequences for camera moves for both film and video. BBC OU programmes from the video studio were transmitted in black and white, whereas all film programmes and inserts were in colour. Early television receivers were not capable of distinguishing a wide range of tones, so the designer was required to understand this limitation. To translate the colour palette into black and white required a system that could be relied on. This was known as a 'greyscale', where tonal values related to colours. So, artwork in colour could be distinguished in black and white.

In the early 1970s the reproduction and legibility of type on television were paramount for the BBC OU Graphic Design Studio when designing for large amounts of educational content. Also important was the designer's 'aesthetic' of function for effective communication. Compared to print design, legible fonts for television were limited for prime information content, so part of the motion designer's skill was taking into consideration time-based media and television resolution versus type size, font and layout.

Transfer lettering (Letraset) was used across a whole range of design solutions. Although time-consuming to use, it had a choice of fonts and was of print-quality reproduction. Hot transfer printing was another means of creating type. A thin foil of plastic-based material is laid onto a heated lead type set in a press. Put under extreme pressure, the foil melts where the type design is set, leaving a permanent impression on the cardboard or celluloid caption. The Character Generator was developed by BBC Engineering through consultation with the Graphic Design Studio, and the first model was basically an electronic typewriter limited to a standard fixed font and without letter spacing or kerning functions. Later research led to BBC Engineering being instrumental in developing the first Aston character generator together with Aston Electronics.

In the television studio a whole range of basic graphic equipment was available. Caption Stands were ubiquitous. Mainly 12×9-inch captions, photographs, text or diagrams were placed onto caption stands for filming as cutaways. Selected cameras could then alternate and captions changed by hand, creating a simple sequence of images. Strap Easels were bigger stands used for larger captions and sequences. The locked-off studio camera faced horizontally at the stand. These 'pull caption' sequences became an art form in cardboard construction. Several layers of black cards were pinned together. Each layer contained graphic information in its final sequence. Layers on top had cut-out windows revealing this information but are hidden by strips of black card that can slide to reveal each sequential layer. The picture output is given a higher contrast from the gallery, so the graphic information is seen clearly on a black background. These step-by-step black sliders were then pulled open by an operator, revealing each element of the sequence.

The Roller Caption Stand comprised of a variable-speed motor driving two rollers. A roll of paper containing text or artwork is wrapped around both rollers in the television aspect ratio. The lined-up studio camera remains fixed horizontally as the rollers rotate, top to bottom or side to side, revealing the moving sequence. This device was also commonly used for end credits moving on screen, which could then be superimposed over a live-action background as required.

Large Display Boards were used extensively in the Video Studio. Their use involved close collaboration with the set designer to reflect the identity of the specific faculty course. Display Boards could be any size from 4×3, 12×6 feet or wrapped around the studio as flattage. They were used for an eclectic mix of artwork such as maps, formulae and PBUs (photographic blow-ups). Mainly a wooden construction they could be surfaced with paint, plastic or painted thin plate so magnetic strips could be used. This hands-on technique was used a lot. On camera the presenter placed or took away magnetic captions onto the board's surface, building a sequence to their commentary. Like the 'pull caption' this magnetic board technique became a design challenge for the graphic designer and led to some highly creative design solutions.

The Caption Scanner consisted of twin carriers containing 30, 35mm slides in each. The designer could create artwork up to sixty frames of animation. These are then copied onto 35mm transparencies and loaded alternatively into the twin carriers. Operated from the studio gallery, a projector scans from one carrier slide to the other, so a sequence of sixty full-screen images can be recorded.

Tools of the trade: Film

For animation or special effects work, although expensive, 35mm film was preferred over 16mm due to higher resolution when employing opticals, cel (clear acetate sheets) animation or multiple exposure work. Although opening title design was very limited for the BBC OU designer, frame-by-frame cel animation with complex sequences was produced. Budget considerations, tight schedules and video studio output were always a didactic challenge.

The Animation Stand comes in all shapes and sizes, from a basic rig to a professionally designed multipurpose system. The camera, looking down, can travel vertically up and down a column to magnify or travel away from the artwork on the base table, which can move independently north/south, east/west and rotate. Depending on the type of stand, the movement over the artwork would be either hand-cranked frame by frame, electronically powered or, later, under computer control. Lights on either side of the stand provide even illumination. An animation camera will have the ability to create fades and dissolves in the camera, as well as shooting in reverse and multiple exposure sequences for effects work.

Aerial Imaging was a technique that used a film projector in sync with the camera. The projected image (live action or animation) was, via a 45-degree mirror, projected onto the underside of the compound through a condenser lens. Type or animation on clear cels could then be placed on top and both captured on film, frame by frame. This system could also be used for rotoscoping, where the projected live action could be copied frame-by-frame drawing on cels in the required style.

Multiplane was created to add depth to cel animation by the Walt Disney Studio. Several sheets of glass are mounted at different distances under the camera. Each glass level holds different cel artwork, building the total required scene. Panning across these glass planes at different speeds and exploring depth of field focus by pulling from one layer to another would give a convincing impression of depth.

Multiple Exposure is an 'in camera' technique where the same film frames are exposed more than once in order to combine two or more visual elements. Using black mattes and masks, the camera films one pass is then wound in reverse, ready to accept the next pass. Commonly, this technique was used for combining animation with live action.

Motion Control was advanced in Stanley Kubrick's film *2001: A Space Odyssey* (1968), which pioneered precise mechanically repeatable moves for both camera rig and model. Further advances were made by George Lucas for *Star Wars* (1977), using a digitally controlled camera to perform complex and repeatable moves. It was a few years later that motion control became affordable and popular, with a choice of rig sizes. Before computerization, filming large models frame by frame in a studio required manually shooting subjects horizontally using a camera connected to a tracking dolly. Camera tape was applied to the dolly's track and on the handles, steering each axis of movement such as pans, tilts and rotations. The number of frames required for each sequence was calculated, and each frame was marked onto the tapes. Allowance had to be made for speeding up and down to obtain smooth movement. Although this was a labour-intensive process, it worked extremely well. An example of this technique was used for the BBC Sutton Hoo documentary series.

Sutton Hoo was a major Anglo-Saxon archaeological site in the United Kingdom. A recurring bird motif found at the dig was chosen to be incorporated as a decorative element into the 'S' of the series title (see Figure 13.1). This motif, as if growing out of rock and discovering the past, was the concept. The bird illustration was traced frame by frame onto a limestone block. An out-of-shot stone mason then cut out each segment frame by frame, while the dolly (each frame calibrated on tape) tracked and rotated back from close-up to a wide shot of the whole title. This 35mm twenty-second sequence was all filmed in camera without additional opticals.

Later mobile rigs were also built for filming in any location. It would be several years before realism using computer modelling would become a serious alternative to motion control filming. It had to first go through the CGI (Computer Generated Image) solid-shaded infancy of 'flying logos' that invaded our screens in the early 1980s. Motion control has continued to evolve, expanding the creative possibilities for filmmakers.

Illustration and artwork

For both video and film different styles of illustration were commissioned for modules across the faculties. The science faculty tended to use air brushing as it mimicked three-dimensional imagery (i.e. molecules and atoms), whether on 12×9-inch captions, large studio boards or animation. The maths faculty's illustration was, in the main, flat graphic solutions with typographic equations and formulae (see Figure 13.2). Large areas of Pantone-coloured paper or paint together with thin-coloured tapes were used to create these images, which to the uninitiated eye looked like abstract art. Arts and social science faculties tended towards a more realistic illustration approach. If relevant to the solution, any illustration technique was employed from pen to paint, charcoal to collage. When developing ideas, the designer had a number of freelance illustrators with a variety of skills to call upon.

Figure 13.1 *Sutton Hoo* (1987) title sequence logo. Courtesy BBC.

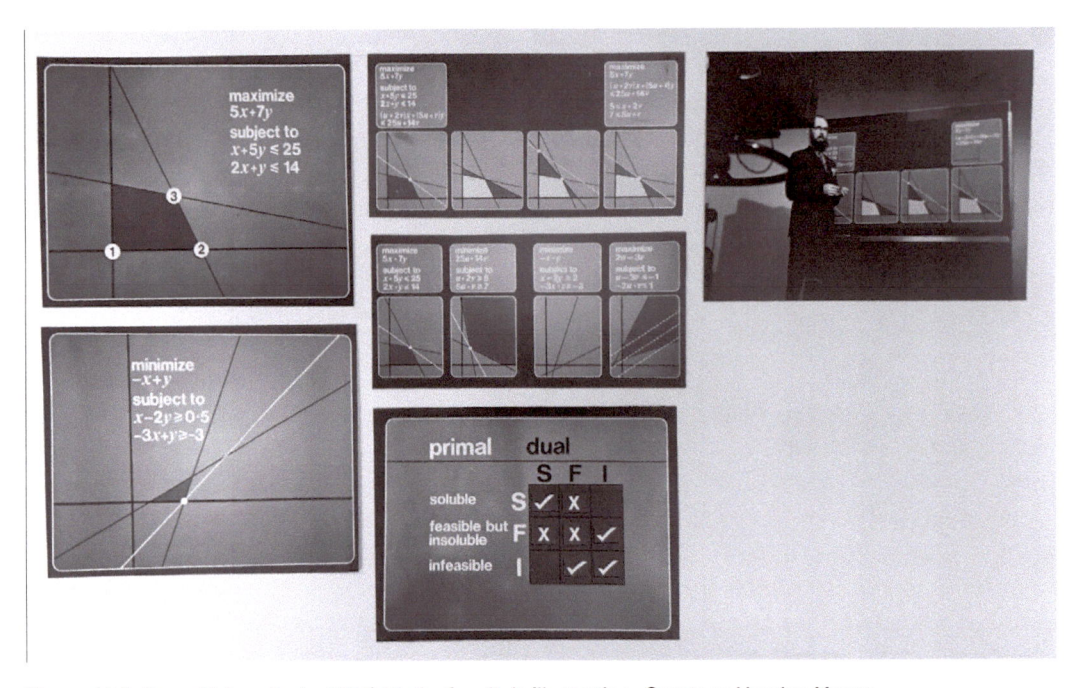

Figure 13.2 Open University (*c*. 1970) Maths faculty's illustration. Courtesy Haydon Young.

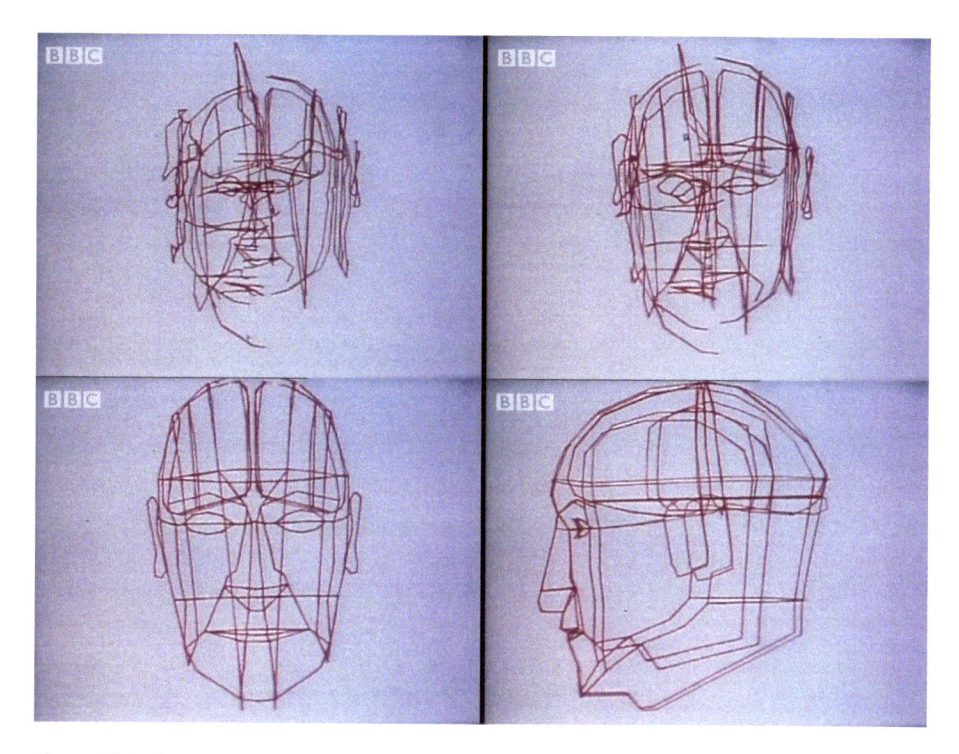

Figure 13.3 Open University (1976) *Personality and Learning* title sequence. Courtesy BBC.

Sound wasn't such an important tool for the educational designer as in general broadcast design. Few title sequences requiring music were created, and the programme content was mainly led by programme presenters in the video studio with film inserts. In those cases where the film sound was the responsibility of the designer, they would work closely with the in-house editor. Sound, whether narration, music or effects, would be recorded onto magnetic film sound stock. The exact timings can be worked out frame by frame from that soundtrack in order to prepare a 'dope sheet'. This paper document showed several columns, actions and camera instructions. Accurate written details were entered in so when filming the animation sequence, it would accurately sync together with the sound.

An example of a hybrid of early digital computer graphics and an analogue recording is the title sequence for *Personality & Learning* (1976) (see Figure 13.3). Using photo portraits of a variety of individuals, combined with a rotating linear everyman image, gave the opening a strong sense of the educational authority for this social science series and was one of the first computer-aided title sequences ever produced at the OU. A vector computer system created by Professor John Vince, then of Brunel University, was used to create the wire frames and to interpolate between one image and the next before drawing the line drawings onto cels with a Rotring pen and a plotter. The cels were registered, painted and then filmed on a rostrum camera.

During the 1980s as television technology advanced, the video recorder allowed students to record overnight on BBC2. In 1982 the BBC OU left Ally Pally to move into a new purpose-built OU Production Centre at the Walton Hall complex in Milton Keynes. This was an up-to-date facility with much-enlarged video and film resources able to develop the new emerging educational systems. Audio-visual material for courses was made directly by the university and sent to students on CDs, then later on DVDs.

Moving from education to information

In the middle of the 1970s, moving from the lucid, didactic world of educational design at the OU to general broadcast television at the BBC Television Centre presented a different challenge for any ambitious motion designer. There was a drain of talent that moved across, such as John Aston, John Cook, Darrel Pockett and Michael Graham-Smith, amongst others, who in turn made space for other up-and-coming graphic design graduates and juniors at OU. Being released from strict academic design discipline to a whole plethora of programme genres was both refreshing and rewarding. It opened up a rich vein of creative possibilities, from sports and drama, news and children's shows to comedy and arts programming. One important difference was the competitive nature of the broadcast designer compared to the educational designer. Healthy interdepartmental and interchannel rivalry played an important factor in the high standard of work created. Television industry design awards were submitted too and creatively fought over. The daily press and TV reviewers would often write about the quality of design work in productions. The allocation of projects became a cross to bear as to who would get the best drama, comedy or sports project brief. The BBC Television Centre was like a small city where the motion designer could pick up the internal telephone, knowing somewhere an individual or department could help with his or her creative problem-solving. At that time in the mid-1970s it employed 600 people in the BBC Design Group alone.

This high standard progressed into the 1980s and was the catalyst for new technology to dominate television, as exemplified by the growth and widespread use of video. Video technology was expanding and so was its marriage partner, the computer. Analogue still prevailed, but digital was making inroads into television.

Tomorrow's World

My transition from Ally Pally to Television Centre was smooth and extremely rewarding. As in OU, social and science-based projects tended to remain my main diet, though I did work on a wider variety of genres. I was also fortunate to work on the visionary science and technology flagship weekly series *Tomorrow's World* for several years. It was primarily a live studio-based series with film inserts shot wherever the latest developments in science and technology were happening. Live broadcasting was fraught with various problems, such as guest innovators and their inventions going badly wrong in the studio. Several presenters became household names while working on the show, from the original Raymond Baxter and James Burke to Judith Hann, Michael Rodd and Maggie Philbin. It also ran live exhibitions, often based in London's Earls Court. These were open to the public and featured a variety of the latest scientific innovations. The series ran from 1965 to 2003. In the 1970s and 1980s it was watched by over 10 million viewers and was said to have inspired generations of children to become scientists.

I produced opening titles for *Tomorrow's World* in 1980 (see Figure 13.5), which replaced the iconic 1976 award-winning titles by Pauline Talbot (Carter) (see Figure 13.4), another ex-BBC OU motion designer. This 'Brain Planet' concept imagery, intercut with abstract flashes of current technology, conveyed a strong sense of science fantasy and fact. The brain-planetary physical models were filmed at Oxford Scientific Films using one of the latest motion control rigs under mechanical control. This very large but well-balanced fingertip control 'Galactorscope' rig with various axes of movement utilized a fibre-optic snorkel lens attachment. This enabled the camera to travel down the model's smoke-filled brain valleys smoothly in slow motion. This footage was then edited together with the current technological live action.

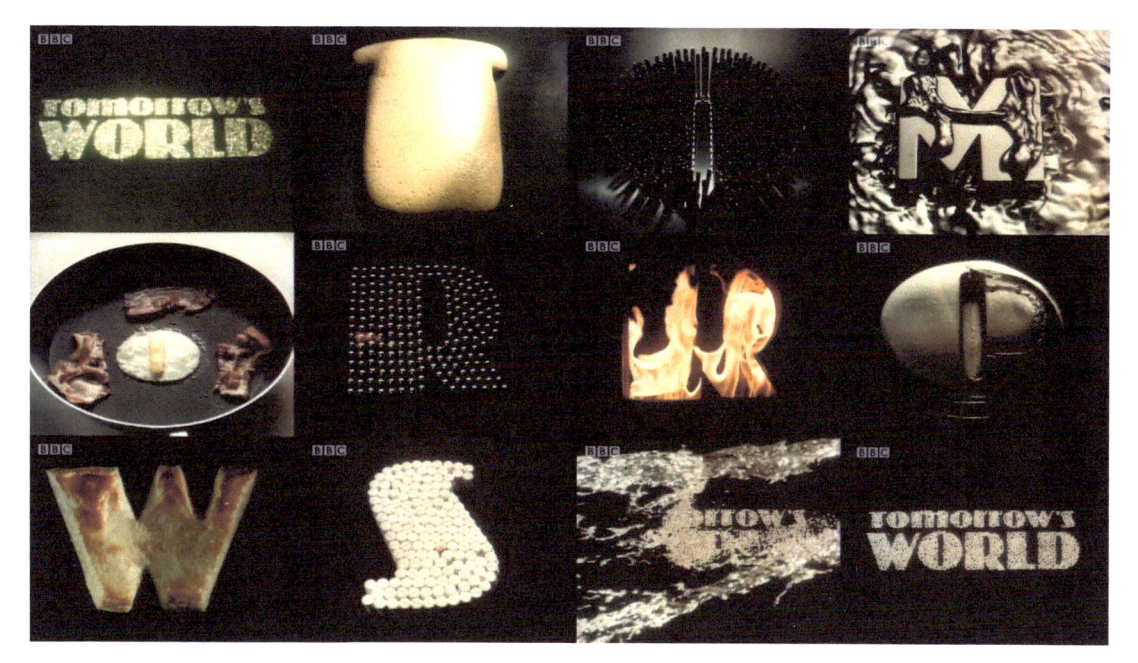

Figure 13.4 *Tomorrow's World* (1976) title sequence. Courtesy BBC.

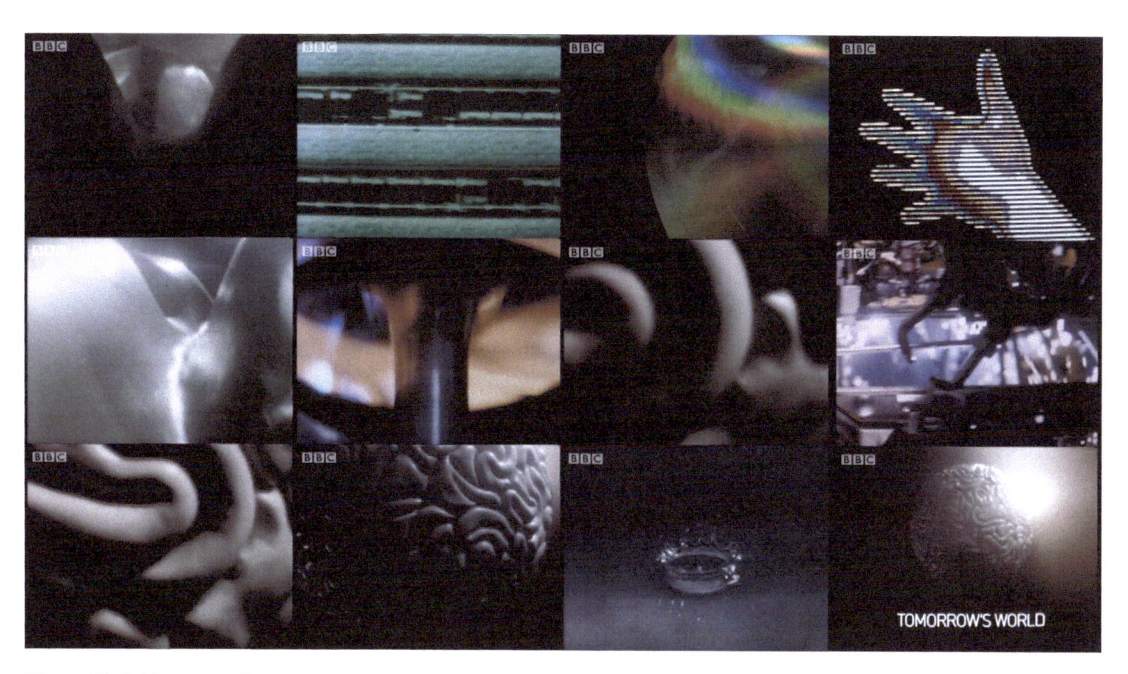

Figure 13.5 *Tomorrow's World* (1980) title sequence. Courtesy BBC.

In 1984 the incoming executive producer invited me to create a new identity, which reflected evolving digital technology and emerging scientific insights. After some research and head-wrestling, I presented an identity that was approved.

Virtual reality

The original rationale for the opening titles was based on the idea of virtual reality (VR), which at the time was the domain of science-fiction writers, although tests were underway in America. I wanted to begin the sequence with someone wearing a stylized VR headset. After discussions with the series editor, we agreed this first image should become the symbol for the series, so we began with zooming into a huge blue dimpled sphere. The sphere is full of water, with real goldfish swimming within a television screen. BBC Engineering created this by actually putting the live TV into a tank of water, suitably waterproofed, while playing the goldfish clip on the TV. Small objects (computer chips) fall through the water together with the fish. This was, I'm afraid, my little private 'fish and chips' joke! The fish clip wipes through to a black-and-white clip of Charlie Chaplin. At that time an American production company was digitally adding colour to black-and-white films, so we commissioned them to produce this clip. Through a wipe Charlie turns into colour as a stream of bubbles float through the screen. This screen animates to a rotating, close-up of a computer-generated head. Solid, shaded complex 3D imagery was still in its infancy at this time, as vector graphics was the computer design standard. To achieve this image, I employed a prosthetic makeup designer (see Figure 13.6).

After some testing a bald actor's head was covered with rubber bicycle patches, then painted and lacquered for a gloss finish. The actor was then filmed rotating and talking on a turntable. It was flattering to be told shortly after transmission that this clip was already on the showreel of one of the leading American computer graphics production companies, purporting to show how good they were at solid shading. I sent them a photograph of my actor in full makeup and asked them to take it off their reel. As the talking face rotates around to the back of the head, it appears to morph into blue and white flowers. This transition employed frame-by-frame plasticine animation, the flowers matching into a real bouquet of blue and white flowers in the form of the resolving TW symbol. We transition

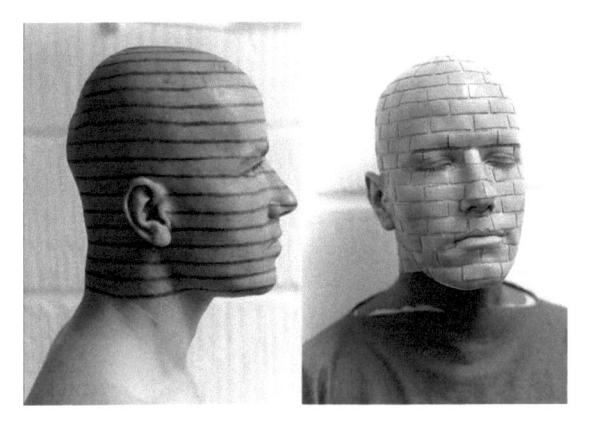

Figure 13.6 *Tomorrow's World* (1984) Prosthetic makeup for the title sequence. Courtesy Haydon Young.

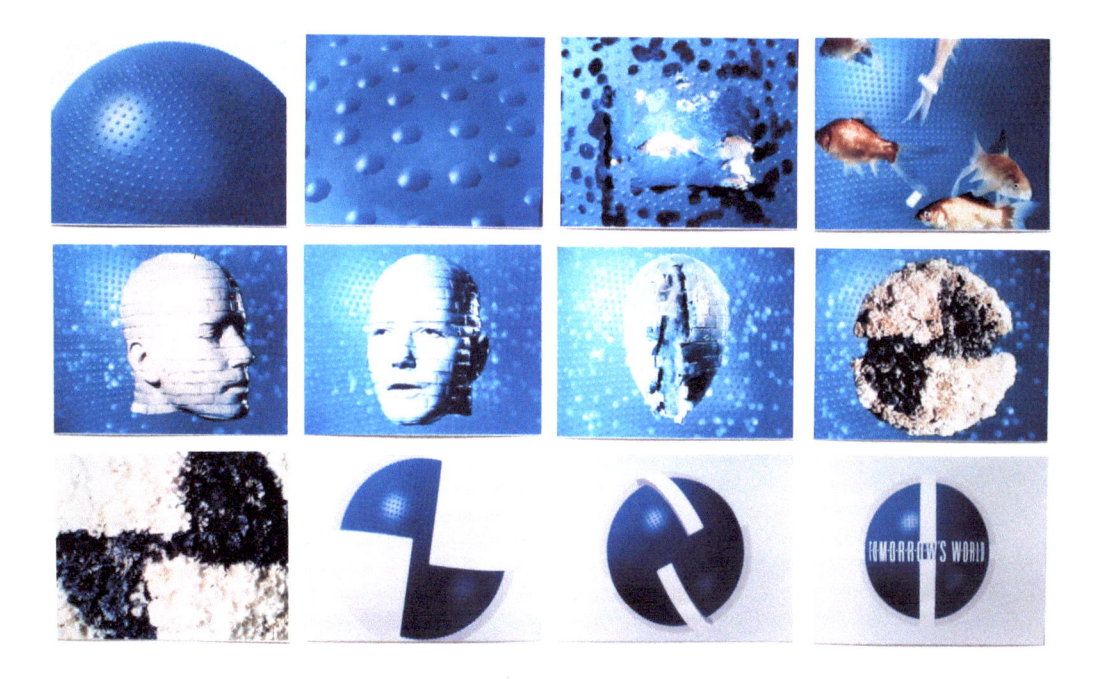

Figure 13.7 *Tomorrow's World* (1984) title sequence. Courtesy BBC.

through to the blue 3D globe encased in the two white outer layers. These rotate around to reveal the symbol T and W encasing the blue sphere as *Tomorrow's World* animates around the centre of the sphere. These elements of 35mm filming and 3D computer modelling were brought into the BBC Video Rostrum Unit. This early pioneering digital manipulation system developed by BBC Engineering achieved exceptional quality chroma keying, animation and an array of potential special effects – a forerunner of the digital revolution yet to come (see Figure 13.7).

Conclusion

Today, the OU is still the largest academic institution in the United Kingdom and a world leader in flexible distance learning. Since 1971 it has taught more than 2 million students worldwide. It has been in partnership with the BBC since its inception and today creates award-winning co-productions for TV, radio and digital.

The BBC, since its inception, has held the high ground in terrestrial television. It has had to change and adapt to market forces and prepare for the digital age with competition from home and abroad. With a global reach, its commercial arm, BBC Studios, now has a revenue of £1.4 billion.

The motion designer has adapted from those early analogue video days to a vast array of digital screen-based media. They require computer and digital technology skills to work in areas such as interactive, web and mobile technologies, as well as film and television. Hopefully, creativity will not be traded or eroded using emerging technologies, but rather enhanced by it.

I have very fond memories of my time at the BBC and all the talented people I worked alongside.

14 Digital pathfinders

The BBC Computer Graphics Workshop 1980 to 1987

BILL GARDNER MBE

Introduction

In this chapter I provide a personal account of a ground-breaking period in the development of computer graphics in UK television, in particular discuss the development of the BBC Computer Graphics Workshop (CGW) at Television Centre, London. I began at the BBC in 1980 and founded the BBC CGW the same year and then went on to manage the department until 1987. Through this period the department oversaw some of the most significant changes to graphics technology, inventing and implementing new ways of producing text and visual graphics for BBC Television programmes.

Think of a number

Within the BBC amongst engineers and programme makers, there have always been the brightest minds and appetite to advance broadcasting technology. My first foray into this world was in 1979 when the BBC Bristol production team from Johnny Ball's *Think of a Number* spotted colour graphic animations at a trade fair that I had created for Tektronix Inc. While working as a research fellow in Computer Aided Design (CAD) and user interface design at the ABACUS Computer Aided Architecture research group at Strathclyde University, I made a rudimentary computer graphic colour paint system and some simple animations. This system was put together using a Tektronix 4027 colour terminal (Gardner 1980) linked to a Hewlett Packard digitizer and an HP9845 desktop computer, which I programmed in Basic. Johnny Ball and his producer wanted to include my graphics in a computer-themed episode of the show and invited me down to see the programme being made. This was my first look behind the scenes of television broadcasting.

When I watched the BBC and ITN coverage of the November 1979 UK General Election later that year, I saw how both channels were using computer graphics to illustrate the overnight results. A little later, a colleague of mine at ABACUS suggested that I have a look at an interesting BBC job advertised in the *Guardian*'s media page – for a senior systems analyst, who would be tasked with developing computer graphics for BBC Television. Intrigued, I applied, sending in a U-Matic showreel, wrapped in tinfoil, in a Jiffy bag along with my application. At the interview conducted by Ron Neil, *Newsnight* producer, and Terry Smith, head of BBC Computer Services, both laughed and said they thought I'd sent in a pack of sandwiches with my form!

The job was based at BBC Television Centre (TVC) in Shepherd's Bush, initially on a two-year contract. The brief I was given by TV senior management was to expand television productions' use of the existing Digital Equipment Corporation (DEC) PDP 11/40 minicomputer, which had been bought from Logica Ltd., along with a custom-designed graphic device called ICON (Logica 1980) and all the data processing software to present the 1979 General Election results. This contract was awarded to Logica in 1977–8, to a tender specification written by Chris Long, a BBC senior systems analyst, who reported to Terry Smith. This system was procured and installed by BBC's Studio Capital Projects Department on the sixth floor of TVC. Immediately after the 1979 General Election, Chris was headhunted by ITN to develop their live news graphics service using their new VT80 graphic device, operated by a team of computer programmers.

Digital type on screen

In March 1980, the total BBC TV computer graphic assets consisted of myself, as senior systems analyst, and programmers Robin Vinson and Ewen MacLaine, who had started the same day as me. After the 1979 General Election, this DEC/ICON system had been 'blacked' by industrial action by BBC engineers until about the early spring of 1980. When I started in my new post, the system was being used on a TV series, *Russian Language and People*, to display large Cyrillic characters. The graphic designer for the programme was Charles McGhie, a senior designer in the BBC Graphic Design Department who had also worked on the recent General Election graphics. ICON had been supplied by Logica with only one font, Helvetica, which Charles had helped refine.

In April 1980, the BBC Research Department (RD), BBC Engineering Designs Department (EDD) and BBC Graphic Design Department organized a weekend typographic workshop at a hotel at Windermere in the Lake District, which brought together BBC design and engineering staff and various external typographic and computer experts, including Neil Wiseman from Cambridge University. The workshop explored the problems of rendering many different typefaces for television and made a huge impression on me. At that time in the early 1980s, TV graphic designers were almost exclusively using hot press foil printing or Letraset on cardboard, or wet photographic processes, including 16mm black-and-white film for making programme graphics, roller-end titles and information graphics, along with captions and maps. An early electronic character generator, made by Ryley, had recently been introduced at BBC but was not liked by designers as it was limited to one typeface.

At the Windermere Workshop, one of the main technical talks was given by Nick Tanton, a research engineer at BBC RD's Kingswood Warren labs. Nick had been investigating the problems of aliasing (i.e. flickering, etc.), which interfered with the accurate rendering of the fine detail needed to display classic typefaces, as well as complicating adaptable letter spacing. These problems were particularly compounded by United Kingdom's 625-line interlaced television at 50 Hz. This workshop explained many of these issues to the BBC graphic designers in particular, but no immediate practical technical solutions were proposed for working designers. Nonetheless, this special workshop made me realize that improved anti-aliasing techniques would be a key technology in any new computer graphics systems that would be needed at BBC TVC, especially for typography, maps and diagrams in information graphics.

In the late spring of 1980, I embarked on a round of introductory meetings with various production departments to assess what the present ICON system could reasonably provide, working with a select number of graphic designers and producers. Our first major customer was the Sunday Night *Money Programme*, and we serviced this with information graphics and captions for two series, working mainly with George Daulby and Howard Moses, both graphic designers who worked within current affairs (based at Lime Grove, West London). Both George and Howard had also worked on by-elections and budgets programmes and were quick to adapt to the new technology of the DEC and ICON.

By the summer of 1980, I began to realize that both the DEC PDP 11/40, and the ICON were almost obsolete and that new systems were needed to enable further programme areas to benefit. It was also clear we needed to start providing design tools that graphic designers could use directly – a quite different approach from that taken then by ITN.

Apart from servicing television programmes, we also provided a data processing service to BBC EDD, which made customized 'black boxes' for electronic on air clocks, captions and material for branding BBC and Open University programmes. This graphic material was created as run-length datasets and transferred on magnetic tape to EDD.

In July 1980 I persuaded Ron Neil, a senior producer on *Newsnight*, to fund a trip to ACM SIGGRAPH, the main US computer graphics conference, held that year in Seattle. This was an eye-opener for anyone from the UK computer graphics community and a rare chance to see into the future of computer graphics. The conference featured papers by Ed Catmull, James Clark, Alvy Ray Smith, Jim Blinn of NASA's JPL and included a very relevant paper on anti-aliased typefaces on raster displays by John Warnock (who later invented Postscript and co-founded the Adobe Company). This paper was the breakthrough that was needed and that we could exploit in any new systems. The insight from that summer's 1980 SIGGRAPH Conference thus helped me set the direction for future systems for computer graphics on BBC Television.

The BBC Computer Graphics Workshop

After SIGGRAPH I decided to coin the term 'BBC Computer Graphic Workshop' (CGW), in homage to the famous BBC Radiophonic Workshop, whose staff had suggested that we create our own branding and identity within BBC Graphic Design. With the support and encouragement of Manager John Aston, our small computer team of three moved successfully from BBC Computer Services to the Graphic Design Department. Previously I had requested that our small computer team of three move from BBC Computer Services to Graphic Design Department, and their Head of Department Brian Tregidden was very supportive.

In early 1981, I started to search for new graphic devices that might suit our rather specialist requirements for TV quality graphics, in particular, 'smart' frame-stores – that is, memory stores that had multi-plane storage, with at least 8-bits per plane, and able to render full-colour images and graphics. The most advanced systems at SIGGRAPH 1980 had 3×8-bit frame-stores, capable of displaying images in 16 million colours. Ideally such a system would include a microcomputer, peripherals and backup storage. We needed to be able to connect, by direct memory transfer (DMA), to larger computers, such as DEC's VAX 11/750, seen as a logical upgrade from our DEC PDP 11/40. Such a system also needed to host up to fifty data input data terminals for large projects such as general elections and the Olympic Games.

I developed an outline specification and a management case paper (Gardner 1981) to justify the likely high cost of a new main computer, its installation and any attached new peripherals, including new computer graphic devices. My paper estimated the likely total cost to be about £500,000 for these new systems (Gardner 1981). This scale of investment necessitated making presentations to both the chief engineer of BBC Television and the then director general Alastair Milne.

These requirements were agreed with BBC Studio Capital Projects Department (SCPD), and the specification for the new 'smart' frame-store graphic devices was sent out to several companies, including Sigma, Spaceward, SGI and Quantel. The winning bid was made by Quantel, who were surprised how close my specification was to their newly launched Paintbox, which had a Motorola 68000 micro-processor and multiple full TV-spec frame-stores, as well as an attached disc drive capability, but sadly lacked the DMA of our newly ordered DEC VAX 11/750. Instead, the Quantel would have to speak to the VAX via a fast 9600-baud RS232 serial line. What Quantel finally delivered was their own development rig, for the Paintbox and an application programmer's toolkit that allowed us to build our own software routines within the Paintbox. As part of the deal with Richard Taylor (managing director of Quantel), the BBC CGW staff were required to sign non-disclosure agreements regarding Quantel's IP. We ordered three soft Paintboxes for *Election Night*, one of which was earmarked for the proposed BBC TV Weather System.

Life got complicated when SCPD decided the new system would need a new computer room at our base on the sixth floor of TVC. The BBC CGW team, which by mid-1982 had then grown to five people (myself, Robin, Ewen and new recruits Colin Wrey and Tom Hartwell), all had to move to a BBC computer suite at Sulgrave House for three months while the new computer room was built. The new DEC 11/750 was installed originally with 2 MB of main memory and two 60 MB exchangeable multi-platter disc drives, each the size of a large washing machine! The first three of our six 'soft' Quantel Paintboxes were installed in the new machine room. Our refurbished offices had eight workstation positions linked by audio and data lines to our machine room and onward to any studio in TVC. The BBC CGW was now a reality and ready for business (see Figure 14.1).

Once re-established on the sixth floor of TVC, each member of the team specialized in different aspects – myself now as manager, Robin as senior analyst/programmer, Ewen as senior programmer, databases and communications, Colin as the Quantel expert and Tom as the main interface with production teams. Naturally the arrival of the Paintbox in TVC attracted the interest of the graphic designers, and we began to get work from various departments, including *Children in Need*, game show programmes and some sports results areas, as well as our regular work for current affairs via *Newsnight*'s producers.

At SIGGRAPH I had subscribed to the *Seybold Report*, which covered both printing and office systems and contained useful information on workstations and digital type foundries. Using leads from articles in *Seybold* and contacts made at a weeklong Typographic Seminar at Stanford University, I began to acquire commercial typeface databases from URW, ITC, MONOTYPE and other digital typeface suppliers on tape. Colin put these to good use and created downloadable, inbuilt anti-aliased fonts, cached within each 'soft' Quantel Paintbox. This process also included the spacing tables demanded by senior designers Charles McGhie, Alan Jeapes and John Cook.

Figure 14.1 BBC Computer Graphics Workshop mainframes, 1982. Courtesy Bill Gardner.

UK General Election 1983

By late 1982 at the CGW we had most of the components and staff skills needed to create a new General Election System and looked forward to building the new Weather System, which I had previously proposed in a Development Report responding to the head of presentation (Gardner 1982).

Around this time, Peter Snow joined the BBC Current Affairs Department as presenter on *Newsnight*. He had previously worked on ITN's 1979 General Election programme. Peter needed a device to allow him to easily request specific election results analyses. In response, I designed a novel touchscreen terminal, which allowed presenters and producers to call up any one of 300 different animated results graphics, using a maximum of 4 'touches'. At ITN Peter had had to remember some 200 three-digit numbers to be able to call up different results graphic sequences via a standard keypad. The production team could not believe that this touchscreen terminal had originally been made by a company called John Fluke Inc. for flight engineers onboard Boeing 747s!

Apart from four touch-screen terminals, the DEC 11/750 was linked to 40 DEC VT100 input terminals, via thick wire Ethernet, to input results data on the night, phoned in from each Constituency count. All the control and database software, as well as the computer graphic software, was programmed by CGW staff using PASCAL compilers. I managed the overall progress of the computer project, with Robin as systems analyst, Ewen as the central database developer and Colin working on the Paintboxes. Rehearsals were always fun but could be tense when bugs crept in. However, David Dimbleby, the main political presenter, was always calm and polite and got on well with all the computer team (see Figure 14.2).

On election night itself, for the first time we were able to use very detailed maps of each constituency, which had been carefully traced by a Glasgow University Masters student intern onto Kodatrace and then subsequently scanned by LASERSCAN in Cambridge, using their unique line following scanner. The line data supplied was then formed into polygons, which then had to be rendered as anti-aliased fonts in the Quantels.

During the General Election development period, the CGW expanded again, with new programmers Chris Cony, Paul Doherty and Steve Walmsley joining the team, recruited via the *Guardian* and *New Scientist*. Our output with producers and graphic designers began to diversify into Quiz programmes, *Children in Need*, UK Budgets, US Elections, and regular slots in *Newsnight*. In spring 1984 we took on a contract to produce all the Los Angeles Olympic Games' medal tables and individual competition results for hundreds of events.

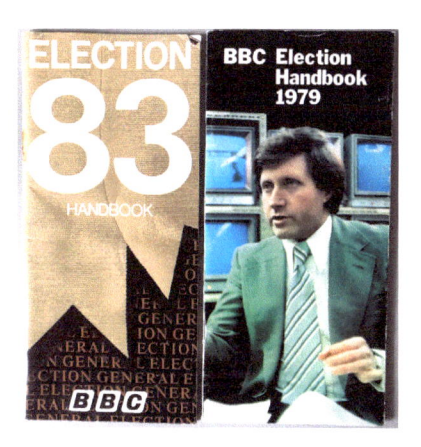

Figure 14.2 BBC Graphics Handbooks for Election 1979 and 1983. Courtesy Bill Gardner.

After the Olympics we started work on two new projects linked to the planned relaunch of BBC1 ident in early 1985. One project was to create a production weather system working with Liz Jones (Varrall), graphic designer, assisted by Sue Worthy, and the Meteorological Office Bracknell computer team. This request came from John Teather, the senior producer, in charge of BBC's weather programmes, who was under pressure to respond to BBC TV's move into Breakfast Television, based at Lime Grove. Led by Editor Ron Neil, the team there had purchased an early Quantel Paintbox, specifically for weather graphics. The other project was to work with Senior Graphic Designer Oliver Elmes and Brian Mason of BBC EDD, on a new BBC Globe station ident for BBC1 (see Figure 1.14).

BBC1 Globe

In 1984 the BBC1 ident was still generated using a mechanical device from a design by BBC senior graphic designer Sid Sutton in 1969 (see Figure 1.24). To revamp the BBC1 ident, another senior graphic designer, Oliver Elmes, envisaged a shaded see-through globe, which was capable of being stored in a dedicated hardware unit, designed by Brian Mason, a senior engineer at BBC EDD. Using my existing contacts with Professor Gordon Petrie at University of Glasgow, I swapped a new Apple Mac in exchange for a globe dataset of continental outlines.

Robin, Ewen and Colin at the CGW processed the high-resolution geographical data on our VAX to make a 5-second, 300 TV fields (*not* frames) anti-aliased, spinning, see-through globe resplendent in shaded gold against a blue background. This animation dataset was then compressed using a run-length encoding scheme, designed by Brian, written to magnetic tape on our VAX and then burnt onto EPROM storage at BBC EDD, along with suitable captioning for the regional variations. The field animated electronic rendition of the spinning globe was ultra-smooth and possibly a first within British television. It went live on the same day in February 1985, along with the first episode of *EastEnders* and the newly built CGW BBC TV Weather System. Later, we also built an animated BBC2 ident, designed by Alan Jeapes, which was also stored in a similar storage scheme.

BBC Weather

Way back in 1980, about a month or two after I joined the BBC, I let the BBC/Meteorological Office weathermen, Jack Scott and Bill Giles, know that I had an idea to replace their long-established, metal-backed maps, magnetic rubber strips (used as isobars), and their well-loved magnetic stick-on clouds, suns, temperature, rain and snow symbols. Until 1980 there were very few computer graphic devices that could generate detailed maps at TV resolution. The BBC's original Logica ICON device would not be a viable production system, but it could allow some prototyping. My proposal involved using both rear projection and Chromakey (CSO). This intrigued the production team, and I was told to book a studio and the large and expensive General Electric Light Valve monochrome video projector. This was a somewhat rare device but had a regular slot in *Top of Pops* to provide video effects on stage for the house dance group, 'Pan's People'.

Today weather reports can be broadcast from a corner office, but that day in May 1980 I was allocated TVC Studio 1, the biggest in Television Centre, to test the prototype weather system. An audience of about forty curious staff, designers, producers and engineers, as well as the BBC weathermen, turned up for the test. John Teather insisted that there had to be a presenter in vision and that they should relate naturally to the graphic background maps and graphics.

In my presentation I showed a set of schematics, explaining how the system components could work operationally. I followed up by introducing Jack Scott, the senior Meteorological Office weatherman. Jack was given a dummy forecast and he could see it on a blue-tinted weather map of the United Kingdom, created by a monochrome GE rear projector on a transparent rear projection screen with some blue lighting spilled on it. This was just clear enough for Jack to be able to convincingly point to places and symbols on the map. The Colour Separation Overlay (also known as Chromakey) electronics desk in the Studio Gallery inserted the map output from the ICON as a full-colour background, while the studio colour camera portrayed Jack in full colour too.

So, three years later in 1983, I was finally asked by John Teather and the then head of presentation at BBC TV to develop a production weather editing and presentation system. It had to be robust and easy enough to use for the duty Weatherman to compose their 'slide' presentations in their office and when they were delivering live presentations in studio. It was envisaged that the main Atlantic charts would come to TVC from the MET Office as metadata files, or compressed images, twice a day by BT KILOSTREAM and that the symbol map sequences would be manually composed by the Weatherman himself on an editing system and be broadcast live from the Presentation Studio several times a day.

Initial thoughts were to adapt two Quantel Paintboxes, but having had a preview of the new Apple Lisa system and seen how easy it was to use, we decided to adopt Lisa's as the user workstations, with a Quantel as the output device (see Figure 14.3). The composed graphic files were sent via the VAX to a soft Quantel Paintbox dedicated to weather output. My blue screen CSO Projection Presentation method was adopted, plus augmented by John Teather's useful suggestion of also displaying the man in vision image on an Autocue mirror on the front of the main studio camera. Tom Hartwell of the CGW and others trained the weathermen on the Lisa software, which had been written in Pascal by Paul Doherty and Steve Walmsley, CGW's youngest programmers.

The system was a resounding success and was voted the best computer system in Britain in 1985 by the British Computer Society in the Public Benefit category. We were rewarded with a splendid dinner in the Dorchester Hotel, where the award ceremony was held. In return I had to give a live demonstration and lecture about the system, with Robin showing how the editing system worked, in the Royal Society's main lecture theatre in the Mall, London, to an invited audience from representatives of many of Britain's learned societies (Gardner 1985a).

Figure 14.3 BBC Weather Presentation Apple Mac XL micro. Courtesy Bill Gardner.

Rapid change and development/animation aspirations

By 1985, the CGW now comprised about ten staff, including our resident graphic designer, Maeve Stephens, and my supportive PA, Toni Groves. A new recruit, Bryan Girdler, experimented with a free copy of MOVIE.BYU, from Brigham Young University in Utah, which was sourced from ZTH in Zurich. Later the CGW used this package for Charles McGhie's title sequence for *Tripods*, a science-fiction drama.

To capture the animation we adapted a high-quality Dunn/Honeywell video to film device by adding a FOROX stop-frame film animation camera to capture the images rendered on the VAX and the Quantel. Colin Wray also used the same kit on the titles for *Birds of Prey 11*, a quirky crime drama on how to steal from hole in the wall Bank terminals! (Gardner 1984).

At that time, our output of 3D material was severely limited due to the lack of a commercially available stop-frame video recorder and the necessary animation software, such as Wavefront or Alias, which were then becoming available in the United States. At the same time, the BBC's corporate management, under pressure from the government, were introducing a policy called 'Producer's Choice'. This policy encouraged producers and designers to bypass internal BBC Service Departments and buy on the emerging commercial marketplace, mainly from facility houses in Soho, who worked on commercials and cinema productions.

Despite this challenge we acquired more customers, and we began to port some of the production applications, such as weather, to cheaper, smaller DEC MicroVAXes each with a dedicated Paintbox.

As we entered 1986 another General Election loomed, with the opportunity to perhaps invest in newer technologies, which would allow producers, the CGW and BBC's graphic designers to service new areas, such as sports, 3D titles and other in-programme content. To bring this requirement for new computers and graphic devices to the attention of senior management, I produced another Development Report (Gardner 1985b).

Other new systems were appearing: first, the PIXAR computer imaging device; second, the MEIKO transputer-based device and third, the BenchMark GIP, all three very powerful graphic processors. I visited PIXAR in California, but it seems they were reluctant to deal with the BBC, as they mistrusted our closeness to Quantel. I worried that the parallel nature of the MEIKO would be tricky and so it turned out to be. Until that point, I had been in sole charge of the technical decisions regarding staff recruitment and all our development systems, software and computer equipment within the CGW. I was totally against buying the MEIKO system, so much so I resigned when it was selected against my advice, arguing it's complexity just wasn't suitable.

End note

After I left BBC in August 1986, it was to take four OCCAM programmers from BBC's Research Department for a total of sixteen-man months to programme the General Election's so-called 'Battleground' display alone, for Peter Snow to front up, while the main CGW staff worked on the rest of the results database and other parts of the graphic results system. The leader of the BBC RD team, Jim Easterbrook, enjoyed his time in the CGW but later admitted to me that the MEIKO had been a computing dead end. The £250,000 MEIKO device was hardly, if ever, used again after the 1987 General Election.

My role as manager of the CGW was temporarily held by my deputy, Robin Vinson, for a year or so, and then subsequently by Ewen MacLaine for several more years, before he joined Siemens. After the great BBC/Siemens Digital Media debacle of the early 2000s the remnants of the CGW were subsumed into RED BEE Media, along with most of BBC Graphic Design.

15 BBC Sport of dash and dare
STEVEN ASPINALL

Introduction

At times of collective national sporting events, particularly World Cups and Olympic Games, UK television viewers have generally chosen BBC Sport as their preferred broadcaster, demonstrating the power of free-to-air (McCaskill 2023). Throughout its history, the corporation has made a significant contribution to the evolution of broadcast sport pioneering many original approaches and creative techniques.

In the following chapter I examine work spanning the last fifty years of BBC Sport, looking at a selection of case studies and hearing stories of memorable projects from that period, including my own. It is written from my personal perspective, based on my observations and experiences as the lead graphic designer for BBC Sport between 1995 and 2000. The role gave me an eye-opening insight into the complex infrastructure, politics and day-to-day chaos that the department was in at that time. It was the last knocking of the monopolistic state-broadcaster age before the world of sports rights digitally fragmented and was taken up by several broadcasters, notably Sky and an emboldened Independent Television (ITV).

I worked across many BBC Sport properties, having been poached from BBC News and Current Affairs, where I had spent the previous six years. The role was a culture shock that became a thrilling, chaotic, scary, creative and ultimately rewarding period of my career.

Grandstand

In the history of live sports coverage, *Grandstand* was a significant pioneer. Launched in 1958 using the latest outside broadcast technical advances to offer a comprehensive selection of Saturday afternoon live sports coverage, culminating in the *Final Score* section, which featured the live scores coming in via the 'teleprinter' which was actually just a live feed of scores as they were being typed out. Followed by the classified football results, where Len Martin, with his distinctive comforting voice, read out all the day's scores over full-frame graphic captions, Martin did this from the very beginning in 1958 until he passed away in 1995. In the days where most matches kicked off at 3.00 pm, these graphics would be in view for more than six minutes. In the pre-digital age these were made of cards, and the studio cameras would simply be pointed at them and locked into position.

Caption cards were very much part of the design process in the 1960s. Title sequences were often clip-based with a simple endcard, sometimes with the title logo superimposed over an action shot.

In 1978, BBC Graphic Designer Pauline Talbot (Carter) elevated the art when she created a memorable and award-winning title sequence for *Match of the Day (MOTD)*. The concept was inspired by images of large-scale card-flashing displays often seen at state events in China – an appropriate and powerful analogy for spectator participation in a football stadium.

After experiencing some initial reticence, Talbot eventually convinced the BBC Sport production chiefs that the concept could work. Permission was obtained for the use of Queens Park Rangers' Loftus Road Stadium for the shoot, within earshot of the Television Centre. A 'crowd' would be required to hold up the cards. To this end, head teachers of local West London schools were approached for help, and they agreed to release the number of children and staff required for the shoot.

Once the stadium seating plan had been studied, Talbot worked out the required size that the cards needed to be in order to align when held up by each child, thereby forming a complete image. A contractor was commissioned to make and supply the cards cut to size. They were made of lightweight corrugated board faced with white paper suitable for painting on.

She gave a briefing to the all-school assemblies of the children involved, explaining the concept, showing them images of Chinese card-flashing and demonstrating how the cards were to be held and turned.

There were several images that needed to appear on the cards – a goalkeeper, a referee, two players heading the ball, players tackling, trophies, the programme presenter Jimmy Hill and Talbot's newly designed programme logo (see Figure 15.1). These were commissioned from illustrator Bob Cosford, whose final pieces were photographed and transparencies made so they could be projected onto the blank cards.

The cards were numbered according to the stadium seating plan and then pinned up on a studio wall by Graham Barkley, the scenic artist, so that he could paint them full size from Cosford's projected images.

The sequence's finale meant that the final card containing Jimmy Hill and the logo needed to be two-sided so it could be rotated in vision to cleverly reveal the programme title. This involved a complex process of removing, rotating and rehanging the cards. The finale was also problematic to film, requiring visual checks from the opposite side of the stadium where the crew sat, addressing the children over the PA system.

In preparation for the shoot, Talbot laid out all 5,500 finished painted and numbered cards out on the floor at the BBC's Lime Grove Studios and collated them into packs of 7, 1 pack for each child. The packs

Figure 15.1 Match of the Day (c. 1971) original artwork for cards shot for the title sequence. Courtesy Pauline Carter.

were distributed on to the seats that the children and teachers would occupy on shoot day. All participants received goodie bags and drinks as a thank you for their efforts.

She recalls that the holding up of the single images was relatively straightforward to film, but perfection was harder to achieve. Rehearsals were filmed and the best shots selected in the edit along with the fifteen live-action clips, all cut to that iconic music.

Although the title sequence went slightly over budget, it was a great success and stood out amongst the pedestrian, dull, clip-based sports graphic design of the time. For this reason, it deservedly won a prestigious Design and Art Direction (D&AD) Silver Award for the most outstanding Sports Title Sequence. The BBC Sports Production team were elated.

Talbot's work set a new benchmark for sports title sequences and is often lovingly recalled by football fans of a certain age. The idea has also been replicated, as evidenced in the 2012 London Olympics, where the technique was used to turn the stands into a giant screen. Those of us who followed in Polly Talbot (Carter)'s footsteps had a lot to live up to.

When the digital revolution began in the 1980s, Designer Darrell Pockett managed to persuade BBC Sport to embrace this change. His *Sportsnight* title sequence in 1985 was the first computer-generated title sequence created by a BBC graphic designer. At the time Computer Graphics (CG) animation was in its infancy and rendering times were super slow. There would be consternation amongst the traditionally reticent BBC Sport production team as on-air deadlines would be threatened. Pockett's sequence, however, was fresh, dynamic and proved to be proper leap forward both creatively and technically (see Figure 15.2).

Figure 15.2 *Sportsnight* (1985) Storyboard and 3D images. Courtesy BBC.

Branding sport

In 1988 BBC Sport introduced a branding element to its coverage. Graphic Designer Peter Clayton was briefed to design a 'brand sting' that would preface all sports broadcasts and act as a signal to the viewers that they were now in the company of BBC Sport.

Jonathan Martin, head of sport in 1988, was inspired by a trophy he had on his desk, featuring a football in orbit around the planet. It was a compelling statement, reminiscent of a nuclear power symbol. This fed into the design brief. The idea of a globe was prevalent in branding at that time, and everyone wanted one; it demonstrated a scale of ambition. For BBC Sport this was not an overreach. They had rights to cover World Cup football, rugby, tennis, cricket, golf and athletics, as well as Olympics and Commonwealth Games, from all parts of the known world.

Football is perhaps the most popular game, but there were many more sports to represent. Images of shuttlecocks, horseshoes, golf balls and ice skates, all rattling around the planet like so much space junk would have been ridiculous. Icons were reduced to a single generic white ball encompassing the entirety of sporting endeavour in pursuit of an elusive point or target. Visually it most closely resembled the cue ball in snooker, which, of course, the BBC did broadcast many hours of.

3D computer animation was still a relatively new medium for designers, and the natural default for rotation of the spherical object – representing Mother Earth – was clockwise. It was only after transmission that scientifically minded students of Copernicus commented that 'in the real solar system' Earth, seen from above the northern hemisphere, rotates anti-clockwise; otherwise the morning sun would rise in the west. Some urgent revision/conceptual retrofitting was required; it was agreed that the ident was meant to 'hold up a mirror on the world', which seemed to placate the BBC guardians of corporate identity and save the cost of remaking the whole thing.

As part of his long BBC career, Graphic Designer Rod Ellis spent ten years working on many different projects for BBC Sport. This period covered two Olympic Games and three World Cups, including the iconic and memorable *Nessun Dorma* Pavarotti title sequence – a Botticelli/Florentine Renaissance-inspired *Primavera* work that Ellis says is 'the best, craziest thing' he ever designed.

In 1992 the BBC core presentation branding was overhauled, and BBC Sport's look and feel were starting to look dated. Rod Ellis found himself in the hot seat as senior graphic designer with responsibility for sport and events, and it became his turn to conjure an aesthetic for the next four-year cycle of Olympic and other sports coverage.

Already significantly invested in the globe, satellite, atomic power concepts for the ident, Ellis's challenge was to make the ident more engaging and more flexible for use across a huge range of programmes and sports coverage.

Ellis took the animation brief to a company called Infynity Graphics, under the supervision of the late Chris Fynes – a former BBC designer and pioneer of CG, a 'legend of Lime Grove' who had created his own bespoke CGI system, infinitely flexible in terms of modelling, lighting and choreography. Sadly, Fynes passed away in January 2023, leaving an astonishing legacy of work.

Texture and subtleties were added to the globe, with the flat blue background replaced by elements within a plum-coloured cosmos, a 'Milky Way of Rhubarb and space dust'. The concentric circles sweeping around the globe were given 'vapour trails' to enhance the sense of movement, creating waves of energy.

The corporate BBC logo still carried the blue, red and green underscore tags (thought by some to represent the RGB primary light colours and by others to allude to the national flags of Scotland, England

and Wales). The idea was to give each of the tags a luminescence, so they cast subtle up-lighting within the scene.

In the family of BBC Sport, *Grandstand* was still the senior sibling, so it made sense to tie the new departmental ident into the Grandstand titles and programme content, so they became one and the same thing. Different colour combinations of the ident were rendered to provide options for other programmes and outside broadcasts, including a gold version reserved for World Cups and major events. The new idents were first broadcast before the opening ceremony of the Barcelona Olympics, also designed by Rod Ellis.

From the mid-1990s, perhaps as a direct result of former London Weekend Television (LWT) producer John Birt's accession to director general and his subsequent desire for modernization, the BBC seemed to develop a more heightened creative culture around branding. Marketing departments, whom designers had previously rarely encountered, now seemed to be growing in influence. Programme makers were always the brief holders and decision-makers, but now marketers have begun to assert creative authority.

At the same time the fledgling Sky Sports was beginning to seriously challenge the BBC/ITV sports monopoly. *Nike* was in the ascendancy, with its progressive advertising, endorsements by sports stars and growing rivalry with *Adidas* beginning to make waves. Footballers, in particular, were beginning to feel and behave like glamorous pop stars. The game was changing. In light of all this it was clear that the look and feel, and perhaps approach, of BBC Sport needed freshening up.

The challenges of working for sports programme makers were, and probably still are, manyfold. There was always a massive cultural difference from the rest of the broadcast clients. Sport production moves super fast, with programme makers often set in their ways; a senior BBC Sport producer once said to me, 'This is the way we've always done it, we don't go in for any of that arty-farty rubbish.' It wasn't very helpful.

With the high stress/long hours of covering sport, production teams were tightly knit and would view designers coming in from outside with suspicion. Producers were more trusting and reliant on their technical operators than they were on graphic designers. From my time in this world, I remember making concerted efforts to gain the trust of both producers and operators – often sitting down with them in Television Centre tea bars to discuss ideas and projects.

1996 was a big year for BBC Sport. Along with the usual *Grandstand/MOTD/Sportsnight/Racing* output, there were also the twin behemoths of the *Olympic Games* and *Euro '96* to contend with. The latter was the first international football tournament to be held in England for thirty years.

The role of lead graphic designer is to take a creative lead while also delegating and managing work allocation across the team. When I was lead, that team comprised of just myself and freelance designers who serviced *Grandstand* in Television Centre Studio 5 (TC5) at weekends. Across the BBC Graphic Design Department, our colleagues in Presentation were raising the standard of motion graphics and channel branding with their multi-award-winning work (see Chapter 2). They set a benchmark that BBC Sport could emulate.

One of my first tasks was to update the BBC Sport branding look and feel. Part of my remit was to redesign the look of the graphic results systems, particularly the classified football results, league tables and associated captioning that played out mainly on *Grandstand* and *MOTD*. To do this effectively I had to navigate, liaise and collaborate with several disparate technical groups, all fiercely guarding their own particular fiefdom. These included the BBC technical operators, unsung heroes who generally worked the captioning systems in BBC Sport Live HQ – TC5 in the Television Centre. Then there were the systems developers/operators also known as the *Computer Graphics Workshop*, and the contractors who had collated and run the classifieds since the early days of *Grandstand*. The latter group had a strong influence on the *Grandstand* leadership team.

Figure 15.3 BBC Sport (1996) Ident. Courtesy BBC.

I updated Ellis's BBC Sport opening sting, intending to freshen things up and use more vibrant colours, akin to the primary palette generally seen in sports events. Part of this refresh involved developing a rich textural animated blue background that I shot on film using moving lights and gobos of the BBC Sport logo. It was also to be used for the classified football results on *Grandstand*. I was very pleased with it. Unfortunately, after it went live, letters arrived from viewers complaining that the movement made them feel sick. I was summoned to the *Grandstand* producer's office and ordered to fix it. We slowed it down and made it slightly darker. All was well in the end and an embarrassing moment was overcome (see Figure 15.3).

Data visualization

The vast and complex technical operation around the data processing of sports information graphics is exemplified by the Saturday tea-time institution that is the classified football results. Legibility is key. The challenge for a graphic designer is to keep it simple and persuade your sports client that they don't need to throw the kitchen sink at the aesthetics. As designers we are used to our work being subject to interference and guidance from different quarters, sometimes it's welcome, sometimes it's a hindrance. At BBC Sport it was no different. Typographically, the classifieds are one of the most challenging briefs in broadcasting. They run for quite a few minutes on screen and need to be easy on the eye.

Up until a certain point in the evolution of sports graphic design, title sequences had traditionally been clip-based. For example, despite Talbot (Carter)'s wonderful work on *MOTD* in 1978, BBC Sport producers would often still want last season's greatest hits put together by a Video Tape (VT) editor with an end caption provided by whichever designer was on duty in the studio.

There was sometimes tension between designers and VT editors at the BBC.

There were some who were graphics allies and some felt that we stood on their toes slightly and made their life more difficult. The challenge for us as designers was always to raise the title sequence to a higher art form. This meant persuading producers to allow us to approach things differently. Having an idea, a visual device that tells a story as opposed to a mere selection of nice shots.

The wider BBC had already started to take branding and marketing more seriously. There were some old-school mandarins within BBC Sport who mistrusted the idea of branding as a BBC Sport-wide entity. There were two distinct production camps in BBC Sport *MOTD* and *Grandstand*, each with their own distinct identity.

Title sequences

In 1997, I was asked to collaborate with *MOTD*'s new producer, Paul McNamara, on the title sequence for the 1997–8 season. This was the first of three title sequences that I designed for the programme. Conceptually, my first thought was to think big. I wanted to tap into football's newfound popularity; I wanted to introduce a shiny new stadium aesthetic, an essence of Britpop. In the 1990s, glamour had become much more of a part of football. A high-end, glossier 'advertising' aesthetic was introduced. Titles were now shot on film. Footballers were starting to gain the kudos of pop stars, and we captured them in beautifully lit vignettes, staring down the lens at their adoring fans (see Figure 15.4).

Figure 15.4 *Match of the Day* (1997, 1998) title sequence. Courtesy BBC.

Shooting on film brought its own challenges; it was expensive and time-consuming and you weren't always sure what you had captured until the rolls were developed and looked at in post-production. It was all in the grade. Title sequences took on the same production values as high-end drama or advertising. Sports stars are an impatient bunch. Having a calm and sympathetic director of photography helped, and still does. Proper production planning had to be factored in. Art direction was crucial. It wasn't a case of a jobbing cameraman quickly knocking off a shot in outside broadcast downtime anymore.

A list of desired footballers was drawn up by the production team. Myself and director of photography, Tim Green, toured the country, filming them in their dressing rooms. I designed a Britpop-inspired logo, abbreviating the programme's title to MOTD and placed it rotating on top of a modern stadium. Our approach rattled a few cages – nobody likes to mess with a classic – and the press were cynical about my new MOTD logo. *MOTD* magazine didn't like it at all. However, once they started using it on their cover, their monthly sales rocketed, and they became the market leader.

In other seasons we created a 'bat signal' version of the logo (see Figure 15.4). Mirroring the distinctive oval shape of the Batman insignia. One evening during the summer of 1998 we filmed the sunset over Arsenal's Highbury stadium. Sitting in the Clock End with the Arsenal chief groundsman regaling us with stories of past players while the time-lapse camera captured the sun slowly setting over the North Bank. It's a lovely memory. We added a projection of the MOTD logo bat signal in post-production at Television Centre. Everyone loved it. Football teams change their stripes every season. There is a high turnover of star players who flit in and out of the spotlight. A programme like *MOTD* is literally about the now.

Editorial stories

Often there would be a request to contribute to a longer editorial piece for, say, *Football Focus* or even a sports documentary. For a graphic designer this can be an opportunity to be very creative. My own news and current affairs background helped on these occasions; I'd often use rostrum shooting techniques to tell a story. There were one or two design-friendly sport producers who would refreshingly always encourage an 'anything goes' approach to graphics. On one occasion I even used an old super eight film camera to create some graphics for a *Football Focus* piece. It was something different and brought a smile to people's faces.

In 1998 I designed the title sequence for the BBCs *France '98 World Cup* coverage. Producer Niall Sloane had dined at a beautifully ornate Parisienne restaurant called the *Julien* and had the idea that it might work as a location for a title sequence. DOP Tim Green and I took the Eurostar over and had a look. I got Green to take lots of photographs, from which I created a visual storyboard. I mapped every shot and worked out exactly where we were going to integrate football footage. We used the restaurant's antique mirrors and it's stained-glass ceiling as screens and created wine labels and Menus, which we also used to track footage in. We shot the whole thing overnight in February. The finished titles were a great success and were nominated for a BAFTA design award (see Figure 15.5).

That same year I worked on a documentary about the life of veteran BBC Sports presenter Jimmy Hill. For the title sequence I felt it would be great to capture Hill's memorably characterful face in an interesting way. Working with producer Susan Roberts, we commissioned Gerald Scarfe, famous illustrator, visual satirist for *The Sunday Times*, painter and designer of Pink Floyd's *The Wall* concept album, to draw Hill. The challenge was to translate this to a compelling sequence. We did this by filming Scarfe drawing Hill in a large white studio space. I hand drew a storyboard and knew I wanted each shot to be a thoughtful composition (see Figure 15.6) – telling the story of Scarfe's mildly savage portrait with a beautifully shot sequence. It was a meeting of cultural polar opposites that worked wonderfully.

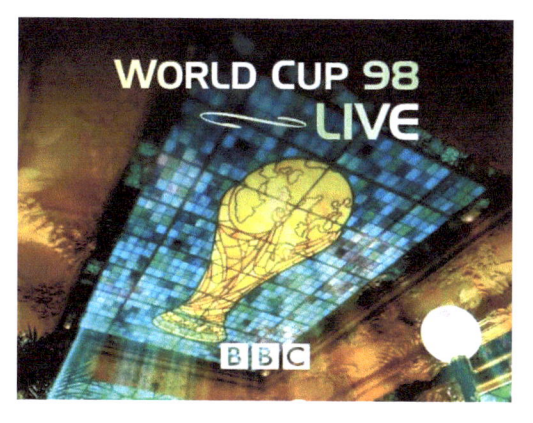

Figure 15.5 *France '98 World Cup* (1998) logo. Courtesy BBC.

Figure 15.6 BBC Sport (1998) Jimmy Hill title sequence. Courtesy BBC.

A new era

Around the turn of the millennium, BBC Graphic Design creative director Jane Fielder was briefed to lead a rebrand of BBC Sport's visual identity. New Director General Greg Dyke saw the department as one of the 'pillars' of the BBC, along with news. For the first time all BBC Sport programmes and marketing activity would share a common approach and a unified look and feel for captions, results and end boards (see Figure 15.7). Along with a hand-picked team including graphic designers Katy Clemmans, Martin Shannon, Victor Martinez and Gregory Millar, Fielder developed two new and simplified results grids based on seventeen lines, for football and the twenty lines of a golf card. Also introduced was a brand colour, yellow, and a mission statement courtesy of new Head of Sport Peter Salmon – *All That Matters in Sport*.

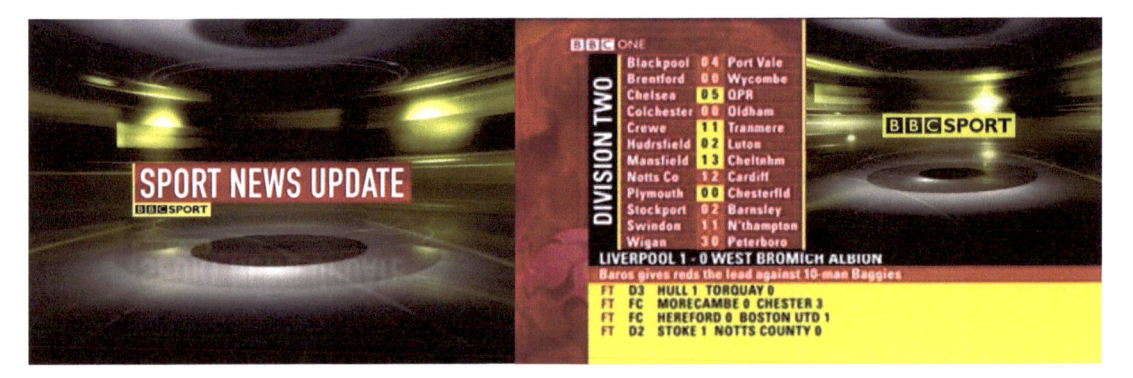

Figure 15.7 BBC Sport (2006). Courtesy BBC.

Paul Mitchell is a renowned Creative Director (CD) and commercials director currently working in Los Angeles, California. In 2001, he was a BBC graphic designer who eventually took his turn in the BBC Sport graphics team. Mitchell joined having worked on *Tomorrow's World* for two years. He cites this as an amazing and intense period of personal growth and felt that working on highvolume graphics content for a science programme was good preparation for the day-to-day demands of servicing BBC Sport's weekly programmes' quick turnaround briefs and short deadlines. The trade-off for a designer in this situation has always been the chance to flex the creative muscles at one of the big prestigious events – *Olympics, World Cup, Euros* and so on. Work that millions of people would see and be excited by.

Post millennium

After pitching the idea to BBC Sport Executive Producer Martin Hopkins and under the guidance of Fielder, Mitchell designed and directed the elegant and dynamic title sequence to the *2002 Commonwealth Games*, hosted in Manchester. This involved filming athletes moving in and around the city's venues on Super 16mm film.

Next for Mitchell was the creation of the titles for *Euro 2004* and the same year's *Olympic Games*. By this time, having several live-action titles under his belt, Mitchell wanted to create a sequence for *Euro 2004*, which used the current generation of superstar footballers. He had done this with *Football Focus* and *Final Score* using players like Steven Gerrard, Wayne Rooney, Rio Ferdinand and Sol Campbell and was now very comfortable directing high-profile talent. However, while making the players a central part of the titles story was ambitious, it was also high-risk as there was no guarantees they would all remain injury-free – as I had found to my cost on *MOTD* a few years earlier.

Along with BBC Sport producer Jason Bernard, Mitchell filmed at several beautiful locations along the length of host nation, Portugal. The purpose of this was to convey the cultural texture of the country while creating sumptuous back plates for the star players to perform on.

Getting access to the superstar footballers proved to be a bigger challenge as their time was very limited. The filming schedule became an epic road trip, taking in London (Thierry Henry, Freddie Ljunberg, Sol Campbell) Liverpool (Michael Owen, Wayne Rooney), Turin (Del Piero, Pavel Nedved) and Barcelona (Patrick Kluivert). Each player was shot against green screen, the idea being that they used the ball to show their silky skills before passing onto the next player. It was a vast undertaking with a mammoth post-production schedule involving 2D and CG animation.

Figure 15.8 BBC Sport, Olympic Games (2004) title sequence. Courtesy BBC.

The 2004 Olympic Games title sequence was also complex – traditionally seen as the pinnacle of sports sequences with a rich history of great titles. This year it was in Greece, the original home of the Olympics which meant that it perhaps carried more meaning and heritage than previous years.

There was a desire to create something as ambitious as the tier one marketing promo; historically this had a lot of money and production time put into it. The BBC in-house team generally never got to work on these. It was decided for the first time that the marketing promo and the title sequence should relate. There hadn't been a direct crossover like that before so there was a lot of pressure on the designer. Two ideas were pitched to BBC director of sport Peter Salmon, who green-lit Mitchell's ambitious vision.

The challenge was to build a sequence that respected Greek history, as well as bringing the games to life. The central idea was to reignite the Olympic Games via the torch. The raising of the torch awakened the Olympic spirits of the games through larger-than-life, epic-scale athletes. A giant swimmer rises up out of the sea with enormous waves. A sprinter sprays dust trails running along the side of Temple of Poseidon. A monumental discus thrower creates a tornado in the ancient Meteora mountains (see Figure 15.8).

Lots of planning and R&D went into the pre- and post-production process. It took time to get permission to film on historic Greek locations, and the BBC name opened a few doors and sourced access to otherwise closed filming locations. Back plates were eventually shot and were matched on a green-screen stage back London. These were key to making the whole thing work, with all the camera data and lighting references combining with CG and practical effects to build and integrate onto the athletes.

The titles were a popular success. A fitting tribute to the spiritual home of the Olympic Games and an appropriate addition to the pantheon of brilliant BBC Graphic Design projects created in the name of BBC Sport.

16 '. . . and now for the News'

Television, probably: The age of cardboard

BRIAN ELEY

BBC News and Current Affairs is one of the keystones of the corporation. It is a trusted global brand that millions of people around the world watch for their news, not only on television but on digital devices as well. How that news is presented visually, illustrated and framed is down to a dedicated team of graphic (motion) designers working around the clock. These chapters reveal insights into the hidden workings of the design team, how they got there and how their typical day is filled with adrenaline and an ever-changing news and technological landscape. This section spans several decades that saw the technological and organizational revolution that started in the 1970s and continues today in a multiplatform delivery.

In this chapter I give a personal account of *Nationwide*, a BBC Current Affairs programme combining regional news, political analysis and discussion with consumer affairs, entertainment and sports reporting. It ran from September 1969 until August 1983. From 1972 it was broadcast each weekday following the national early evening news and allowed the BBC's regions to 'opt-out' before handing back to BBC Lime Grove Studios in London.

I was with *Nationwide* from approximately 1976 until the end of 1979. I joined a team of designers who worked exclusively on *Nationwide* to convey simplified graphic information, such as the location of a derailed train, the size of a party's majority in the House of Commons, the rising curve of the cost of living or simply to mount stills and newspaper headlines for the studio cameras. Graphics would typically be ordered and broadcast on the same day. We might also work on 'strands' within the programme with lead-times of more than a day, for instance, to mark a significant anniversary or current event (e.g. VE Day or the beginning of the racing season).

Our workload was determined by the demands of a team of editors and researchers. These could change dramatically over the course of a working day, with items urgently demanded then abruptly dropped, even while the show was on air.

The road to Siberia

In the summer of 1974, I entered the BBC as a 'graphic artist' (junior design assistant) in the presentation department at TV Centre. I was hired as 'holiday relief' on a limited three-month contract, largely, I suspect, on the strength of an unfinished student film and a storyboard for an imaginary news programme that I had struggled to complete for my diploma show at St Martin's College of Art (now part of the University of the Arts, London).

At BBC Television Centre, I was put to work in the presentation department on the daily production of promotional stills for BBC1 and BBC2, surrounded by some intimidatingly talented and fast-working illustrators. Stills were photographed as 35mm transparencies (known as TJs, for Telejector) and then rephotographed to add typography and channel logos. Occasionally, we might also have the opportunity to work on a moving sequence.

After three months, I was moved to the main graphics department as assistant to senior designers Alan Jeapes and, subsequently, Michael Graham-Smith. Following two consecutive six-month contracts, I was granted a staff position and promptly moved to Lime Grove Studios on the other side of Shepherd's Bush to join the team on *Nationwide*. Colleagues at TV Centre likened this to being sent to 'Siberia'.

Tabloid television

At Lime Grove, TV Centre graphic designers were thought, perhaps unkindly, to look down on those in current affairs, and particularly *Nationwide*. If a programme like *Panorama* was the equivalent of a broadsheet newspaper, *Nationwide* was a tabloid. Our clients were not producers of award-winning dramas, documentaries or arts programmes, needing a designer to provide a title sequence for David Attenborough or Dennis Potter. They were journalists, suspicious of 'artiness' and oblivious to the distinction between serif and sans serif. One of *Nationwide*'s studio directors was even suspected of being colour blind (all BBC graphic designers had to pass a colour test to be employed).

Each weekday, Monday to Friday, at 6.05 pm, *Nationwide* would air, ready or not. It might spend five minutes on an in-depth examination of the exchange rate mechanism, followed by a lengthy interview with a man who promised to show his pet snail enjoying a glass of beer. (The snail died live on camera; a production office inquest concluded that this was either from alcohol poisoning or heat from the studio lights.)

The front page

Lime Grove Studios dated from 1915 and had originally accommodated the Gaumont Film Company. The *Nationwide* production office occupied the entire top floor of one wing and was home to the editorial team, researchers, presenters, secretaries, a stills photographer, photocopiers and stills library. To one side of the main room was the senior editor's office, one of the few private spaces. There were no computers on desktops, just typewriters and a chorus of constantly ringing telephones.

The production office entirely surrounded the *Nationwide* graphics studio, which at times could feel under siege. A distinctive feature of the studio was a serving hatch that overlooked the main office. This was rolled up at the start of the day and rolled down at night, suggesting a mobile hotdog stand. Designers would linger at the hatch and listen to production office chatter for clues about the nature of the day's work.

The interior of the graphics studio was permanently cluttered with tools and materials, all within arm's reach. Our materials were typically sheets of matte black cardboard, white Letraset, Magic Markers, Polaroid cameras, Pantone papers and, of course, sticky-back plastic. Our principal tools were the 10A Swann-Morton scalpel, the Letraset burnisher and black marker pens that would hopefully conceal unwanted white cardboard edges from the studio cameras. Adhesive was usually aerosol 'spray-mount', regarded even then as damaging to lungs; speed demanded it and without a dedicated 'spray booth' we inhaled constantly.

One whole wall was devoted to boxes of Letraset. In theory these were neatly filed according to font and point-size; in practice, it was a constant losing battle to return the sheets to their correct box. For much of the time we worked standing, at benches clad in cutting mats or layers of cardboard scared by scalpel blades. Every surface was permanently coated with a tacky spray-mount film. At the end of a busy day, the floor could be ankle-deep in paper, cards and balls of masking tape. BBC cleaners were barred from attempting to distinguish between 'wanted' and 'unwanted' materials, so we were left to police ourselves.

In the tiny photographic studio next door, designers could commission stills or order them to be enlarged to giant proportions to enhance the studio set downstairs. These photographic blow-ups (PBUs) were generally out-sourced to a specialist studio and returned to Lime Grove by taxi in just a couple of hours. Editorial decisions rapidly became design decisions, with few cost-controls. We were very rarely told that anything was 'too expensive'. The team I joined at *Nationwide* included at various times, Bill Blaik, John Speirs, Mick Gilbert, Liz Jones (Varrall) and Tricia King (Hylton).

You were seldom briefed in writing. Someone would yell instructions from across the room and you would get to work. I loathed the sweat-shop pace, but I will admit to relishing the 'hold the front page' atmosphere.

Anarchy in the United Kingdom

Nationwide owned a specially designed symbol nicknamed 'the Mandala'. This was a distinctive but extremely complex device that worked well enough as a set-design element and was even available as a Letraset symbol; however, it did not reduce well in size and tended to dominate all other information when used as a graphic device on captions. The programme's font was Futura in all its forms, but this could easily vary if the editorial team decided it somehow didn't reflect the character of a particular news item – for instance, appearing 'too modern' or 'not traditional enough' to be appropriate. There was no consistent colour palette. Without a designated 'brand guardian' to defend consistency, results were uneven and speed of delivery was always paramount.

A complex graphic might be commissioned after lunch, once the programme's running order had begun to take shape, be scheduled for transmission, then abruptly dropped to allow for an interview or breaking news story to overrun. It didn't matter. Dead stories were seldom held over for the following day, so were eventually filed away in one of two industrial-sized rubbish bins at the back of the studio.

In this fast-moving environment, with a constantly revolving team of designers, consistency was a major problem. Programme branding was in its infancy, but we were all conscious of the need to maintain a consistent visual style. Without it, each member of the graphics team had to constantly 're-invent the wheel' rather than follow a set of clear guidelines. How did one create a pie-chart? A bar-chart? How did one maintain a consistent style of illustration, for instance, to depict generic nurses, strikers, businessmen, schoolchildren or policemen – a school, a hospital, or nuclear power station? At *Nationwide*, each designer was left to devise their own solution, according to ability, inclination, available reference and the time available. This ran counter to my time with Alan Jeapes and Michael Graham-Smith, designers who demanded precision and taught by example, rarely rushing to judgement over a choice of colour or typeface.

BBC graphic designers trained 'on the job' as assistants to someone senior. At St Martins I had acquired certain television and film-related skills (how to write a dope sheet and how to mark the key beats in a roll of magnetic sound), but art school had left me unprepared for the daily rough and tumble of *Nationwide*.

Faced with a punishing daily schedule, the editorial team craved novelty. Consistency was not a priority for a programme that ranged from serious political commentary to entertaining trivia (performing pets, eccentric grannies and the Nationwide Disco Dancing Competition). Every day was a new day, demanding fresh and novel design solutions. To the editors, attempts to standardize or rationalize graphic design could appear lazy or, worse, boring.

A snapshot of a typical studio day

The working day begins by rolling up the hatch at around 10.00 am. The core team of editors and researchers sit around a white-board at the far end of an otherwise empty office, heads buried in the morning newspapers, trying to conjure a running order for that evening's show. Junior researchers are officially referred to as RATS (Research Assistant Trainees) and are intensely competitive, as the more stories they can get on air, the more likely they are to move on to greater things (future documentary filmmaker Adam Curtis is just one of the *Nationwide* RATs I encounter during this period). At first slowly, then suddenly, the office fills with assistants and secretaries and the white-board acquires a tentative, scribbled running order: 'nurses' – 'nuclear' – 'minister (possible)' – 'skate-boarding duck' – etc. Then the presenters arrive: typically Frank Bough, Sue Lawley and Bob Wellings. Meanwhile, the graphic designers occupy themselves filing sheets of Letraset (see Figure 16.1).

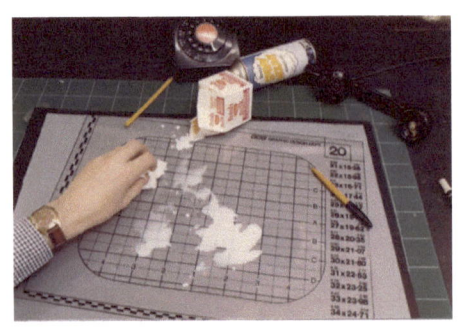

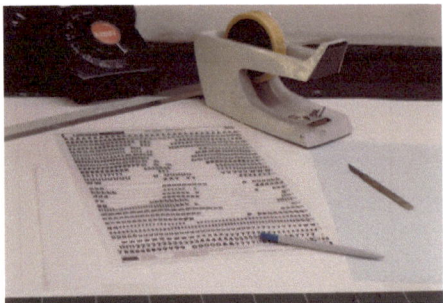

Figure 16.1 Playful visualizations of the United Kingdom using graphic materials of the day. Courtesy Brian Eley.

172 Designing the BBC

At some point before lunch, a research assistant ambles over to the open hatch and asks, 'Any chance of a hanging map today?' The researcher offers you a scribbled sketch. It depicts a presenter standing in front of a map – a four-foot square panel hung from the studio set. The map is to feature symbols to represent proposed nuclear power stations. The researcher asks if, once the power stations had been revealed, they can meltdown and leak nuclear radiation. You ask the researcher if they are really sure about this and if they have the agreement of the editor and the studio director for that day. More often than not, the response from the researcher is: 'Definitely. Probably. I'll go and check.' While he checks, you get to work.

The four-foot square panel is plywood and heavy, with a metal surface and steel hooks at the back, designed to hang from any part of the studio set. The metal surface enables the use of magnetized rubber for icons, lettering or images to be attached or moved around freely by the presenter.

If the panel is to be a map, you apply a roll of adhesive blue material ('sea') to the entire surface. Then, a top coat of green material ('land'). Six-foot-wide rolls of adhesive material in a range of *Nationwide* colours, including green and blue, are arranged on rollers along one wall of the studio. You open an atlas and identify the area you want to copy. You photograph this on Polaroid transparency film, using a rostrum-mounted camera in an alcove at the rear of the cramped studio. The transparency is loaded into a projector and the panel is propped against a convenient wall or door. You focus the image onto the panel, adjusting the scale and composition to allow for a title and any additional information. If there is time, you sketch the coastal outline of the map in pencil.

Nationwide geography is a simplified version of the real world, so you are allowed to take liberties with the coastline. If you are short of time, you draw directly with the point of your scalpel using a new blade, cutting through both layers of adhesive material with one movement. You then rip away unwanted areas of 'land' to reveal the 'sea' beneath. The adhesive material has a matte surface that will appear flawless under studio lights.

You identify key locations by eye and mark them with large adhesive paper dots. Letraset or Letrasign is used to apply place names with the aid of a T-square and sellotaped paper strips. A library photograph of a typical nuclear power station is obtained from the stills library and traced in outline. This is copied and coloured by hand using Magic Markers and backed by magnetic rubber; experience tells you to produce slightly more of these than ordered to allow for studio damage or script changes. Pencil lines are cleaned with a solvent spray. Any air-bubbles are removed by making tiny punctures with a scalpel and squeezing out the air from beneath the material, which is slightly elastic.

Meanwhile, the Editor of the Day is not sure if the item deserves this level of treatment. He examines the map. Why don't the power stations melt down and leak nuclear radiation? You remind the editor that this will require some sort of animation, ideally on film, with a few days advance notice.

The researcher fights their corner and proposes that the presenter bring the map alive by manipulating the magnetic power stations, using appropriate hand gestures and perhaps using explosive vocal effects. The editor is unconvinced. He also knows that presenters regard magnetic graphics as potential boobytraps. Directors didn't like them either, as it complicated their camera set-ups. The editorial team confer, the map is dropped and the item is relegated to three lines in 'other news'. For researcher and graphics team, this is business as usual.

Once the programme is on air, you stay alert for any last-minute changes or additions to the running order. Activity in the production office starts to wind down, and you check the monitors for evidence of your other contributions to the show. You make peace with those researchers whose careers you may have helped or hindered that day and join the general drift towards the BBC Bar. Tomorrow will be another opportunity to get it right.

Leap of faith: 1

Working closely with the *Nationwide* production team could generate friction but also a remarkable degree of trust. Aware that the lack of a consistent graphic style created not only problems but also opportunities, I formed an idea. Sometime in late 1977 I approached the editor responsible for entertainment news with a proposal for a review of the capital's pub-rock music scene, to be called 'London Rock'.

I was an avid reader of the music press and knew that interesting things were happening in small venues across the capital. My proposal was for a quick tour of places where you could hear the new wave of artists who had appeared behind the punk vanguard (Sex Pistols, Damned, etc.) and were beginning to attract attention.

The film would be animated, so entirely under my control. It would be a sort of collage, no more than two minutes in duration; as brief as a seven-inch single and short enough to slip easily into the programme's running order. I would write it, artwork it and find someone to provide a voice-over. It would be a rostrum camera shoot on 16mm. With nothing drawn or written down, my proposal was accepted. I was given less than two weeks to deliver.

I briefed our regular stills photographer, and we combed the music press for venues, regardless of who was performing. We spent three or four nights concentrating on shots of audiences. I persuaded one of *Nationwide*'s younger presenters, Kieran Prendiville, to record a voice-over during his lunch break. The artwork was a mashup of black-and-white stills, band posters, handwriting and pages photocopied from the *London A-to-Z*.

Remarkably, the rostrum shoot at TV Centre took place on the day of transmission. To keep costs low, the film was shot on reversal stock, meaning there would be no negative. This meant that if anything disastrous happened to the print, there would be no backup. Sometime in the afternoon, the undeveloped film was rushed to BBC News Department's laboratory and from there to Lime Grove to be cut into an existing package of films for that evening. There was no chance to check for faults. In fact, given the 'punk' roughness of the animation, it would have been almost impossible to identify a fault. The whole film, from proposal to transmission, was a reckless leap of faith (see Figure 16.2).

Figure 16.2 *London Rock* (1977) image from title sequence. Courtesy Brian Eley.

The film was appropriately abrupt and jumpy and entirely un-*Nationwide*. As far as I'm aware, apart from a few faded transparencies, not a trace of this film survives. It was transmitted once, then promptly disappeared; in that sense, it is a typical example of disposable motion graphics in the age of cardboard.

Leap of faith: 2

Towards the end of my time at *Nationwide*, I was asked by the senior editor to revise the show's opening title sequence. This would be my first opening title, seen by a huge early-evening audience five days a week. It should have been a daunting prospect, but I enjoyed the confidence that comes from not knowing what you don't know. The editor was looking for something 'up to date' and wondered if anything could be done quickly 'using a computer'. I gave him the standard response: 'Definitely. Probably. I'll go and check.'

In an obscure office deep within TV Centre, the corporation's computer experts examined my crude sketches. They broke the news to me as gently as they could; what I wanted was in theory possible but was currently beyond the scope of their department. However, they could offer me a phone number.

What I wanted was a sequence that would emphasize the breadth of *Nationwide*'s national coverage, allowing the viewer to feel like an astronaut, swooping across coastal cliffs, rolling hills, fields and forests, towns and cities and industrial sprawl. I was thinking Star Wars; what we produced was closer to Pac-Man.

I was now armed with that rare thing, a *Nationwide* budget. The phone number I had been given took me to a company a half-hours train journey from London. They specialized in 'architectural walk-throughs', which were wire-frame models of yet-to-be-constructed buildings designed to impress an architect's clients. I asked them to construct both the *Nationwide* logo and a realistic 3D model of the British Isles. They seemed keen. I told them my budget. They laughed.

Lacking a producer to negotiate costs, I went away and revised my storyboard until the green hills of Britain had been ironed flat and only the cliffs remained, running the full length of Britain's coastline at a height of approximately 70 to 80 miles.

As the work progressed, I began to understand what I had agreed to. The animation could be previewed as a wire-frame on the company's screens, but the frames would be output as black-and-white wire-frame drawings, inked onto a single roll of paper. I had dreamed of something radical, but the sequence would follow a long-established Current Affairs template; an opening flourish – a brief 'fly-over' of a toy-like Britain – followed by an assortment of easily updated archive images, followed by a reveal of the programme logo.

I recall shooting a simple animatic sequence on film using storyboard frames in order to check timings against the newly recorded theme music. The roll of black-and-white line drawings were trimmed and numbered. The drawings were copied to traditional animation cels by a commercial animation company and then hand-painted at Lime Grove by a freelance designer, in a process that would have been familiar to any animator from the 1920s onward. The 35mm rostrum shoot was out-sourced to an effects company in London's Soho, who could offer a package deal including a 'rising sun' effect (rising in the North, for some reason) (see Figure 16.3).

I have no memory of previewing the title sequence to *Nationwide*'s senior editor, which probably means it was moderately well received. I was given no notes or demands for changes. In current affairs, if something arrives on time and is more or less on-brief, then you have succeeded. I've no idea how long those titles were in use, but when the final edition of *Nationwide* aired in 1983, it was with an entirely different sequence.

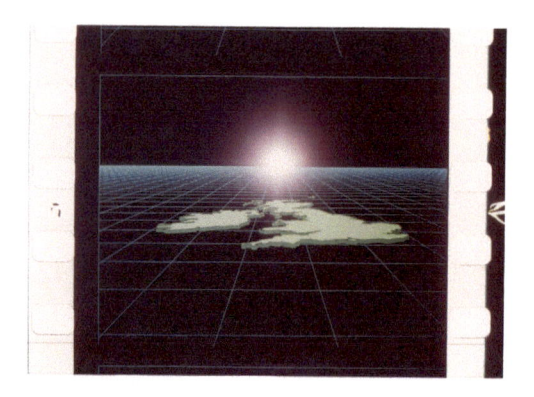

Figure 16.3 *Nationwide* (*c.* 1980) 35mm clip of computer-generated green grid and United Kingdom. Courtesy Brian Eley.

Definitely, Probably

In the early days of computer-aided motion graphics, there was a trend for designs that aped the characteristics of computer screens, without any actual computer being involved, or involved only marginally. The mere sight of a green grid was enough to suggest 'this is the future'. My time at the BBC coincided almost exactly with this period, one which witnessed the release of *Star Wars* (1977), the Sony Walkman and a fashion for digital wristwatches that glowed in the dark. Television was still adjusting to the widespread ownership of colour TVs and digital images were just a rumour. Motion graphics were still in the age of cardboard, but the future of television would definitely arrive soon - probably.

17   *Breakfast Time*

To infinity and beyond

TERRY HYLTON

An unnamed viewer in Surrey said she liked 'the little clock face in the bottom right hand corner of the screen telling you the time all the time', and 'someone going through all the newspapers for you'. (Press Agency UPI / BBC News Website 2013)

There was a lot of favourable press when *Breakfast Time* launched on 17 January 1983. Television graphic design, especially that which originated from News and Current Affairs, has always been somewhat transitory, with content and title sequences being as disposable as daily newspapers, and maybe even more so today as we find ourselves in the 'skip the intro' streaming age. As I write, it coincides with the anniversary of *Breakfast Time*, and the title sequence and graphics I designed have been shown again on national television after forty years, so maybe it's not all that bad!

Beginnings

Being a graphic designer at the BBC was always my vocation and never a chore. I had decided that was the career I had wanted to pursue from about the age of sixteen, and then I spent the next thirteen years trying to get there. After graduating from Norwich School of Art in 1974, I applied for and attended boards for graphic design assistant positions advertised as far afield as Glasgow, Bristol, Birmingham and Alexandra Palace. I obviously did not 'board' well. So as a last ditch attempt to get into television I took a position as a graphic designer at the University of Sheffield in late 1975. The Audio Visual Centre there was a very busy resource akin to the Open University. I gained a lot of confidence and learnt an enormous amount before my BBC career in Current Affairs Graphics at Lime Grove finally began in 1979.

Newsnight, which was originally scheduled to start in September 1979 (but delayed because of a strike), was the first joint News and Current Affairs Programme and utilized both Current Affairs Graphics staff and News Graphics staff (all working independently from their respective studios). It required a large resource in all areas of production. The only daily Current Affairs programme at the time was the early evening *Nationwide*, so a small number of graphic design assistants were employed on three-month contracts, as the *Newsnight* transmission time of 10.45 pm five nights a week from Television Centre was very demanding. Lime Grove Studios were home to all Current Affairs programmes, *Nationwide, Panorama, Newsweek, The Money Programme, That's Life,* Obituaries and Specials such as the Budget.

I began on *Newsweek*, followed with brief periods on *Nationwide*, *Newsnight* and then enjoyed myself on what I perceived as the crown jewel of BBC Current Affairs – *Panorama*, with the ever-creative Howard

Moses. In the Autumn of 1982, a call went out for 'Anybody interested in working on a new daily early morning programme?' It was going to be a mix of News, Current Affairs and lighter items, although this was not mentioned, briefed or discussed at the time. It was just a new daily early morning programme. There were no takers amongst the designers working on the current roster of programmes, and seeing the opportunity to get my teeth into a new project that I could be involved in from the start was a challenge I could not resist. The programme was going to be called *Breakfast Time* and the launch was scheduled for the early part of 1983. I, for one, did not comprehend the significance at the time of Current Affairs Graphic Designers also taking on the role of News Graphic Design, which became the ultimate management plan of amalgamating the departments two years later. As far as I was concerned, it was all daily 'information graphics' (a term that was not to become commonly used until at least twenty years later), and I would be responsible for twelve and a half hours of live graphics output per week.

A new challenge

In those days, new programmes with their associated title sequences were few and far between in Current Affairs. So, I made the titles my first priority, and apart from anything else, I needed to 'get them out of the way' as there was so much else to do. With a programme starting at 6.30 am every weekday morning, I wondered who was going to be awake to watch titles at that time of the day. Ron Neil, the editor, explained that he needed something about fifteen to twenty seconds long that could be used in different iterations throughout the two and a half hours we were going to be on air, so the titles became more important. As all titles end with a four-second hold on the name and any logotype, that helped bring any animation time down, saving valuable frames. So, with such a short sequence to design, I decided that the logical way to approach it was to work backwards with the logo forming in some way.

Ron Neil was a big fan of graphics and saw the importance of giving the programme strong branding. He had spent time in America researching breakfast programmes that were bold and colourful. He had joined the Current Affairs Department in 1969 to become a producer on *Nationwide*, on which he worked until 1976, eventually becoming its output editor. After *Breakfast Time* Ron relaunched the *Six O'Clock News*. He then became overall editor of television news, and then director of news and current affairs in 1988, followed by becoming head of regional broadcasting the next year. He was a member of the BBC's Board of Management for twelve years.

At this time there was only myself, but I was then joined by Tricia King (Hylton) from *Nationwide*, who had been allocated to the programme. I think it was some time in November when I finally found my logo inspiration (now affectionately referred to as 'the Squashed Spider'); Ron always called it a Mandala as the *Nationwide* logo had always been called. It is sometimes when you are 'not designing' that one comes up with a good idea or two, and I recall vividly that mine came when away from work one weekend. When I did get into work on Monday, I tidied up the design and drew up a colour version very quickly. There were to be two versions – one with and one without *Breakfast Time*. The main on-screen title was actually *BBC Breakfast Time* – another first to see 'BBC' branded on an opening sequence which wasn't a news bulletin.

The logo consisted of seven sections, which formed a segmented sun. It ticked all the boxes required for a 'good' Logo; it worked at various sizes in colour and in black and white, and it was easy to create and naturally lend itself to animation. The logo needed to be supported by the programme title. In those days whenever a specific font was required that was not available as a Letraset rubdown, it would be photoset, or failing that if something unique, it would be hand-drawn. I had decided it needed to be an italic font, which, to me, expressed speed, news, urgency and early morning. In my mind there was only one font that would do it, and it was to be found on a box of Corn Flakes! I had assumed the face would be easy to track down but could not find anything even close to it, so I designed the characters I needed and then had them drawn as well as some other letters we would need to use.

My storyboard had quickly come together, and I had already decided its geometric form was best suited to computer animation in some way.

Computer titles and content – A hybrid solution

In November 1982 Channel Four had launched with Martin Lambie-Nairn's ground-breaking idents. Martin, who I later worked with on many occasions, had to go to Los Angeles for his animations, but said his idents had proved very time-consuming, problematical and expensive to achieve. Brian Eley and myself had briefly shared an office at Lime Grove and he had told me he had used computer animation for part of the *Nationwide* titles. I needed a process that could be achieved relatively quickly because we were rapidly approaching Christmas, so I had to look close to home.

As was always the case in current affairs (which sounds unbelievable by today's standards), we did not have a budget for any graphic work and none of the designers had any idea how much anything cost. We were always working against the clock, with transmission times normally within seven days of receiving a brief, and money just didn't come into it.

Music

Ron approved my storyboard and said we needed to meet the composer who was going to be writing our music. Shortly after, I found myself at a very imposing house not far from Television Centre, sitting in front of a grand piano with George Fenton who had already worked on several BBC programmes. I had some rough timings worked out with key drawings. In those days there was not any easy way to make an animatic or get a line test from a computer to show anyone or play a demo track with the picture. George's demo was just what Ron wanted, and I could tell it was going to work well with my animation idea. Ron had lots of ideas for using music 'beds' under news headlines or at other intervals throughout our 2.5 hours, so a lot of incidental music was recorded at the title track session by a small group of musicians.

Titles

When the final mixed track was delivered, I frame-counted and refined my storyboard ideas. I had come across Electronic Arts, one of London's nascent computer graphics companies that had the ability to plot vector/wireframe animations onto animation cels. The technology could not render or work in colour – something taken for granted today. I previewed wire-frame tests on their black-and-white display and then working from my dope sheet, tweaked timings and pushed the button on plotting the outline animation onto cels – about 250 of them in total. We were working in doubles – 2 frames per image =12 images per second – as was the case with traditional cel animation.

But that was just the start of the process; each segment of the logo was to be a different colour. The titles were going to be shot on 35mm film, and I also needed a matte pass for compositing onto different backgrounds (the cels needed to be opaque so they could also be backlit), which meant three coats of cel paint for each colour (twenty-one coats total). We were by now hard up against Christmas, so the job was split between several cel painters from various locations around North London. This all happened 'after hours' as I was totally engrossed with the programme content design during the day. When I had all the cels back in my office, I then had to create the dope sheet for the rostrum shoot. Some cels were to be used in different permutations for different stings, a benefit from having them plotted by computer, so I got good value out of my cel plots. The matte pass meant the sequence could be combined with different backgrounds, one of which was a sunrise over Tower Bridge, which Ron had sent a crew out to shoot on tape. The TK (telecine) transfer of the film to tape to make the final product happened as soon as we were back after the Christmas break on 3 January, which was two weeks before we were going on air. Andy Davy was one of the new intake that started as graphic design assistants on that day; completely new to TV he was dropped right in it, coming with me to the TK transfer session to put the titles onto 1-inch video tape.

Content graphics

As we took briefs for content graphic material that was going to be required for a daily early morning programme, I never considered differentiating between the current affairs and news graphics content styling. This had not been the case when *Newsnight* had launched in 1980, which was the first programme established as news and current affairs working together. Myself being based in Lime Grove, and News at Television Centre being a separate department, meant I had no knowledge or real experience of what might be required or how news graphics operated. Though not being seen as 'creative', news graphics had a tried and tested system for getting maps and diagrams onto the screen very quickly, which we would need to emulate.

While the titles were being created before Christmas, Tricia and I had been focusing on the information content. I wanted to do something that hadn't been seen before, but it needed to be easy to produce and offer variations that could encompass all programme content. That inspiration fell into place very quickly when I opened a new graphic arts catalogue from Mecanorma, which had just appeared from France as a competitor to Letraset. They had a range of graduated papers, with white graduating through to a large range of pastel colours. They were perfect as a background for the sunrise effect of the logo, evocative of light coming upwards, as well as working on their own as branding colours for our news graphics backings for stills and the programme strands. With the titles being a combination of high-tech logo animations with low-tech hand-lettering, the programme content was also going to evolve into a hybrid of analogue paper craft and digital storage and transmission, but none of us appreciated this at the time.

On-screen clock

An on-screen clock also had to be designed (see Figure 17.1). There wasn't really a brief, just a recognition that people would be getting ready to leave the house for work, and the editor wanted them to get the time 'off television' rather than having to look elsewhere. The BBC's in-house engineering resources were considerable in those days, and there was always someone who could help. I briefed the BBC Research and Design Department, and they set about designing and building a clock generator that could offer three colours and a key. It was 8-bit – very low resolution for the PAL 625-line signal. My design had to be somewhat blocky; I wanted it to be a friendly analogue face rather than a digital one, and I believed it would be easier to read from a distance. But where to position it on screen? The bottom of frame is the normal place for text, and English is read left to right. I decided the natural place for something to be on the screen constantly was bottom right; it was always there but didn't interfere with everything else that would appear. That was another

Figure 17.1 *Breakfast Time* (1983) logo and on screen clock with presenter Frank Bough. Courtesy Terry Hylton.

reason why it was an analogue face, because I didn't want numbers next to words. With 16×9 ratios it is less of an issue and *BBC News* still has their digital clock in the same position today. The *Breakfast Time* clock became an anchor for our graphics as it was constantly on screen and we had to design everything else around it. We even stuck paper clocks on our graphics output monitors just in case anybody forgot to allow space for it, and on occasion we had to remind the gallery to switch the clock back in when the vision mixer had forgotten.

While we had been toiling with our coloured paper, logos and film animations, Lime Grove Studios was being transformed into the BBC's Topical Production Centre. On the new production office floor, we were given a graphics studio alongside, similar to the *Nationwide* model but much larger and with better facilities.

Multiple challenges

New workstations

On our return after Christmas, the result of all the engineering and building work (part of which was the new electronic *Breakfast Time* Graphics area) was unveiled to us. It seems totally unbelievable today that something like that could be installed without any input from (or training for) the people who were going to use it. It happened so quickly and to the best of my knowledge even our graphics manager was unaware.

The Electronic Graphics Suite was an L-shaped space approximately seven metres on each side, with graphics transmission on one side and creation on the other. The transmission side consisted of the just-released Quantel DLS 6001 Stills Store and a Riley caption generator that supplied all lower third text.

Design staff were to be responsible for 'playing out' all the material created in that area. Our material appeared as Graphics 1 or 2 on the input of the main mixer in the transmission gallery.

This playing-out role was unexpected and not to everybody's liking; however, it had been thrust upon us, and we took up the challenge. The advantage was that as soon as something had been made, it could be offered to the gallery immediately without any other involvement. The efficiency of this side of the operation evolved when applied to other programmes, even arts programmes like *The Late Show* (1989–95), which also grew out of Lime Grove.

In the design side of the suite, we were presented with an Ikegami HL79 Caption Camera and a Quantel DPB 7001 (which I later christened the Classic Paintbox). This was very soon to become the single device that would have the most significant influence on broadcast television graphics for at least the next fifteen years. With its pen and tablet workstation, it had been very well thought out, operated by a wired pressure-sensitive pen and a 'puck'. The on-screen menu consisted of different functions, and by swiping across the screen, these could be switched 'off' or 'on'.

The simple graphics mixing desk had an input router to enable material to be taken in from external sources – video tape or telecine for example – and the mixer would allow sources to be combined. Considering no designers had been consulted, the Engineering Department had made a pretty good job of giving us most of what we needed. It did inspire my creativity. This original concept was later refined as more programmes 'went digital'. On *Breakfast Time* we very much became the innovators and experimentalists for all sorts of new graphics working practices.

Stills store

Previously all current affairs programmes relied on the Photography Department for 5×4 Polaroids or traditional photo printing etc. With the introduction of the digital Stills Store, suddenly we had the ability to 'grab' images direct from 35mm slides or videotape without any loss of quality, which had not been the case before with analogue recording. This was years before digital cameras. The stills store allocated each image a unique number when digitized, the original 6001 only holding 180×1MB digital images. 'Stacks' of images were built for sequences that could be played out with cuts, dissolves and wipe-downs or sent individually to the gallery for more sophisticated effects. The stills store also offered some creative capability, allowing images to be cropped, combined with others in the system and allocated different coloured borders. We asked Quantel to specially adapt our machine to help tie in with our house style so images could have thinner borders. Our range of backgrounds were all stored, as well as pre-set layouts, which simplified production time and of course guaranteed design continuity. Because of its small capacity we could barely afford to keep images on the system from one programme to the next, and we had to be ruthless with our digital housekeeping. With four teams of three designers or assistants, each working a week of nights once a month, all would have to be completely competent before we could use it live.

Training for launch

So being presented with all this equipment just two weeks away from our launch date, there was understandably a huge amount to take in. Apart from anything else we had many new design assistants who did not have any TV experience at all to make up the twelve staff required for the programme.

We logically focused on the stills store transmission technology first, as we had to get our material into the gallery. Our graduated paper backgrounds were combined with cropped boxed images created inside the stills store. One of its advantages (apart from its speed) was that it was fully digital, so what you saw was exactly what was transmitted. And another immediate improvement was that we could flawlessly produce perfectly pin-registered graphic sequences, which had always been an issue when trying to line up thirty-35mm slides or captions in the studio.

As we started to get to grips with everything, full programme pilots were started; initially they would have been on paper, which did not involve us, but we did stumble through a few 'proper pilots' to the best of our ability. Each one was a learning curve, with more improvements being made from the previous one. Each iteration gave us an indication of what sort of graphic material and volume were going to be required for our news bulletins. This is how we really started to build our house-style library and understand the pressure and expectations of news graphics.

Weather

The weather segments were going to be a major part of the programme and were to be back projected from an Eidophor projector into the studio set, fronted by the presenter, Francis Wilson. The main national weather output from the Television Centre at this time was still employing physical charts with magnetic symbols that the meteorologist walked between. Our solution involved 'digital captions', which were built up using transparent cloud shapes cut from Letraset (rather than symbols) positioned on a master map cut out of Pantone paper and all registered under the camera on an animation peg bar. This technique allowed us to create simple sequences of cloud movement predicted throughout the day, and we also used cel overlays for additional information.

News maps and other information graphics were created using our paper backgrounds and overlays (see Figure 17.2). The maps were cut out to start with, and the stills store gave us the ability to combine other images on top. Other strands included a daily review of some news stories selected by a guest, often a member of Parliament. The papers were delivered to us with the relevant stories outlined in red marker pen and were grabbed through the camera directly into the stills store. That was the basic routine when we went on air.

The current affairs items that required graphics were invariably created by the design staff who were working the day shifts. Such material required design input and creation time, although working generally within our house style, it was not the sort of work that the night shifts allowed or were intended for. The production team who were not working the day shift on the actual programme were referred to as 'Forward Planning'. Graphics might have been recorded from the stills store to tape during the daytime shifts or simply left in the stills store for live playout, as was the case with the Top 20 Chart rundown every Friday morning for example. The production office was quiet in the evenings.

Across the two and a half hours we were on air each weekday, there were five news and weather segments. And while the weather did not change from 6.30 am when we went on air, inevitably the news frequently did. One of the unique selling points of a long-format programme was the fact that it is always

Figure 17.2 Designer John Martin adding Letraset to a news map, 1985. Courtesy Andy Davy.

broadcasting the absolute latest world news, local news and travel. Local travel news was deemed as particularly important, which was a reason to have the television switched on at this time.

When the night shift started at midnight, we started putting the graphic material together as the latest news stories started to trickle in. On the night/TX (transmission) shift, the team worked together in the electronic graphics area. During the daytime shifts, design staff moved between the two areas.

Every night at around 4.00 am after collecting the latest weather data from the MET Office, Francis Wilson would bring in requirements for his 'Window on the Weather' slots, sketched out on paper. We would put it together, and he would come back to check them before going on air. He always started his broadcast in vision in front of the Eidophor, and then the gallery would take the sequence 'clean' as he voiced over – again, something that was not achievable with the way of the traditional Television Centre Weather presentation, but also a way of getting over the limitations of Eidophor displays.

At 6.30 am when the programme went on air, two design staff had the responsibility for the playout, working from a paper script, while the other person handled any developing news graphic requirements (see Figure 17.3). Like an Apollo mission, it is a measure of how important our launch day programme was to Quantel, as they were present to work with us and assist with the playout.

The stills store allowed imagery to be taken in at one workstation in the design area and played out from the other. The respective image file numbers being called across the room, which would then be reviewed and inserted into its appropriate stack. The designer responsible for playing-out material would always have had sight of everything and checked before transmitting.

This was a news programme, and a lot of news happens early in the morning, and so those segments could change considerably during transmission, and there would invariably be new items that required graphics after we had gone on air. As the stories of the day developed, revised news script pages printed on paper were distributed to all.

With a team of twelve graphics staff working over a four-week shift, it became apparent that a Graphics Bible would be extremely necessary and invaluable. This had previously never been the case on other programmes at Lime Grove, which had relied on word of mouth and replication. The style guide was compiled by Andy Davy, who had joined from *Which?* magazine. Andy completely got it from 'day one' and was very tech savvy, as he had experimented with computer graphics while at college. The graphic day shifts provided valuable style and technology training time for the new staff. With such a demanding programme, as soon as we were on air, we did not get to see each other very often, if at all.

Figure 17.3 Filling out a Graphics News Requisition, 1985. Courtesy Andy Davy.

One giant leap

Breakfast Time went on air on 17 January 1983, with considerable coverage in the National Press, and we succeeded in beating our rival *TV-Am* to air, which was one of the BBC's goals. All our graphics content was very well received, and the logo even appeared on the cover and inside of the *Radio Times*.

Shortly after, a union delegation of designers from Television Centre came to meet with us and raise their concern over working practices. The issue being, we were working with new technology with little or no formal training, and we were transmitting it live on air. Perhaps if our respective departments (Scenery Block and Lime Grove) had been closer in both physical and management terms, this could have been avoided. Graphic designers at Lime Grove had little or no union membership, and in retrospect, in our naïveté, we were just keen to learn and excited to experiment, albeit on the job.

There was still the matter of the Quantel Paintbox that we all had to learn, although it had been designed in a very intuitive way. The shift pattern gave staff the opportunity to get to grips with it when not working nights. When we were confident that everybody was competent after the first few weeks, we started developing the house style with the benefit of this new tool.

Maps

The News and Weather were two programme segments that benefitted immensely and immediately. Following on from our original maps cut out from paper, News maps 'Phase 2' were produced from images grabbed in from an atlas and then traced over and colour-filled to make a digital version. While time-consuming, it was still faster than cutting them out of paper and, of course, gave a better result as the Paintbox could add type as well. It was also very easy to create images for a sequence.

Then in Phase 3, to speed things up even more, I came up with the idea of having a set of highly detailed black-and-white world maps drawn up with country borders and laminated (see Figure 17.4). The Paintbox had the ability to make a stencil from a black-and-white image and allowed us to make our map style quite sophisticated. Land masses had a drop shadow and were composed onto our graduated backgrounds. This was a major step forward in terms of speed and consistency, but then Andy Davy improved the process even more: the Paintbox having the ability to record and replay (faster) a 'pen sequence' (like a macro). This meant that after the map artwork was grabbed in, the Paintbox was switched into 'map playback mode',

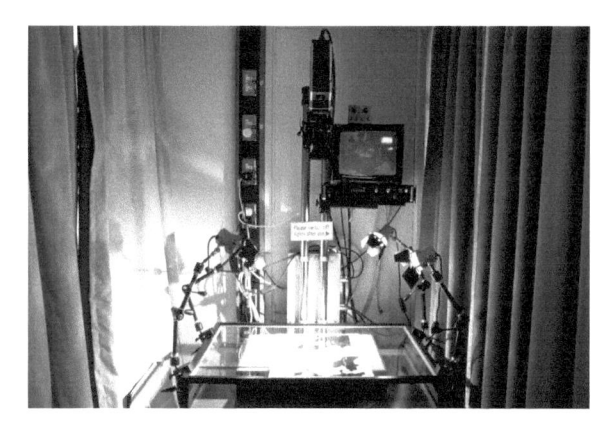

Figure 17.4 News Graphics rostrum with Ikegami camera, 1985. Courtesy Andy Davy.

and it went off on its own, making the stencil, retrieving the land and sea elements out of the library and combining them faster than any human could. This approach became standard practice when the Paintbox arrived in other BBC graphics departments a few years later.

The weather sequence benefitted in particular, with the ability for much more sophisticated and polished sequences to be constructed faster, with wind direction arrows and temperature discs being easily added. It also brought the capability of combining a satellite image that had been faxed over from Imperial College as an overlay onto a UK master map. This had never been done before. Television graphics were going through a radical technological advancement.

Conclusion

On *Breakfast*, I really believe that from a News and Current Affairs Graphics perspective, the designers became more appreciated and recognized for their contribution. This, in turn, made them more motivated and resulted in producing content at a faster pace, which is exactly what the news environment required.

In 1984, David Lloyd had been given the unenviable task of pulling all the regions together to create a replacement for the very popular and long-running *Nationwide*. I was flattered to be summoned to bring that to air, as the hours were going to be better, and I was keen to develop ideas and techniques that had come out from *Breakfast Time*. *60 Minutes* was to share the facility with *Breakfast Time*, which of course did make full Topical Production Centre utilization sense but meant we all had to be better organized with less 'equipment' time to produce more graphics. *60 Minutes* allowed me to push the envelope a bit further with my use of computer technology for titles, as well as creating other bespoke electronic effects for programme content.

Graphics alone do not make a programme. After another six months, in autumn 1984, a new programme was to take that evening slot in the BBC1 schedule, the *Six O'Clock News*, to be edited by Ron Neil. Ron asked for several things that he believed were necessary for the bulletin's success, including having me transferred to news to develop the show. In turn, I asked for Andy Davy to join me. Historically, production were assigned graphics staff; it was not the one thing to ask for a designer to work on your programme. However, things were evolving and the design staff were being noticed.

On reflection, I am grateful to the management for providing us with this new technology, but the success of pioneering new graphics was down to the dedication and time spent by the design team.

Figure 17.5 *Six O'Clock News* electronic graphics suite, 1985. Courtesy Andy Davy.

Joining forces with Andy again, the *Six* really did become the showcase for everything the previous twelve months had taught us; we were extremely adept with the technology by then (see Figure 17.5). Computer Animation technology had progressed considerably from that available for *Breakfast* and *60 Minutes*, with more facilities having opened in London and allowing us to work in colour!

In 1989 *Breakfast Time* was rechristened *BBC Breakfast*, moved to Television Centre and was folded into the corporate styling of all BBC News output. This, of course, made a whole lot of sense as corporate branding became important to all large organizations. Sadly, the strong personality that we had helped create was lost, but that is the ever-changing world of television news.

18 News 24/7

CHYAS BUFFETT, MARK CHAUDOIR, ANDY DAVY, IAN WORMLEIGHTON AND IAIN MACDONALD

The creative departments in BBC News and Current Affairs Design have always been a hive for developing talent. Colloquially referred to as the University of Design, they nurture talent, instilling not just accuracy and purpose but the ability to pique the interest of the casual user. It is this BBC ethos, 'To Engage and Inform', which lies at the heart of the entire output.

Engaged in generation across multiple outputs, from national news bulletins *One, Six (Nine)* and *Ten* to 24 hours News; from high-end political programming *Panorama* and *Question Time* to consumer affairs *Watchdog* and *Working Lunch*. Around the clock, from *Breakfast* to *Newsnight*, the operation never stops, and it's this variety, excitement, sense of meaning and purpose that drives both output and individual to achieve more.

Delivering across multiple creative outputs, the design teams service all creative, from brand and rebrand to experiential activations, from titles and visual language to the purest information design; idea, creative execution and information design brought together to impart knowledge in the most engaging way. All this across multiple channels of broadcast, print, out-of-home advertising (OOH), digital and a seemingly never-ending stream of social outputs requires drive, consistency and creativity second to none, all to the thirty-second deadline of a breaking news story or the thirty-second attention span of the user.

Always the first to embrace and harness new technologies and approaches, the decades have seen change and advance, not just in the tools used but in the ethos behind the direction. From hand-rendered maps using Letraset and copy camera to the earliest 3D graphics, through Quantel Paintbox, Hal and Adobe After Effects, from VR to AR and the latest advances in AI, across TV, laptop and phone screens, to big screens, outdoor screens and touch screens, the technology is always considered on merit and always used as a tool.

Processes evolve from individual creatives working on isolated strands using specialist operational skills and single pieces of kit to multi-skilled generators working in matrix teams to deliver a story. Moving from information design to data visualization to visual journalism to content generators and storytellers, journalists, designers, videographers and creative technologists work together, developing the skills of one another to connect with the user as never before.

All these skills, all this tech and this growth and change in the industry are never more visible than at General Election time, when brands and titles harmonize with the purest visual journalism, when technology is harnessed to best tell the story, when multiple channels impart information in the most engaging manner and when creativity and the idea are never more visible but never get in the way of the news.

News matters and design delivers.

Getting into television

'The brilliant thing about the BBC ad was it was a traineeship, no experience necessary' (Hill interview 2023). The expansion of news programming and the ever-increasing appetite for graphic captions, motion graphics and arresting visuals to illustrate stories have for many decades provided more opportunities to get into television than through other departments. For some designers it was a stepping stone that they graduated from, armed with impressive skills for creating digital and filmed motion graphics. It was in the 1980s and 1990s through the Quantel Paintbox and Hal years that saw the greatest shift and throughput of talent.

The interview

As many as 4,000 people would apply to an advert for BBC News Resources Graphic Designer. Through a shortlisting process, a group of 100 candidates was brought to White City for a series of tests, spotting BBC News graphics from the competition, brainstorming in groups to identify different personality types and a storyboarding test. Kevin Hill recalls:

> I'd never done a storyboard in my life. They showed us a storyboard and they said 'right, you got 15 minutes to storyboard a graphic about lowering the age of consent for gay people', and so I storyboarded this graphic and then they literally walked in and said 'oh, the story has been scrapped, you've got to do another one and you've got 5 minutes'. And so it was just really hard. (Hill 2023)

First day at work

Once employed, the new designer was put on probation and sent on a technical training course for a few weeks.

> What followed was six months of the most intense, the most demanding, the most enjoyable training ever. From 'A Taste of Television' at the old Wood Norton college, introducing us to how it all ties together, to well defined technology modules on the kit we'd use, shadowing multiple teams and programmes and crucially learning from the best in the industry, many of whom still impart their enviable knowledge to current and future generations. We were finally released, cut loose onto our own separate programmes. (Buffett 2023)

Ian Wormleighton joined in 1989; by then, all BBC News bulletins used the Quantel Paintbox since the launch of the *Six O'Clock News* five years earlier. Paintbox only made static graphics, to move them required other equipment and people to operate them. At this point in graphics production, the designer had to work within a team of technicians and vision mixers. Paintbox, Charisma (a picture mover) and Abekas (a digital storage device) were all set up digitally, so there was no image loss between image layers and versions, unlike analogue tape, where the image quality degraded after every pass or version recorded.

> You'd create the stills on the Paintbox, then somebody on the Stills Store would record them, and then you would have to put them in order and put all the mixes in, and then play it live to air from there. When I first joined there was a Stills Coordinator who would help you with all of that. You'd also have an Aston (caption generator) person who would do a lot of the typing that you might need, and sometimes they'd be typing live into the studio or live into an edit suite. . . . So you'd be playing out live to the gallery from

there, and then in the middle there were the Graphic Vision Mixers with the Abekas and Charisma. (Wormleighton 2023)

At one end of the design suite was the *Six O'Clock*, and at the other in mirror was the *One O'Clock* graphics team. Chyaz Buffett began his career in 1994 on *BBC Breakfast*.

> I'll never forget my first on-air graphic: a Paintbox and Charisma construct of seaside highlights on Breakfast News, it took the whole 8-hour shift to build, making air by the skin of our teeth. What followed was a year of experimentation (out of sight?), pushing creative boundaries, seeing what we could get away with and this time remains some of the most radical on-air information design I've been involved with. A multiple award-winning team and great times . . . Night shifts forge strong bonds and the closeness of these colleagues will never be surpassed. (Buffett 2023)

A typical day

The day shift would begin with one of the design team, which in the early 1990s comprised of a lead designer and two assistants, attending the editorial meeting for a briefing on the news stories of the day. Once briefed, an assistant would gather images and maps from the digital storage drive and prepare the solo Paintbox for the *Six O'Clock News* to create the list of images. If the *Newsnight* Paintbox was vacant, that could be harnessed by the team to double the work capacity while it was available. At that time there was no integrated brand strategy, each News programme had its own editor, or 'news baron', that controlled output and visual identity.

> At that time, the *One O'clock*, the *Six O'clock, the Nine O'clock, Newsnight*, and everything all had completely different styles and everything. So everything had to be done again. And so whatever the *One O'clock* news did before us, whether that was a map, any graphic, anything, had to be completely redone from scratch for the *Six O'Clock* and the same happened again for what was then the *Nine O'clock News*, at which, you know, in 2023, looks like madness. (Wormleighton 2023)

During quiet periods designers used the time to practice their skills and learn new techniques on the 'kit'. 'It's a bit like being in the fire brigade' (Wormleighton 2023). The adrenaline rush of making a graphic while the programme was live on air was hard to beat. The stakes are high because when mistakes happen, everyone sees it, and hard lessons are learnt in the glare of the studio gallery. 'It's very easy to make a spelling mistake, and you've got to be really detail minded' (Wormleighton 2023). But at the end of day, 'the slate is wiped clean' (Davy 2023).

At the cusp of change: Old guard, new tricks

> There were people who were older, and I remember some of them were people who had been there for years and talked about when the Falklands War was on, and how they would be camping out there through the night . . . making models and doing artwork for it. (Wormleighton 2023)

Andy Davy, head of news graphics (1985–9), remembers when the first digital graphics system, the Quantel Paintbox, was introduced. 'A number of the existing staff were really quite wary about this, and didn't like the way this was going, whereas the newcomers came in with no preconceptions' (Davy 2023). They came in straight from art college and at the same time learning cardboard graphics, which was an extension of what they learnt at college, and also picking up digital skills, thinking, 'oh well this is this is how you do telly . . . and took to it like a duck to water' (Davy 2023).

He remembers sitting next to an older designer, who had been an illustrator pre-BBC, watching him complete what the older colleague considered a finished piece of work.

> It was not very good at all, but he was completely satisfied, and what I realised was that when you're familiar with a technology or craft, you have that point where you think 'I've achieved my goal'. In design terms, you know it's not good enough. And for him that had gone out the window, because it was surmounting the *technology* barrier that gave him that sense of 'I've finished'. And I remember thinking, that's interesting, he's lost his design hurdle and he's replaced it with a technology hurdle. . . . But during that learning curve design standards often went out the window in a way to simply get anything done. (Davy 2023)

Davy had a professional respect for the particular craft skills of the older lettering artists, many of whom were in their fifties and had come from BBC News at Alexander Palace in the 1960s.

> These guys had all grown old together. . . . They weren't designers as we might now recognise and they thought we were a bit weird with our graphics degrees. . . . They could do a painted map remarkably quickly . . . they could produce that much quicker than we could on a Paintbox because they could reach in (to their physical archive filing system), find one, get a cel overlay, get the lettering out and it would be done really quickly. (Davy 2023)

The first news programme to use digital graphics was the *Six O'Clock* in September 1984, and this was then followed by a redesigned *Nine O'Clock* news programme. Digital resources and new studios were designed and built in Television Centre (see Figure 16.4). Building on the earlier *Breakfast Time* set up by Terry Hylton (see chapter 17), Davy worked with colleagues in engineering to develop a new workflow of graphics into the news gallery. During this transition period two very different pools of knowledge co-existed, though rarely mixed and interacted. A generation gap was aggravated by different attitudes to technology and self-identity. Older designers that managed to bridge the gap were unusual. Lime Grove was now abandoned, but not until after a special August Bank Holiday series of tributes made by the BBC2 flagship arts programme *The Late Show* in 1991.

And then there was one

The new digital environment and workflow had its teething problems. At one point a bottleneck of work formed around the limited number of available Paintboxes. As a result if stories did not have the graphics to support them, they were frequently dropped. Davy was concerned: 'We shouldn't be controlling what the viewers are seeing based on what we were able to produce' (Davy 2023). So graphics producers were introduced to manage and become the conduit between graphics and editorial. When the Quantel Paintbox was superseded by Hal and Harriet, designers now had the capacity to build motion graphics with enough digital storage for eleven-seconds of animation, thus removing the reliance on the Charisma and Abekas operators. They could work solo. News producers now had an insatiable appetite for motion graphics.

At a news editorial level, it wasn't until 1997 that a universal brand approach to BBC News was established with 'Concept News' brought in by director of news, Tony Hall. This was to be rolled across the regions as well as every news bulletin throughout the day. At every step there were vested interests and old practices that had to be overcome to unify a brand identity that could compete on a stage that had moved from regional, national to international and satellite broadcasting.

BBC News countdown

In 2003 designer and director Mark Chaudoir was commissioned to create four ninety-second countdown sequences to precede BBC News 24. He filmed around United Kingdom using time-lapse photography, showing wide and far-reaching set of subject matter. In 2005 BBC News again commissioned Mark to produce a new set of countdown films as they wanted to show more of a global reach and news gathering.

> I said, well, the one thing you never see when you watch the news is you never see the camera and you never see the satellite truck. You only see the presenter. Yeah, you only see the news reader saying over to you. You never see what's behind that. I said why don't we just go and film the actual news gathering and use the red and white lines from titles sequence to actually show the news going back to the BBC. (Chaudoir 2023)

He then produced a treatment and storyboards with a set of ideas that were generic news stories but seen from a fresh perspective with a correspondent and cameraperson: newsgathering in action. He then briefed numerous BBC News cameraman to gather footage in the more extreme war zones and natural disaster areas, sending them storyboards and extensive direction and talking to them and their news correspondent. He also set out to get brand synergy with Martin Lambie-Nairn's *BBC News* titles, which featured red lines and Dave Lowe's music.

The joy of the project meant he got to travel the world filming BBC Correspondents and worked with each bureau to set up filming and locations, 'for example the Indian BBC Bureau set up the correspondent on the BBC Bureau roof with satellite dishes, on a busy Delhi street corner; in Thailand we put Andrew Harding into a boat going through Bangkok canals; we took the African correspondent into a school' (Chaudoir 2023) (see Figure 18.1).

Chaudoir gathered over twenty-four hours of footage, which he edited into four ninety-second countdowns.

> We also developed sweeping time-lapses and posted in the red News lines. Clive Norman the cameraman, devised an ingenious clockwork device which allowed the camera to rotate filming time-lapse, rather than the usual static time-lapse. In post house VTR we put in the red lines. (Chaudoir 2023)

The countdown is still on air with a different set of graphics but still in the style of countdowns created by Mark in 2005. The longevity Mark believes is that the countdowns have captured the public's interest in BBC News gathering and seeing correspondents out in the field with camerapersons and seeing how news is gathered. A huge part of the success is also the news and countdown music composed by Dave Lowe, which has become iconic and is widely popular. 'For me there's a sense of pride in that 18 years later, they're still going out. Of course it's been upgraded, but countdowns go out 24 times a day, 8,760 times a year, so it's gone out nearly 160,000 times' (Chaudoir 2023).

Figure 18.1 *BBC News 24 Top the Hour Countdown* (2005) photos from shoot and tickets. Courtesy Mark Chaudoir.

Conclusion

The accounts of Brian Eley, Terry Hylton, Ian Wormleighton, Chyaz Buffett, Mark Chaudoir and Andy Davy illustrate the revolution in television news production that turned cardboard graphics into motion graphics. Since the 1970s broadcasting across the globe has created a voracious appetite for news bulletins and magazines that has had a profound effect on the development of graphics technology and working practices. The production economy of motion graphics saw the replacement and redundancy of many skills as equipment was superseded by more efficient technologies. Each new generation of designer that was recruited accepted new technology as their norm, only to find in a few years that they too had to adapt and upskill in response to further changes, be it in production or platform of delivery to the audience.

> A decade on and off, I left news on multiple occasions, but have often been drawn back by the energy, the creativity, the meaning and purpose. Nowhere is the growth so rapid; nowhere is the creative challenge greater; nowhere are friendships so forged by intensity and adversity, wrapped in the news of triumph and tragedy. Plus, where else do you get to change jobs every six months?
>
> And where has this career taken us? From my cohort, one has worked in New York for the biggest creative teams, one runs their own agency, one is a multiple Emmy Award-winning title designer, and I brand the UK around the world.
>
> News is the university of design and we all graduated with honours. Thank you BBC. (Buffett 2023)

Epilogue
FOR MICHAEL GRAHAM-SMITH

With the support of a small group of BBC alumni, Ex-BBC senior graphic designer Michael Graham-Smith has spent many years tirelessly collating and establishing the BBC Motion Graphics Archive, which has been the stimulus for this book.

Coming from an academic background, he attained a degree in German and French. His interest in design was developed during a course at *The London College of Printing*, which led to various jobs in print and film design before starting work for the *Open University* at Alexandra Place in 1972. He remained a designer with the BBC until 1994.

During later years, he was also a respected mentor to many who followed him into the design department. His skills as a quietly consistent, intelligent and good-humoured teacher continued into a professorship of media arts in Cologne, Germany. He won the Prix d'Or with his students at the Annecy Student Animation Festival before retiring in 2004. Ever the Polymath, it was at this stage in 'retirement' that Michael's abilities focused upon the creation of the archive.

Without his perseverance over many years to see the archive delivered, much of the metadata, many of the artefacts and memories would have been lost or buried. He recognized the importance of creating a legacy that not only celebrates the past but informs and inspires current and future designers to contextualize their practice and value their contribution as part of a future legacy in the ever-evolving art that is motion graphics.

Appendix

1936	BBC transmit first television pictures from Alexandra Palace, London
1953	First BBC 'Television Symbol', designed by Abram Games, who had designed brand identity for Festival of Britain in 1952
1954	BBC Graphic Design Department formed and employ their first art school-trained graphic designer, John Sewell RCA
1955	ITV begins broadcasting as commercial alternative to BBC, the United Kingdom now have two television channels
1959	Bernard Lodge RCA joins BBC
1963	First episode of *Dr Who*, titles designed by Bernard Lodge, music by Delia Derbyshire at BBC Radiophonic Workshop
	BBC1 spinning globe identity launched
1964	BBC2 launched and UK television improves resolution from 405 to 625 lines
1969	Colour transmission begins in United Kingdom
1970	United Kingdom has 200,000 colour televisions and 1 million monochrome
1971	First episode of *Old Grey Whistle Test*, designed by Roger Ferrin, animation all shot in camera on a film-rostrum on 16mm Eastman colour
1973	Bernard Lodge updates *Dr Who* titles using slit-scan technology on 35mm film
1974	BBC1 globe ident redesigned in blue and yellow by Sid Sutton
1976	Match of the Day titles designed by Pauline Carter, shot live action in a stadium with hundreds of people holding up coloured cards to create an image across the stands.
1979	BBC2 ident, designed by Oliver Elmes, played out from digital solid-state hard-drive developed by BBC Computer Graphic Workshop
1981	Michael Blakstad, a BBC programme director, spoke at European Broadcasting Union conference urging television graphic designers to be 'more thrusting and ambitious' in defining programme visual identity
	First generation Quantel Paintbox, digital painting system launched with hard-drive, tablet, stylus and keyboard
1982	Quantel Mirage is first 3D picture manipulator
	Lambie-Nairn's Channel 4 logo changes the landscape of UK television branding

	Graham McCallum designed animated backgrounds using chromakey to combine live action for drama series *Jane*, based on a newspaper cartoon
1983	BBC1 ident, designed by Alan Jeapes, replaces mechanical model globe with a computer generated animating gold globe playing from a digital hard-drive
	BBC Video Rostrum developed in-house as a digital storage system with editing and video camera capability
1984	Motion-control camera at Moving Picture Company developed by Peter Truckle
1985	First episode of *EastEnders*, titles designed by Alan Jeapes
	Quantel Harry launched, a digital moving image editing, layering and manipulation tool to replace analogue video and film opticals
	BBC Weather maps go digital, replacing magnetic symbols on a studio map
1988	BBC News outsource title design to Lambie-Nairn, designed by Daniel Barber
	Red Nose Day first Comic Relief telethon with titles designed by Daniel Frick and Paul D'Auria
1989	Sky TV begins broadcasting by satellite heralding multichannel revolution in UK television
	First programme of *The Late Show* a live late night arts review with a dedicated graphics team for BBC2
1991	BBC2 rebranded by Lambie-Nairn, designed by Daniel Barber
	BBC1 rebranded by Lambie-Nairn, designed by Daniel Barber
1992	Quantel Henry provides greater levels of digital moving image layering and manipulation
1997	BBC1 globe returns as a live-action hot air balloon over UK landscapes
1998	First digital widescreen broadcasts using 14:9 ratio
1999	Hard-drive digital video recorders introduced allowing viewers to pause live tv
2000	BBC HD broadcasts high-definition 16:9
2001	BBC1 rebranded with dancers replacing globe for new controller Lorraine Heggessey
2002	BBC Graphic Design Department becomes part of BBC Broadcast
2005	BBC Broadcast becomes Red Bee Media
	Red Bee win pitch for new ITV idents
2006	BBC1 redesign by Red Bee, using circular devices echoing globe
2007	BBC2 redesign by Red Bee
	BBC iPlayer launched as digital streaming service
2014	*Doctor Who* titles designed by a fan, Steven Moffat from his bedroom
2016	BBC3 launched as an online only service
2017	BBC1 rebranded showing groups of real people across the United Kingdom, *Oneness*
2018	BBC2 rebrand by BBC Creative and Superunion using a variety of motion graphics studios
	BBC Weather redesigned across broadcast and digital platforms
2020	BBC1 rebranded showing audience generated video during lockdown across the United Kingdom

References

Introduction

Hendy, D. (2022), *The BBC: A People's History*, London: Profile Books
Herdeg, W. and Halas, J. (1967), *Film & Tv Graphics*, Zurich: The Graphis Press.
Hesmondhalgh, D. (2007), *The Culture Industries*, 2nd edn, London: Sage.
Higgins, C. (2015), *This New Noise*, London: Guardian 7, 63–4.
Lambie-Nairn, M. (1997), *Brand Identity for Television*, London: Phaidon.
Laughton, R. (1966), *TV Graphics*, London: Studio Vista; New York: Reinhold Pub.
Macdonald, I. (2014), 'Cultural Change in the Creative Industries: A Case Study of BBC Graphic Design from 1990-2011', *Visual Communication*, 13 (1): 31–49.

Chapter 1

Merritt, D. (1993), *Graphic Design in Television*, Oxford: Focal Press.
Merritt, D. (1987), *Television Graphic Design: From Pencil to Pixel*, London: Trefoil.
About the BBC (2023), 'Mission, Values and Public Ppurposes'. Available online: https://www.bbc.com/aboutthebbc/governance/mission (Accessed September 2023)
Adams, P. C. (1992), Television as a Gathering Place. *Annals of the Association of American Geographers*, 82 (1): 117–35.
Aston, J. (1997), in M. Lambie-Nairn, *Brand Identity for Television; With Knobs on,* London: Phaidon Press.
BBC (2023a), 'The Television Symbol the Story of Abram Games's batwings logo'. Available online: https://www.bbc.com/historyofthebbc/research/bbc-idents/television-symbol/ (Accessed September 2023).
BBC (2023b), 'Into the New Millennium: BBC One's Identity Post-1997'. Available online: https://www.bbc.com/historyofthebbc/research/bbc-idents/into-the-new-millennium/ (Accessed September 2023).
Blauvelt, A. (2011), 'Brand New Worlds: Corporate Makeovers and Dead Logos'. Available online: https://walkerart.org/magazine/brand-new-worlds-corporate-makeovers-and-dead (Accessed September 2023).
Bryant, A. and Mawer, C. (2016), *The TV Brand Builders: How to Win Audiences and Influence Viewers*, London: Kogan Page.
Chaudoir, M. (2023), interview with the authors, May 2023 [online].
Cole. N. (2023), interview with the authors, March 2023 [online].
Creative Review (2015), 'How to Successfully Mix Business and Creativity by Martin Lambie-Nairn'. Available online: https://www.creativereview.co.uk/successfully-mix-business-and-creativity-by-martin-lambie-nairn/ (Accessed September 2023).
Davies, S. (2023), interview with the authors, March 2023 [in person].
Davenport, T. H. and Beck, J. C. (2001), *The Attention Economy*, Boston: Harvard Business School Press.
Emin, T. (2006), 'Tracey Emin: My Life In A Column'. Available online:https://www.independent.co.uk/voices/columnists/tracey-emin/tracey-emin-my-life-in-a-column-429604.html (Accessed September 2023).

Fielder, J. (2023) interview with the authors, August 2023 [online].
Gouldie, M. (2023), interview with the authors, May 2023 [online].
Grainge, P. (2021), 'From Idents to Influencers: The Promotional Screen Industries', *The Routledge Companion to Media Industries*, Abingdon: Routledge.
Green, L. (2010), 'Rory Sutherland's Quiet Behavioural Revolution Gives the Status Quo Bias a Nudge'. Available online: https://www.telegraph.co.uk/finance/newsbysector/mediatechnologyandtelecoms/media/8023044/Rory-Sutherlands-quiet-behavioural-revolution-gives-the-status-quo-bias-a-nudge-think-tank.html (Accessed September 2023).
Hodgson, J. (2002), 'BBC1 Drops Globe in Multicultural Rebranding Exercise'. Available online: https://www.theguardian.com/media/2002/mar/26/marketingandpr.broadcasting (Accessed September 2023).
Losasso, M. (2023), interview with the authors, May 2023 [email].
Masters, P. (2023), interview with the authors, March 2023 [online].
Mawer, C. (2023), interview with the authors, March 2023 [online].
McLuhan, M. (1964), *Understanding Media: The Extensions of Man*, London: Routledge Classics.
Merritt, D. (1993), *Graphic Design in Television*, Oxford: Focal Press.
Moran, J. (2013), *Armchair Nation: An Intimate History of Britain in Front of the TV,* London: Profile Books.
Morton, M. (2022), 'Graphic Design, Music and Sound in the BBC's Channel Idents, 1991–2021' Available online: https://journals.sagepub.com/doi/full/10.1177/17496020211067736 (Accessed September 2023).
Nairn, M. L. (2015), In Creative Review: How to Successfully Mix Business and Creativity by Martin Lambie-Nairn. Available online: https://www.creativereview.co.uk/successfully-mix-business-and-creativity-by-martin-lambie-nairn/ (Accessed September 2023).
Ofcom (2019), *Ofcom's Annual Report on the BBC*. London: Ofcom. Available online: https://www.ofcom.org.uk/__data/assets/pdf_file/0026/173735/second-bbc-annual-report.pdf (Accessed 30 August 2023).
Platt, T (2023), interview with the authors, May 2023 [online].
Philips, A. (2012), In 'Knowledge at Warton: Transmedia Storytelling, Fan Culture and the Future of Marketing'. Available online: https://knowledge.wharton.upenn.edu/article/transmedia-storytelling-fan-culture-and-the-future-of-marketing/ (Accessed September 2023).
Ritson, M. (2004), 'Mark Ritson on Branding: Why are Brand Positionings Made So Complex?' Available online: https://www.campaignlive.co.uk/article/mark-ritson-branding-why-brand-positionings-made-so-complex/228959 (Accessed September 2023.)
Seiter, E. (1987), *Television and Contemporary Criticism: Channels of Discourse*, London: Methuen & Co Ltd.
Thompson, M (2004), 'Speech Given at the MediaGuardian Edinburgh International Television Festival 2004 - Defining Public Value'. Available online: https://www.bbc.co.uk/pressoffice/speeches/stories/thompson_edinburgh04.shtml (Accessed 2023).
Williams, P. (2023), interview with the author, March 2023 [online].
Williams, R. (1974), *Television, Technology and Cultural Form*, London: Fontana/ Collins.
WIRED (2021), 'Jony Ive & Anna Wintour in Conversation - RE:WIRED 2021: Designing for the Future We Want to Inhabit'. Available online: https://www.youtube.com/watch?v=piCuW2wSSTA (Accessed September 2023).
Wyatt-Brooks, J. (2023), interview with the authors, March 2023 [in person].

BBC Motion Graphics Archive Links

Introduction

https://www.ravensbourne.ac.uk/bbc-motion-graphics-archive/sid-sutton
https://www.ravensbourne.ac.uk/bbc-motion-graphics-archive/1953-bbc-bats-wings-identity

THE ROLE OF IDENTS
https://www.ravensbourne.ac.uk/bbc-motion-graphics-archive/bbc-archive-search?querybbc=bbc+one+globe
https://www.ravensbourne.ac.uk/bbc-motion-graphics-archive/bbc-archive-search?querybbc=bbc+clock
https://www.ravensbourne.ac.uk/bbc-motion-graphics-archive/bbc-one-hippos-long-ident-2006
https://www.ravensbourne.ac.uk/bbc-motion-graphics-archive/1991-bbc2-rebrand-paint-ident

IDENTS AS A MARKETING TOOL
https://www.ravensbourne.ac.uk/bbc-motion-graphics-archive/bbc2-flowers-ident-1991
https://www.ravensbourne.ac.uk/bbc-motion-graphics-archive/bbc2-mars-ident-1997
https://www.ravensbourne.ac.uk/bbc-motion-graphics-archive/bbc-two-india-ident
https://www.ravensbourne.ac.uk/bbc-motion-graphics-archive/bbc2-cell-ident-1993
https://www.ravensbourne.ac.uk/bbc-motion-graphics-archive/bbc-two-50th-cactus-sting-2014
https://www.ravensbourne.ac.uk/bbc-motion-graphics-archive/euro-2000-championships-ident-2000
https://www.ravensbourne.ac.uk/bbc-motion-graphics-archive/bbc-one-mission-control-long-ident-2007
https://www.ravensbourne.ac.uk/bbc-motion-graphics-archive/bbc-one-strictly-come-dancing-ident-2010
https://www.ravensbourne.ac.uk/bbc-motion-graphics-archive/bbc-one-bang-goes-theory-ident-2009
https://www.ravensbourne.ac.uk/bbc-motion-graphics-archive/bbc-two-winter-daleks-ident-2000
https://www.ravensbourne.ac.uk/bbc-motion-graphics-archive/wallace-and-gromit-christmas-slipper-ident-1995
https://www.ravensbourne.ac.uk/bbc-motion-graphics-archive/cbbc-shaun-sheep-ident-version-2-2007

REFLECTING THE NATION
https://www.ravensbourne.ac.uk/bbc-motion-graphics-archive/bbc-archive-search?querybbc=bbc+one+globe
https://www.ravensbourne.ac.uk/bbc-motion-graphics-archive/balloon-above-needles-ident-1998
https://www.ravensbourne.ac.uk/bbc-motion-graphics-archive/balloon-above-angel-north-ident-1998
https://www.ravensbourne.ac.uk/bbc-motion-graphics-archive/bbc-one-bikes-short-ident-2006
https://www.ravensbourne.ac.uk/bbc-motion-graphics-archive/bbc-one-rhythm-movement-wheelchair-dancers-ident-2002

CHRISTMAS MAGIC
https://www.ravensbourne.ac.uk/bbc-motion-graphics-archive/bbc1-christmas-wizard-ident-1-1990
https://www.ravensbourne.ac.uk/bbc-motion-graphics-archive/bbc1-christmas-wizard-ident-2-1990
https://www.ravensbourne.ac.uk/bbc-motion-graphics-archive/bbc-one-christmas-gruffalo-ident-2011
https://www.ravensbourne.ac.uk/bbc-motion-graphics-archive/bbc2-christmas-campaign-wild-fairies-cracker-sting-1998
https://www.ravensbourne.ac.uk/bbc-motion-graphics-archive/bbc2-christmas-tin-toy-ident-1993
https://www.ravensbourne.ac.uk/bbc-motion-graphics-archive/bbc-one-christmas-hot-air-balloon-ident-1999
https://www.ravensbourne.ac.uk/bbc-motion-graphics-archive/bbc-one-christmas-ident-1-2001
https://www.ravensbourne.ac.uk/bbc-motion-graphics-archive/bbc2-christmas-gift-sting-2-reeves-mortimer-1997

BEYOND CHRISTMAS
https://www.ravensbourne.ac.uk/bbc-motion-graphics-archive/1991-bbc2-rebrand-paint-ident
https://www.ravensbourne.ac.uk/bbc-motion-graphics-archive/bbc2-winter-promotion-slinky-1994
https://www.ravensbourne.ac.uk/bbc-motion-graphics-archive/bbc2-winter-promotion-magnet-1-1994
https://www.ravensbourne.ac.uk/bbc-motion-graphics-archive/bbc-one-idents-compilation-2015

TECHNOLOGY

https://www.ravensbourne.ac.uk/bbc-motion-graphics-archive/bbc2-winter-promotion-bungee-1994
https://www.ravensbourne.ac.uk/bbc-motion-graphics-archive/1969-bbc1-mirrored-globe-1
https://www.ravensbourne.ac.uk/bbc-motion-graphics-archive/1991-bbc1-virtual-globe-0
https://www.ravensbourne.ac.uk/bbc-motion-graphics-archive/balloon-above-eilean-donan-castle-ident-1997
https://www.ravensbourne.ac.uk/bbc-motion-graphics-archive/bbc-one-penguins-ident-2007
https://www.ravensbourne.ac.uk/bbc-motion-graphics-archive/bbc-one-magical-forest-long-ident-2007
https://www.ravensbourne.ac.uk/bbc-motion-graphics-archive/bbc-archive-search?querybbc=curve&page=1
https://www.ravensbourne.ac.uk/bbc-motion-graphics-archive/1974-bbc2-colour-ident-4
https://www.ravensbourne.ac.uk/bbc-motion-graphics-archive/bbc-two-curve-punchy-ident-2019

Chapter 2

Baranowski, A. (2018), 'Anatomy of a Soundscape'. https://vimeo.com/322756903 (Accessed 11 November 2022).
Baranowski, A. (2020), interview with the authors, November 2020 [online].
Bashford, S. (2002), 'BBC Four Reveals "Sophisticated" Identity'. https://www.campaignlive.co.uk/article/branding-bbc-four-reveals-sophisticated-identity/139077 (Accessed 11 November 2022).
BBC. (2013), 'The Story of BBC Television Idents'. https://www.bbc.com/historyofthebbc/research/bbc-idents/ (Accessed 11 November 2022).
Betancourt, M. (2013), *The History of Motion Graphics: From Avant-Garde to Industry in the United States*, Rockville, Md.: Wildside Press.
Born, G. (2005), *Uncertain Vision: Birt, Dyke and the Reinvention of the BBC*, London: Vintage.
Brownie, B. (2013), 'Modular Construction and Anamorphosis in Channel 4 Idents: Past and Present', *Journal of Media Practice*, 14 (2): 93–109.
Brownie, B. (2015), 'Fluid Typography: Transforming Letterforms in Television Idents', *Arts and the Market*, 5 (2): 154–67.
Brownrigg, M. and Meech, P. (1999), 'Strike Up the Brand! The Aural Aspects of UK Television Channel', *Media Education Journal,* 27: 29–31.
Brownrigg, M. and Meech, P. (2002), 'From Fanfare to Funfair: The Changing Sound World of Uk Television Idents', *Popular Music*, 21(3): 345–55.
Brownrigg, M. and Meech, P. (2011), '"Music is Half the Picture": The Soundworld of UK Television Idents', Ephemeral Media. P. Grainge. London: BFI: 70–87.
Bryant, A. and Mawer, C. (2016), *The TV Brand Builders: How to Win Audiences and Influence Viewers*, London, Philadelphia: Kogan Page.
Chion, M. (1994), *Audio-Vision: Sound on Screen*, ed. and trans. Claudia Gorbman, foreword by Walter Murch, New York: Columbia University Press.
Crook, G. (1986), *The Changing Image: Television Graphics From Caption Card to Computer*, London, Built by Robots.
Davison, A. (2013), 'Title Sequences for Contemporary Television Serials', in Claudia Gorbman, Carol Vernallis, John Richardson (eds), *The Oxford Handbook of New Audiovisual Aesthetics*, Oxford: Oxford University Press.
Johnson, C. (2013a), 'From Brand Congruence to the 'Virtuous Circle': Branding and the Commercialization of Public Service Broadcasting', *Media, Culture & Society,* 35 (3): 314–31.
Johnson, C. (2013b), 'The Continuity of 'Continuity': Flow and the Changing Experience of Watching Broadcast Television', *Key Words: A Journal of Cultural Materialism*, (11): 27–43.
Keeley, J. (2020), interview with the authors, November 2020 [online].
Lambie-Nairn, M. (1997), *Brand Identity for Television: With Knobs On*, London: Phaidon.

Lambie-Nairn, M. (2020), interview with the authors, September 2020 [phonecall].
Laughton, R. (1966), *TV Ggraphics*. London, Studio Vista.
Light, J. J. (2004), 'Television Channel Identity: The Role of Channels in the Delivery of Public Service Television in Britain, 1996-2002' [Unpublished PhD thesis]. University of Glasgow.
Macdonald, I. (2014), 'Cultural Change in the Creative Industries: A Case Study of BBC Graphic Design From 1990–2011', *Visual Communication,* 13 (1): 31–49.
Macdonald, I. (2015), 'Designing to Engage a Television Audience: How are Different Media Used in TV Ident Creation?' *Arts and the Market,* 5 (2): 139–53.
Macdonald, I. (2016), *Hybrid Practices in Moving Image Design: Methods of Heritage and Digital Production in Motion Graphics*, Cham: Springer International Publishing AG.
Mollaghan, A. (2015), *The Visual Music Film,* Basingstoke, Palgrave Macmillan.
Morton, M. (2022), 'Graphic Design, Music and Sound in the BBC's Channel Idents, 1991–2021', *Critical Studies in Television*, 17 (2): 117–34.
Morton, M. (2023), '"A Hidden Art Form" the Value of Sound in UK Television Idents (1982-2022)' [Unpublished doctoral thesis]. University of Edinburgh. https://era.ed.ac.uk/handle/1842/40722
OED Online. (2022), *Improvisation*, Oxford University Press. https://www-oed-com.ezproxy.is.ed.ac.uk/view/Entry/92872?redirectedFrom=improvisation (Accessed 21 November 2022).
Pasler, J. (2001), *Impressionism, Grove Music Online*, Oxford University Press. https://www-oxfordmusiconline-com.ezproxy.is.ed.ac.uk/grovemusic/view/10.1093/gmo/9781561592630.001.0001/omo-9781561592630-e-0000050026 (Accessed 11 November 2022).
Sadler, T. and Sadler, G. (2020), interview with the authors, October 2020 [online].
Superunion (2019). 'BBC Two Rebrand.' https://sites.wpp.com/wppedcream/2019/design-and-branding/broadcast_design-animation/bbc-two-rebrand (Accessed 27 August 2024).
Tang, M. (2020), 'Interdisciplinarity and Creativity', in Elias G. Carayannis (ed.), *Encyclopaedia of Creativity,* 678–84, London, Springer.

Chapter 3

BBC (2014b) 'Top of the Pops Trivia'. Available online: https://www.bbc.co.uk/totp2/trivia/logos/ (Accessed 12 April 2023).
Blaxill, R. (2023), interview with authors.
Cowey, C. (2023), interview with authors.
The Guardian (2004), 'Top of the Pops through the Decades'. Available online: https://www.theguardian.com/music/2004/nov/29/popandrock.television (Accessed 24 March 2023).
Harvey, M. (2023), interview with authors.
Kale, S. (2021), 'We All Cringe Together': The Unlikely Afterlife of Top of the Pops', *The Guardian*. Available online: https://www.theguardian.com/music/2021/apr/30/chart-music-top-of-the-pops-nostalgia (Accessed 13 April 2023).
Ortmans, M. (2023), interview with authors.
Top of the Pops late 1970s Opening Titles (no author, n.d.). Available online: https://www.youtube.com/watch?v=K0PiVpHvXd0 (Accessed 2 July 2023).
TOTP Titles 1981 (no author, n.d.). Available online: https://vimeo.com/206124136 (Accessed 20 April 2023).
Ure, M. OBE (2023), interview with authors.
Williams, P. (2023), interview with authors.
Westbrook, C. (2016), 'Here's a Very Young Boy George in the Audience of Top of the Pops in 1981…', *Metro*. Available online: https://metro.co.uk/2016/01/09/heres-a-very-young-boy-george-in-the-audience-of-the-pops-in-1981-5612169/ (Accessed 15 June 2023).

BBC Motion Graphics Archive Links

Ray of Light

https://www.ravensbourne.ac.uk/bbc-motion-graphics-archive/top-pops-1981
https://www.ravensbourne.ac.uk/bbc-motion-graphics-archive/top-pops-1983
https://www.ravensbourne.ac.uk/bbc-motion-graphics-archive/top-pops-1985

DIGITAL AND ANALOGUE GEOMETRY

https://www.ravensbourne.ac.uk/bbc-motion-graphics-archive/top-pops-1988
https://www.ravensbourne.ac.uk/bbc-motion-graphics-archive/top-pops-1989

FLEXIBLE COHERENCE

https://www.ravensbourne.ac.uk/bbc-motion-graphics-archive/top-pops-1995
https://www.ravensbourne.ac.uk/bbc-motion-graphics-archive/top-pops-2-1994

BACK TO BASICS

https://www.ravensbourne.ac.uk/bbc-motion-graphics-archive/top-pops-1998

Chapter 4

Baxter, B. and E. Barnes (1989), *Blue Peter: The Inside Story*, Dorking: Ringpress Books.
Buckingham, D. (2005), 'A Apecial Audience? Children and Television', in J. Wasko (ed.), *A Companion to Television*, 468–88, Oxford: Blackwell Publishing.
Evans, E. (2023), interview with the author, April 2023 [online].
Hendy, D. (2022), *The BBC: A People's History*, London: Profile Books.
Hill, K. (2023), interview with the author, March 2023 [online].
Vinnicombe, E. (2023), interview with the author, February 2023 [online].

BBC Motion Graphics Archive links

https://www.ravensbourne.ac.uk/bbc-motion-graphics-archive/blue-peter-1963
https://www.ravensbourne.ac.uk/bbc-motion-graphics-archive/blue-peter-1995
https://www.ravensbourne.ac.uk/bbc-motion-graphics-archive/blue-peter-1999
https://www.ravensbourne.ac.uk/bbc-motion-graphics-archive/blue-peter-2000
https://www.ravensbourne.ac.uk/bbc-motion-graphics-archive/blue-peter-2004
https://www.ravensbourne.ac.uk/bbc-motion-graphics-archive/blue-peter-2021

Chapter 5

Bass, J. and P. Kirkham (2011), *Saul Bass: A Life in Film & Design*, London: Laurence King.
Buttner, C. (2023), email correspondence with authors, May 2023.
Jeapes, A. (1985), personal communication, [letter].
Jeapes, A. (1998), personal communication to Matthew Robinson, [letter].
Kemistry (2004), *Timeframes*, London: Kemistry Gallery.
Laughton, R. (1966), *TV Graphics*, London: Studio Vista; New York: Reinhold Pub.

Merritt, D. (1987), *Television Graphic Design: From Pencil to Pixel*, London: Trefoil.
Merritt, D. (1993), *Graphic Design in Television*, Oxford: Focal Press.
Minghella, A. (1989), *Truly Madly Deeply,* UK: BBC Films.
Sutton, S. (2023), interview with the authors, May 2023 [online].

BBC Motion Graphics Archive links

https://www.ravensbourne.ac.uk/bbc-motion-graphics-archive/hitch-hikers-guide-galaxy-1981
https://www.ravensbourne.ac.uk/bbc-motion-graphics-archive/i-claudius-1976
https://www.ravensbourne.ac.uk/bbc-motion-graphics-archive/eastenders-1985
https://www.ravensbourne.ac.uk/bbc-motion-graphics-archive/eastenders-1999
https://www.ravensbourne.ac.uk/bbc-motion-graphics-archive/eastenders-2021
https://www.ravensbourne.ac.uk/bbc-motion-graphics-archive/sense-guilt-1990
https://www.ravensbourne.ac.uk/bbc-motion-graphics-archive/between-lines-1992
https://www.ravensbourne.ac.uk/bbc-motion-graphics-archive/life-and-loves-she-devil-1986
https://www.ravensbourne.ac.uk/bbc-motion-graphics-archive/casualty-1986
https://www.ravensbourne.ac.uk/bbc-motion-graphics-archive/play-today-1977

Chapter 6

Art-of-the-title (2013), 'Doctor Who 50 years of main Title Design'. Available online: https://www.artofthetitle.com/feature/doctor-who-50-years-of-main-title-design/ (Accessed 30 August 2023).
John Smith VFX (2018), 'Way Back in 2010'. Available online: https://m.facebook.com/JohnSmithVFX/photos/way-back-in-2010-i-was-sixteen-years-old-and-had-just-started-learning-how-to-us/1899488486810865/ (Accessed 30 August 2023).
Laughton, R. (1966), *TV Graphics*, London: Studio Vista; New York: Reinhold Pub.
Lodge, B. (2019), Interview Recorded by Mark Craig [video].
Lodge, B. (2023), email correspondence, May 2023.
Losasso, M. (2023), email correspondence, May 2023.
Macdonald, I. (2015), 'How to Make a Doctor Who Title Sequence'. Available online: https://theconversation.com/how-to-make-a-doctor-who-title-sequence-at-home-a-masterclass-47729 (Accessed 30 August 2023).
Merritt, D. (1987), *Television Graphic Design: From Pencil to Pixel*, London: Trefoil.
Myerson, J. and Vickers, G. (2002), *Rewind. Forty Years of Design and Advertising,* London, New York: Phaidon.
Ofcom (2019), *Ofcom's Annual Report on the BBC*. London: Ofcom. Available online: https://www.ofcom.org.uk/__data/assets/pdf_file/0026/173735/second-bbc-annual-report.pdf (Accessed 30 August 2023).
Radio Times (2017), 'Another Doctor Who Fan has been Hired to Work on the Series'. Available online: https://www.radiotimes.com/tv/sci-fi/doctor-who-fan-hired-john-smith/ (Accessed 30 August 2023).
Sutton, S. (2023), email correspondence, May 2023.
Yates, D. and J. Price. (2015), *Communication Design: Insights from the Creative Industries*, London: Bloomsbury Publishing.

BBC Motion Graphics Archive links

https://www.ravensbourne.ac.uk/bbc-motion-graphics-archive/doctor-who-1963-0
https://www.ravensbourne.ac.uk/bbc-motion-graphics-archive/doctor-who-1967
https://www.ravensbourne.ac.uk/bbc-motion-graphics-archive/doctor-who-1970

https://www.ravensbourne.ac.uk/bbc-motion-graphics-archive/doctor-who-1973
https://www.ravensbourne.ac.uk/bbc-motion-graphics-archive/doctor-who-version-5-slitscan-1974
https://www.ravensbourne.ac.uk/bbc-motion-graphics-archive/doctor-who-1980
https://www.ravensbourne.ac.uk/bbc-motion-graphics-archive/doctor-who-2020

Chapter 7

Burke, A. (2019), *Hinterland Remixed: Media, Memory, and the Canadian 1970s*, Montreal and Kingston: McGill-Queen's University Press.
Canadian Broadcasting Corporation Graphic Standards Manual / Société Radio-Canada Manuel des norms graphiques, (1975), CBC/SRC.
Durrell, G. (2008), *Kramer: Burton Kramer | Identities | A Half Century of Graphic Design | 1958-2008*, Bolton, ON: Lulu.
Fallan, K. and Lees-Maffei, G. (2016), 'Introduction', in *Designing Worlds: National Design Histories in an Age of Globalization*, 1–21, New York and Oxford: Berghahn.
Hadlaw, J. (2019), 'Design Nationalism, Technological Pragmatism and the Performance of Canadian-ness: The Case of the Contempra Telephone', *Journal of Design History*, 32 (3): 240–62.
'Hubert Tison', *Société des designers graphiques du Québec*. Available online: https://www.sdgq.ca/sdgq-members/hubert
Newman, S. (2017), *Head of Drama: The Memoir of Sydney Newman*, Toronto: ECW Press.
Poyner, R. (2004), 'Penguin Crime', *Eye*, 53 (14). Available online: https://www.eyemagazine.com/feature/article/penguin-crime-text-in-full
Psychedelitypes (1968), New York: Photo-Lettering Inc.
Treyvaud, J.-J. (1966), 'Du dessin animé au papillon de Radio-Canada', *Culture Information: Ici Radio-Canada*, 1 (7): 4–7.
Williams, R. (1974), *Television: Technology and Cultural Form*, London: Fontana.

BBC Motion Graphics Archive Links

https://www.ravensbourne.ac.uk/bbc-motion-graphics-archive/doctor-who-1967
https://www.ravensbourne.ac.uk/bbc-motion-graphics-archive/maigret-1961
https://www.ravensbourne.ac.uk/bbc-motion-graphics-archive/forsyte-saga-1967
https://www.ravensbourne.ac.uk/bbc-motion-graphics-archive/civilisation-1969
https://www.ravensbourne.ac.uk/bbc-motion-graphics-archive/i-claudius-1976
https://www.ravensbourne.ac.uk/bbc-motion-graphics-archive/barchester-chronicles-1982
https://www.ravensbourne.ac.uk/bbc-motion-graphics-archive/goodies-1970
https://www.ravensbourne.ac.uk/bbc-motion-graphics-archive/two-ronnies-1977
https://www.ravensbourne.ac.uk/bbc-motion-graphics-archive/1969-bbc1-mirrored-globe-1
https://www.ravensbourne.ac.uk/bbc-motion-graphics-archive/1967-bbc2-cube-colour-ident-1

Chapter 8

Almeida, M. (2023), interview with the author, February 2023 [online].
Anonymized (2023), 'Multiculturalism In The BBC'. Interview by Omeiza Haruna [MS Teams], 01 March 2023.

Back, L. (1996), *New Ethnicities and Urban Culture: Racisms and Multicultural in Young Lives,* London: UCL Press Ltd.

BBC (n.d.), *Charter and Agreement*. Available online: https://www.bbc.com/aboutthebbc/governance/charter (Accessed September 2023).

Carroll, N. (2014), *Humour: A Very Short Introduction*, Gosport: Ashford Colour Press Ltd.

Da Costa, C. (2007), *Racial Stereotyping and Selective Positioning in Contemporary British Animation*, PhD thesis. Brighton University. Available online: https://ethos.bl.uk/OrderDetails.do?did=1&uin=uk.bl.ethos.499066 (Accessed September 2023).

Design Council (2018), *The Design Economy 2018*. Available online: https://www.designcouncil.org.uk/fileadmin/uploads/dc/Documents/Design_Economy_2018_exec_summary.pdf (Accessed September 2023).

Hall, S. (2003), 'The Whites of Their Eyes', in G. Dines and J. M. Humez (eds), *Gender, Race and Class in Media: A Text-Reader,* 89–93, London: SAGE.

Hall, S., J. Evans and S. Nixon, eds. (2013), *Representation*, London: SAGE Publications Ltd.

Hamed, R. (2023), interview with the author, January 2023 [online].

Hendy, D. (2022), *The BBC: A People's History*, London: Profile Books.

Henry, L. (1992), 'Lenny Henry', in J. Pines (ed.), *Black and White in Colour: Black People in British Television Since 1936,* 209–20, London: British Film Institute.

Herbert, J. (2023), interview with the author, March 2023 [online].

Lury, K. (2001), *British Youth Television: Cynicism and Enchantment,* Oxford: Clarendon Press.

Malik, S. (2002), *Representing Black Britain: Black and Asian Images on Television,* London: SAGE Publications.

Medhurst, A. (1989), 'The Lenny Henry Show', in T. Daniels and J. Gerson (eds), *The Colour Black,* 55–9, London: British Film Institute.

Mitchell, P. (2023) interview with the author, February 2023 [online].

Office for National Statistics (2022), *Ethnic Groups, England and Wales 2021*. Available online: https://www.ons.gov.uk/peoplepopulationandcommunity/culturalidentity/ethnicity/bulletins/ethnicgroupenglandandwales/census2021 (Accessed September 2023).

Shohat, E. and Stam, R. (2014), *Unthinking Eurocentrism: Multiculturalism and the Media,* London: Routledge.

Timeshift: Black and White Minstrels Revisited (2005), [TV programme] BBC Four, 8 August.

Twitchin, J., ed. (1978), 'Introduction', in *BBC Television Further Education: Five Views of Multi-Racial Britain,* 5–7, London: Commission for Racial Equality.

UK Screen Alliance (2019), *Inclusion & Diversity in UK: Visual Effects, Animation and Post-Production.* Available online: https://www.ukscreenalliance.co.uk/wp-content/uploads/2019/09/UK-Screen-Alliance-Inclusio

Walters, M. (2023), interview with the author, March 2023 [online].

BBC Motion Graphics Archive links

https://www.ravensbourne.ac.uk/bbc-motion-graphics-archive/lenny-henry-show-1985

https://www.ravensbourne.ac.uk/bbc-motion-graphics-archive/lenny-henry-show-1987

https://www.ravensbourne.ac.uk/bbc-motion-graphics-archive/def-ii-1988

https://www.ravensbourne.ac.uk/bbc-motion-graphics-archive/def-ii-1990

https://www.ravensbourne.ac.uk/bbc-motion-graphics-archive/gardeners-world-1993

https://www.ravensbourne.ac.uk/bbc-motion-graphics-archive/qed-1995

https://www.ravensbourne.ac.uk/bbc-motion-graphics-archive/sportsnight-1990

https://www.ravensbourne.ac.uk/bbc-motion-graphics-archive/juke-box-jury-1990

https://www.ravensbourne.ac.uk/bbc-motion-graphics-archive/bbc-sport-olympic-games-2004

Chapter 9

1965. 'How Delia Derbyshire made the Doctor Who theme | Tomorrow's World | Music | BBC Archive'. Available at: https://www.youtube.com/watch?v=qsRuhCflRyg (Accessed September 2023).

BBC Media Centre. *'BBC One to Air a One-off Special of the EastEnders Credits for Frozen Planet II'*. Available at: https://www.bbc.com/mediacentre/2022/eastenders-credits-frozen-planet-ii (Accessed September 2023).

BBC Motion Graphics Archive Links

Forces of Design

https://www.ravensbourne.ac.uk/bbc-motion-graphics-archive/eastenders-1985

Chapter 10

Macdonald, I. (2014), 'Cultural Change in the Creative Industries: a case study of BBC Graphic Design from 1990-2011', *Visual Communication*, 13 (1): 39–45.

Macdonald, I. (2016), *Hybrid Practices in Moving Image Design - Methods of Heritage and Digital Production in Motion Graphics*, London: Palgrave Macmillan

Manovich, L. (2013), *Software Takes Command*, London: Bloomsbury.

Martinez, M. (2023), Personal Correspondence with author, May 2023 [online].

Chapter 12

Laughton, R. (1966), *TV Graphics*, London: Studio Vista; New York: Reinhold Pub.

Merritt, D. (1993), *Graphic Design in Television*, Oxford: Focal Press.

Queen (1991), *Inuendo* [Pop Video], UK. Available online: https://www.youtube.com/watch?v=g2N0TkfrQhY (Accessed September 2023)

BBC Motion Graphics Archive links

https://www.ravensbourne.ac.uk/bbc-motion-graphics-archive/grange-hill-1978
https://www.ravensbourne.ac.uk/bbc-motion-graphics-archive/soldiers-1985
https://www.ravensbourne.ac.uk/bbc-motion-graphics-archive/soldiers-programme-inserts-1985
https://www.ravensbourne.ac.uk/bbc-motion-graphics-archive/soldiers-closing-titles-1985
https://www.ravensbourne.ac.uk/bbc-motion-graphics-archive/dorothy-l-sayers-mystery-1987
https://www.ravensbourne.ac.uk/bbc-motion-graphics-archive/de-bonos-thinking-course-1982
https://www.ravensbourne.ac.uk/bbc-motion-graphics-archive/ken-homs-chinese-cookery-1984
https://www.ravensbourne.ac.uk/bbc-motion-graphics-archive/italians-1984
https://www.ravensbourne.ac.uk/bbc-motion-graphics-archive/war-korea-1988
https://www.ravensbourne.ac.uk/bbc-motion-graphics-archive/war-korea-programme-inserts-1988
https://www.ravensbourne.ac.uk/bbc-motion-graphics-archive/chronicle-1989

Chapter 13

Clarke, B. (1974), *Graphic Design in Educational Television*, New York: Watson-Guptill Publications.

BBC Motion Graphics Archive links

Tools of the Trade: Film

https://www.ravensbourne.ac.uk/bbc-motion-graphics-archive/sutton-hoo-1987

ILLUSTRATION & ARTWORK

https://www.ravensbourne.ac.uk/bbc-motion-graphics-archive/ou-personality-and-learning-1976

TOMORROWS WORLD

https://docs.google.com/document/d/1guSmR4ZWFdWL9p9aBc8S_5BbPFLXr-H7/edit
https://www.ravensbourne.ac.uk/bbc-motion-graphics-archive/tomorrows-world-1980

Chapter 14

Gardner, W. (1980), 'Interactive Techniques for the Tektronix 4027 Colour Terminal', *Displays*, 2 (1): 47–55.
Gardner, W. (1981), 'The Case for a New Graphic Display Device', BBC Internal Report.
Gardner, W. (1982), 'Tomorrow's Weather', BBC Internal Report.
Gardner, W. (1984), 'BBC Television Computer Graphics', in BBC Engineering Directorate Brochure, Track Forward 84.
Gardner, W. (1985a), 'The BBC Television Weather System', British Computer Society; *Computer Bulletin*, 1 (4).
Gardner, W. (1985b), 'Additional Computer Graphics Resources'. BBC Internal Report.
Logica Ltd. (1980), ICON Brochure.

BBC Motion Graphics Archive links

https://www.ravensbourne.ac.uk/bbc-motion-graphics-archive/1985-bbc1-globe-computer-originated-world
https://www.ravensbourne.ac.uk/bbc-motion-graphics-archive/1986-bbc2-computer-animated-two
https://www.ravensbourne.ac.uk/bbc-motion-graphics-archive/bbc-weather
https://www.ravensbourne.ac.uk/bbc-motion-graphics-archive/bbc-weather-forecast-1985
https://www.ravensbourne.ac.uk/bbc-motion-graphics-archive/tripods-1985

Chapter 15

McCaskill, S. (2023), *BBC Sport's Barbara Slater on the Power of Free-to-Air, Making Difficult Choices, and How PSBs can Help Sports Grow in the Digital Era.* Available online: https://www.sportspromedia.com/analysis/bbc-sport-barbara-slater-interview-womens-sports-fta-broadcasting-iplayer/?zephr_sso_ott=WhqnbU (accessed September 2023).

External Links

Grandstand

https://www.youtube.com/watch?v=QCPz9zygKEo

BBC Motion Graphic Archive Links

Grandstand

https://www.youtube.com/watch?v=Z0x31VGYikI
https://www.ravensbourne.ac.uk/bbc-motion-graphics-archive/sportsnight-1985

BRANDING SPORT

https://www.ravensbourne.ac.uk/bbc-motion-graphics-archive/bbc-sport-ident-1996

POST MILLENNIUM

https://www.ravensbourne.ac.uk/bbc-motion-graphics-archive/bbc-sport-olympic-games-2004

Chapter 16

BBC Motion Graphics Archive links

https://www.ravensbourne.ac.uk/bbc-motion-graphics-archive/nationwide-1969

Chapter 17

Press Agency UPI / BBC News Website 17 January 2013.

BBC Motion Graphics Archive links

https://www.ravensbourne.ac.uk/bbc-motion-graphics-archive/breakfast-time-1984
https://www.ravensbourne.ac.uk/bbc-motion-graphics-archive/bbc-six-oclock-news-1984
https://www.ravensbourne.ac.uk/bbc-motion-graphics-archive/bbc-breakfast-news-1989

Chapter 18

Buffett, C. (2023), email correspondence, May 2023.
Chaudoir, M. (2023), email correspondence, June 2023.
Davy, A. (2023), interview with authors, May 2023 [online].
Hill, K. (2023), interview with authors, May 2023 [online].
Wormleighton, I. (2023), interview with authors, May 2023 [online].

BBC Motion Graphics Archive links

https://www.ravensbourne.ac.uk/bbc-motion-graphics-archive/nine-oclock-news-1985
https://www.ravensbourne.ac.uk/bbc-motion-graphics-archive/bbc-one-oclock-news-1986
https://www.ravensbourne.ac.uk/bbc-motion-graphics-archive/bbc-news-countdown-trail-2003
https://www.ravensbourne.ac.uk/bbc-motion-graphics-archive/bbc-news-countdown-trail-2003-0

Index

3D effects   32, 33, 48, 103, 156
   animation   84, 160
   creating in Paintbox   124
3Peach   26, 31
35mm film   68, 74, 129, 140
280 Useful Ideas from Japan
   logo design   127
   title sequence   126
2001: A Space Odyssey   80, 141
2004 Olympic Games title sequence   166, 167

Aardman Animation   18
Academy Award   68
ACM SIGGRAPH Conference   151, 152
Adobe After Effects   117
aerial imaging   140
After Effects   82–3
Akinwolere, Ayo   62
Alexandra Palace   137–9, 192, *see also* Open University
Almeida, Morgan   101, 103
American Cinematographer   79–80
animation   5, 31, 54, 68, 69, 71, 74, 75, 112, 149, 160, *see also* film; motion graphics
   3D   84, 160
   bumper   29
   butterfly   91, 92
   caption scanner   140
   cel   130, 132, 133, 140, 179
   computer   37, 135, 179
   Doctor Who title sequence   81, 82
   'flickbook' effect   125
   hand drawing   134–5
   line drawings   175
   logo   77
   'moods'   41
   music venue tour   174–5
   non-linear editing   42
   plasticine   146, 147
   'smarty ship'   59
   spinning globe   154
   stand   140
   stop-frame   26, 132, 133, 156
   typography   72
   Virtual Globe   31, 32
   wireframe   135, 143, 175, 179
anti-aliasing   150, 151, 153
Apple   21
   Lisa   155
   Mac   127–8, 154
appointment viewing   76
apps   45, 64
Argent, Rod   133
Ariel image system   113
Arnold, Dave   60, 62
art/artwork   41
   Open University   143
   scenic   110
ARTEM   31, 49
artificial intelligence (AI)   5, 34–5
Aspinall, Tim   69
Aston, John   10, 138, 151
attention economy   21
audience   3, 4, 34
   BBC   20–1
   Blue Peter   57, 63
   engagement   63–5
   Top of the Pops   45, 47
   virtual community   20
awards
   BAFTA   18, 43, 68, 105
   D&AD Wood Pencil   49, 133
Ayton, Susan   19

badge, *Blue Peter*   64–5
Bailey, Dick   71, 87
Baker, Colin   81
Baker, Tom   80
Ball, Johnny   149
Bang Goes the Theory   15
Baranowski, Alex   41–3
'Barnacle Bill'   58

Barnes, Edward   57
Barthes, Roland   20
Bass, Saul   67, 69, 71, 112
Baxter, Biddy   57, 64, 65
BBC, *see* Open University
   audience   20–1
   charter   95, 106
   Computer Graphics Workshop (CGW) (*see* Computer Graphics Workshop)
   Graphic Department   1, 4
   logos   13 (*see also* logo)
   Motion Graphics Archive   1, 85, 86, 93, 128
   News and Current Affairs   5
   news correspondents   193
   News Graphics   122
   Presentation Design team   9, 10
   'Producer's Choice' policy   156
   Radiophonic Workshop   151
   rebranding   13 (*see also* rebranding)
   Scenery Block   110, 111, 114
   Studio Capital Projects Department (SCPD)   151–2
   Television Centre   137, 144, 149, 169–70
   'Television Symbol'   9
   tuning symbol   19
BBC Breakfast   187
BBC Four   39–40
   idents   39–41
   music   40
BBC One   3
   Balloon   21, 22, 27
   'Circles' ident   15
   colour broadcasting   31
   ident   10, 21–3, 154
BBC Sport   157, *see also* Grandstand; *Match of the Day* (MOTD)
   branding   160–3
   data visualization   162–3
   editorial stories   164
   rebranding   165, 166
   title sequence   163
BBC Three   39–40
BBC Two   3, 11, 40
   Doctor Who Night   16
   idents   14, 40–3
   launch idents   28–9
Beale, Janice   21
Bernard, Jason   166
Betancourt, Michael   41
binge-watching   76
Birt, John   161
Black and White Minstrel Show, The   95
Blagden, Bob   75
Blakstad, Lucy   99

Blaxill, Ric   51–2, 55
Blue Peter   4, 57, 63
   audience engagement   63–5
   badge   64–5
   branding   60–3
   end credits   63
   logo   57, 60–1, 64
   logotype   65
   music   62
   presenters   60, 62
   production design   60
   set redesign   64–5
   'smarty ship'   59
   theme tune   64
   title sequence   57, 60–4
   viewership   62
blurring effect   75
Bonaccorsi, Matthew   84
books, graphic design   73
Boy George   55
branding   3, 5, 21, 34, *see also* ident/s
   BBC Sport   160–3
   BBC 'Television Symbol'   9
   Blue Peter   60–3
   Breakfast Time   178
   channel   37
   digital   11
   'one company'   13
   programme   171
   re-   13, 21, 22, 25, 39–40
   Top of the Pops   55
Breakfast Time   177, 185, 186
   branding   178
   content graphics   180
   logo   178–80
   news maps   185
   news segments   183, 184
   on-screen clock   180, 181
   title sequence   178–80
   training for launch   182–3
   weather segments   183, 184
British Academy of Film and Television Arts (BAFTA)   18, 43, 68, 105
British Film Institute (BFI)   77
Britishness   95
broadcast design   40
Brooker, Charlie   19
Brooks, Tom   118
budget
   BBC   136
   CGI   135
   drama production   76
   live-action shoot   76

Nationwide title sequence   175
   title sequence   71, 126, 129–30, 132
bumper, animation   29
Bungee ident   30
butterfly, animation   91
Buttner, Christine   73, 74

camera   71
   aerial imaging   140
   animation   140
   caption   182
   fly-through   49
   howlround effect   77
   motion control   69, 141, 144
   multiplane   141
   Paintbox   124
   rostrum   79–81, 118, 130, 132, 135, 143, 147, 164, 174, 175
   television studio   139–40
   tracking dolly   80
cameramen   193
Canada   4
   modernization   85
   motion graphics   85
   television   86
Canadian Broadcasting Corporation (CBC)   4, 85
   BBC influence   86
   debut of Doctor Who   86
   logo   91–3
   motion graphics   92–3
   presentations of BBC material   87–9
   visual identity   91, 92
Capaldi, Peter   82
caption cards   157–8
caption scanner   140
caption stand   139–40
Cassandre, Adolphe   134
Casualty   74–5
CBBC   19
CDs   49
cel animation   140
   Breakfast Time title sequence   179–80
   Grange Hill title sequence   130
   multiplane camera   141
   painting   132, 134
   Soldiers title sequence   130, 132
   wireframe   143
channel   22, 161
   branding   37
   digital   20–1
   flag   13
   frame   13
   ident   37
   rebranding   40
Chapman, Ben   55
Chapman, Celia   22
character generator   139, 150
Charged   42
Chaudoir, Mark   30, 193
Chibnall, Chris   83
Chinyangagya, Radzi   62
choreography, title sequence   133
Christmas idents   24–8
Chromakey   154–5
circle ident   15, 23, 28, 29, 32
'Circles' identity   15
Clarke, Vince   53
classified football results   157, 162
Clayton, Peter   160
Clemmans, Katy   165
clip-based title sequence   162
Cload, Ted   134
closed-circuit television   137
collaboration   41, 43, 115, 125, 140
Collective Consciousness Society   55
Collinson, Phil   82
colour   105, 146
   BBC Sport opening sequence   162
   Blue Peter logo   64
   Blue Peter title sequence   61
   Doctor Who title sequence   81
   frame-store   151
   television   113
comedy   89
comics   130, *see also* cel animation
commissioning process, graphic design   67–8
computer animation   37, 59, 135, 179, *see also* CGI
computer graphics   150
   ACM SIGGRAPH Conference   151
   anti-aliasing   150, 151, 153
   colour paint system   149
   DEC/ICON system   150, 151
   direct memory transfer (DMA)   151
   General Election System   153
   MEIKO   156
   PIXAR   156
   'smart' frame-store   151–2
   Sportsnight title sequence   159
   weather   154–5
Computer Graphics Workshop (CGW)   5, 149, 153, 156, 161
computer-generated imagery (CGI)   30, 69, 74, 134
   Blue Peter title sequence   61
   budget   135
   maps   135
   wireframe   135

'Concept News'   192–3
Connections, opening sequence   87
Contempra   93
continuity announcer   90
Cony, Chris   153
Cook, Abby   62
Cooke, Alistair   89
copyright
   film   132
   title sequence   68
Cosford, Bob   130, 158
countdown sequence   193
Covid-19   24
Cowey, Chris   53–6
Cramer, Felix   71
creativity   5, 14, 119, 124
crotales   38, 39
culture/cultural
   memory   4, 85
      youth   96, 99
Current Affairs, graphic design   178
'Curve'   32, 33

D&AD Wood Pencil   49, 133
Dallas, Rosalind   103, 104
dance   22
dancefloor movement   95
Daulby, George   150
D'Auria, Paul   97, 113–14, 122
Davies, Russell T   82
Davies, Sarah   13, 32
Davy, Andy   180, 184, 186, 187, 191–2
Dawburn, Graham   110
De Bono's Thinking Course   134
Deck, Barry   52
DEF II   99
   multiculturalism   101, 106
   title sequence   98, 99
Dempster, Ross   60
Derbyshire, Delia   78, 79, 112
design nationalism   4, 85, 93
Dibb, Emma   64
digital branding   11
digital channel   39
   idents   19
digital drawing machine   109, 113
Digital Equipment Corporation (DEC)   153, 156
   PDP 11/40 minicomputer   149–51
   VAX 11/750   151
Dimbleby, David   153
direct memory transfer (DMA)   151–2
directing
   2002 Commonwealth Games title sequence   166

   live action   133–4
display board   140
distance learning, *see* Open University
diversity   96, 98, 101, 103–5, *see also* representation
Doctor Who   4, 28, 80, 83, 112
   2005 reboot   81–2
   CBC debut   86
   Dalek ident   16
   fanbase   82–4
   franchise   82
   logo   79–82
   music   78–9
   Royal Mint medals   84
   Series 7   79
   Series 11   79–80
   Series 18   80
   title sequence   77–80, 82–3
documentary   95–6, 132
Doherty, Paul   153, 155
dope sheet   130, 179, 180
Dorothy L. Sayers Mysteries   133
Dorrington, Harry   99
drama serial   71, 73
drama title   4, 76
   35mm stills shot   68
   animation   68, 71, 75
   graphic design   67–8
   'gripping'   42–3
   moodboard presentation   68
   photography   69–71, 75
   typography   72
drawing/s   5, 121–2, *see also* digital drawing machine
   animation   134–5
   Escher   71, 72
   line   175
   rapidograph   135
Dudley, Anne   126

EastEnders   4, 17, 69
   logo   69
   title sequence   111
Easterbrook, Jim   156
editing
   DEF II title sequence   99, 101
   non-linear   42
educational television   138–9, *see also* Open University
Electronic Arts   179
electronic programme guide (EPG)   105
Eley, Brian   179
Ellis, Roderick   103, 160–2
Elmes, Oliver   37, 81, 154
Emin, Tracey   10

end credits   63, 68
English, Bob   121
Eric   109, 113
Escher, M.C.   71, 72
Euro '96   161
Euro 2004   166
Evans, Ellen   64, 65
Eve, Trevor   71, 72
experimentation
   graphic design   129
   Quantel Paintbox   118, 125
   sound design   40–1
exploding pizza   92–3

fandom, *Whovians*   83
Farley, Dave   68, 132, 134
Farnon, Robert   71
Fenton, George   179
Fielder, Jane   21, 26, 30, 165, 166
film/filmmaking   141
   35mm   129, 140
   compositing   113
   documentary   95–6, 132
   editing   68
   Kodalith   81
   mobile rigs   141
   multiple exposure   141
   music venue tour   174–5
   poster   69
   title sequence   68–9
Fincham, Peter   22
Fischinger, Oskar, *An Optical Poem*   41
flag channel   13
Fleming, Allan   91
'flickbook'   125
Florence, Peter   135
football   161
Forsyte Saga   87
Forsyth, Frederick   130
Foster, Doug   31, 118
Fox, Paul   13, 31
frame channel   13
frame-store   151–2
franchise, *Doctor Who*   82
Friedman, Liz   31, 76
Frozen Planet II   111
Frutiger, Adrian   48
Futura   171
Fynes, Chris   160
Fywell, Tim   71

Gall, Linda   103
Games, Abram   3, 9, 37

Gardeners' World   101
Garnett, Tony   72
Gau, John   132
Gavin, Pat   134
General Election System
   'Battleground' display   156
   DEC 11/750   153
   maps   153
   touchscreen terminals   153
Genghis Cohen   69
Giles, Bill   154
Gill, Rosemary   57
Ginger, Dan   112
Girdler, Bryan   156
Glaister, Gerald   71
Glasman, Joe   40–1
globe ident   10, 19, 21, 22, 25, 31, 32, 90, 154, 160–1
Glory Enough for All, opening sequence   89
Gold, Murray   62
Good Life, The   124
Goodies, The, title sequence   89, 90
Goossens, Sidonie   37
Gorey, Edward   89
Gouldie, Maylin   26
Graham-Smith, Michael   73, 74, 171, 195
Grainer, Ron   78
Grainge, Paul   22
Grandstand   161
   classified football results   157, 162
   Final Score section   157
   globe ident   161
Grange Hill   68
   caption cards   157
   music   130
   title sequence   31, 130
graphic design   2, 49, 115, 170, 191–2, *see also* computer graphics; logo; motion graphics; Quantel Paintbox; title sequence
   books   73
   collaboration   125
   commissioning process   67–8
   Current Affairs   178
   digital drawing machine   109, 113
   drawing   121–2
   experimentation   129
   first day at work   190–1
   invisible graphics   74
   lead designer   161
   news   180
   Newsnight   177
   on-the-job training   171
   Open University   137–9

Quantel Paintbox   113
sketching   124–5
sport information graphics   162
storyboard   117, 190
style guide   184
tech integration   123
test card   37
time constraints   123
training   190
typical day   191
typography   111–12
'visual music'   41
graticule   139
Green, Tim   164
Greenway, Iain   26, 71, 74
greyscale   139
Gripping   42–3
Groves, Toni   156
Guardian   23
Guardian, The   53, 153

Hadlaw, Jan   4, 85, 93
HAL   31
Hall, Tony   192–3
Hamid, Ruhi   101
Hanshaw, Billy   82–3
Harding, Andrew   193
Harnett, Ollie   19
harp motif, *Silk*   39
Harris, Jack   112
Hart, Tony   57, 58, 61
Hastings, Max   135
Hayman, David   74
HBO   76
Head, Sally   73
Heggessey, Larraine   22
Hendy, D.   1
Henry, Lenny   97
Herbert, John   103, 104
Herdeg, W.   1
Hey, Stan   97
Heyes, Bernard   51
Hibbert, Jerry   132
high-definition television broadcasting   68, 105
Hill, Jimmy   158, 164
Hill, Kevin   58–61
hip-hop   98
historical drama   89
Hocking, Steve   58, 60
Hockney, David   116
Hodge, Patricia   73
Hopkins, Martin   166

Horrocks, Margaret   48–9, 51
howlround effect   77–9, 82, 84, 112
humour, *The Lenny Henry Show*   97
Huq, Konnie   62

I, Claudius   71
ICON   150, 151, 154
ident/s   3, 9, 34, 179
    balloon   21, 22
    BBC Four   19, 39–41
    BBC One   10, 21–3, 154
    BBC Two   28–9, 40–3
    Bungee   30
    CBC   93
    channel   37
    Charged   42
    Christmas   24–8
    circle   15, 23, 28, 29, 32
    Crate   28
    'Curve'   32, 33
    digital channel   19
    globe   10, 11, 19, 25, 31, 90, 160–1
    hot air balloon   21, 22
    'Improvisation'   40–1
    inclusivity   23, 24
    'lockdown'   24
    Magic Forest   17
    as marketing tool   14–19
    meta   14, 15
    Paint   38
    rebranding   40
    'Rhythm and Movement'   22, 23
    seasonality   24–30
    Silk   38–9
    sonic aspects   37–8
    storytelling   10, 20
    technology   30, 31
    ticking clock   10
    Wallace and Gromit   18, 19
    Water   39
illustration
    cel animation   130, 132, 134
    Open University   141
immigration   95
'Improvisation'   40–1
improvisation   42–3
inclusivity   23, 24, 62
information graphics   13, 115, 150–1, 162, 178, 183,
    see also maps
invisible graphics   74
ITN   149, 150, 153
ITV   37
Ive, Jonathan   21, 22

216   Index

Jackson, Michael   14, 18
Jeapes, Alan   67, 69, 71, 110–12, 154, 171
Jeffrey, Allison   60
Jervis, Dave   60

on-the-job training   171
Johnson, Catherine   37, 40
Jones, Liz   154
Jordan, Diane-Louise   62
Juke Box Jury   103, 104

Keating, Roly   40
Keeley, Jason   40–1, 43
Kemp, Alan   72
Kes   72
Kodalith   81, 135
Korea, CGI map   135
Kramer, Burton   4, 92

Lambert, Verity   77
Lambie-Nairn, Martin   1, 2, 11, 13, 21, 22, 32, 38, 40, 41, 110–11, 121, 179
language   20
Laughton, Roy   1, 129
lead graphic designer   161
Led Zeppelin, *Whole Lotta Love*   55
Lenny Henry Show, The
    humour   97
    multiculturalism   97, 98, 105–6
    title sequence   96–8
Letraset   150, 170–3, 183, 189
Levell, Tim   63
Life in Cold Blood   17
lighting   42, 118
    ray tracing   70
    Top of the Pops   52
Lime Grove Studios   170–1, 177, 181
line drawings   175
Between the Lines   72
Liszt, Franz, *Second Hungarian Rhapsody*   41
live action   72, 166
    DEF II title sequence   99
    directing   133–4
    Lenny Henry Show title sequence   97, 98
    Play for Today title sequence   75–6
    rotoscope   132, 133
live broadcasting   144
Lloyd, David   186
Loach, Ken   72
'lockdown' idents   24
Lodge, Bernard   67–9, 77, 79, 81, 82, 112
Logica

graphics generator   37
ICON   150
logo   73
    280 Useful Ideas from Japan   127
    animated   77
    Blue Peter   57, 60–1, 64
    Breakfast Time   180
    Canadian Broadcasting Corporation (CBC)   91–3
    Canadian National Railways   91
    Doctor Who   79–82
    EastEnders   69
    globe   19
    Match of the Day (MOTD)   164
    phototypesetting   178
    Sportsnight   125
    Top of the Pops   46–9, 52
    Top of the Pops 2   52–4
Long, Chris   150
Losasso, Matthew   30, 82, 118
Loves and Lives of a She-Devil, The   73–4
Lowe, Dave   193
Lucas, George   80
Lynott, Phil, 'Yellow Pearl'   46

Macdonald, Iain   68
MacLaine, Ewen   150, 156
Madame Bovary   71
Magic Forest ident   17
Maigret   86, 87
Mainframe   42
Man Who Fell To Earth, The   121
'Mandala, the'   171, 178
Manovich, Lev   115, 117
maps   189
    General Election System   153
    Korea   135
    meteorological   154–5, 183
    news   185
    symbols   172–3
Marber Grid   86, 87
Mark One Group   105
marketing, idents   14–19
Marson, Richard   62
Martin, Geoffrey   86, 87
Martin, Jonathan   160
Martin, Len   157
Martinez, Mina   115
Martinez, Victor   165
Maseeley Press   112
Mason, Brian   154
Masterpiece Theatre   88, 89
Masters, Pam   13, 22, 31, 32
Match of the Day (MOTD)   162

logo   164
title sequence   157–9, 163, 164
Mawer, Charlie   14, 15, 22
Maxwell, Robert   113–14
May, Simon   69
McGee, Mike   72, 74
McGhie, Charles   115, 150, 156
McKenzie, Everol   48
McLaren, Norman   41
McNamara, Andy   59
McNamara, Paul   163
McWatt, John   112
Mecanorma   180
MEIKO   156
Merritt, Douglas   1
meta idents   14, 15
metaphor   71, 74
metaphorical space   40
Mill, The   82
Millar, Gregory   165
Miller, Mary Jane   86
Minghella, Anthony   68
Ministry of Sound   52
Mirrored Globe   31
Mitchell, Paul   104–5, 166
mnemonics   3
modernization, Canada   85
Moffat, Steven   83
Money Programme   150
Montagnon, Peter   138
Monty Python's Flying Circus
   continuity announcer   90–1
   motion graphics   90
moodboard   68, 134
mood/s   74
   Gripping   43
   programming   41
   title sequence   69
Moran, Joe   20
Moses, Howard   150, 177–8
Moshinsky, Elijah   69
moth, symbolism   71
motion control camera   69, 141, 144
motion graphics   1, 4, 69, 85, 86, 129, 161,
    see also animation; Open University;
    title sequence
   Canadian Broadcasting Corporation   92–3
   The Goodies title sequence   89, 90
   Grange Hill title sequence   130
   Lenny Henry Show title sequence   98
   Monty Python's Flying Circus   90
   news   192
   Open University   139

Top of the Pops title sequence   46–8
'visual music'   41
Mudenda, Mwaksi   62
multiculturalism   96–8, 101, 105–6
multiplane camera   141
multiple exposure   141
music   3, 104, 174, *see also Top of the Pops*
   BBC Four   40
   Blue Peter   62, 64
   Breakfast Time title sequence   179
   countdown   193
   Doctor Who   78–9
   downloads   45
   Grange Hill title sequence   130
   Gripping   42–3
   hip-hop   98
   improvisation   40–3
   Paint   38
   Silk   39
   Soldiers title sequence   133
   title sequence   68, 71
   venue tour animation   174–5
   'visual'   41
Myerson, Jeremy   79
Mylod, Mark   15
Mystery!   89

Nationwide   169, 177
   branding   171
   graphics studio   170–1
   Lime Grove Studios   170
   'the Mandala'   171, 178
   maps   173
   photographic studio   171
   production team   174
   Research Assistant Trainees (RATS)   172–3
   title sequence   175
Neil, Ron   149, 151, 154, 178, 186
Netflix   41
Network 7   98
news   194
news maps   185
Newsnight, graphic design   177
Nickolds, Andrew   97
Nolan, Sidney   116
non-linear editing   42
Olympic Games   159, 161, 166, 167
on-screen clock, *Breakfast Time*   180, 181
Open University   5, 147, *see also* video studio
   cel animation sequences   140
   graphic design   137–9
   illustration   141
   motion design   139

presenter   140
    Production Centre   143
    sound design   143
    summer schools   138
    title sequence   143
    transfer lettering   139
opening sequence   75, *see also* title sequence
    BBC Sport   162
    Connections   87
    Glory Enough for All   89
    virtual reality (VR)   146
opening titles   1
Ortmans, Marc   45–6, 49, 51
Our World   112

Paint, sound design   38
painting, cel animation   132
Painting with Light   116
Palin, Michael   90
Palmer, Ben   77, 79
Palmer, Tom   126
Panorama   177–8
Park, Nick   18
Passmore, Simon   71
PDP 11/40 minicomputer   149–50
Pearson, Neil   72
'Pedigree Comedy' campaign   14, 15
Penguin Crime   86, 87
Personality & Learning   143
Pertwee, Jon   79
Peter Anderson Studio   82
Philips, Andrea   14
photography   74
    blurring effect   75
    Howlround effect   78
    stills   68, 170, 174
    time-lapse   193
    title sequence   69–71
Photoshop   70–1
phototypesetting   113, 134, 178
Pickles, Ben   83–4
pirate radio   98
PIXAR   156
plasticine animation   146, 147
Platt, Tim   103
Play for Today   75–6
Pockett, Darrell   159
policy, 'Producer's Choice'   156
politics   95, 97
Pollock, Anthony   132
pop music   3
poster, film   69
Prendiville, Kieran   174

Presentation Design team   9, 10, 28–31
presenters, *Blue Peter*   62
Prix Pixel   136
'Producer's Choice' policy   156
production design   5, 60, 110
programming   3, 9, 10, 40
    Christmas   25–30
    continuity announcer   90
    idents   14
    international circulation   90–1
    moods   41
    race relations   95–6
    young adult   98
    youth   96
PromaxBDA   105
promotional content   22, *see also* ident/s
promotional stills   169–70
props   73, 110
Pstrowski, Stephan   71
public service channels   37
pull caption sequence   140

Quantel Harry   114, 126
Quantel Henry   75
Quantel Paintbox   5, 31, 49, 74, 113–14, 122, 152, 154–6, 182, 190–2
    advantages and drawbacks   124
    animation   125
    in-camera work   118
    collaboration   125
    experimentation   118, 125
    interface   123
    logo design   125
    pen and tablet   115, 123
    stencil   124
    tablet workstation   118
    training   185
    unofficial apprenticeship   116–17
    weather sequence   185, 186

race/racial
    discrimination   95
    relations   95–6, 101
radio, pirate   98
rapidograph   135
ray tracing   70
rebranding   13, 21, 22, 25, 39–40, 162–3
    BBC Sport   165, 166
    BBC Two   41
    Blue Peter   60–3
Red Bee Creative   14, 28, 82
Reed, Owen   60
representation   4

diverse   101
multicultural   96–8, 101, 105–6
progressive   96
racialized minority   95–6, 98, 103
Research Assistant Trainees (RATS)   172–3
'Rhythm and Movement' ident   22, 23
Richard Purdum Productions   134
Rickman, Alan   68
Ritson, Mark   23
Roberts, Susan   164
roller caption stand   140
Root, Jane   40
rostrum camera   79–81, 118, 130, 132, 135, 143, 147, 164, 174, 175, 180
rotating globe   11
rotoscope   132, 133
Royal Mint, *Doctor Who* medals   84
Rutherford, Paul   86

Sadler, Gaynor   38, 39, 43
Sadler, Tony   38, 39, 43
Salmon, Peter   165
satire   90
Saville, Philip   73
Scarfe, Gerald   164
Scenery Block   110, 111, 114
scenic art   110
Scott, Jack   154, 155
Screenwipe   19
seasonal idents, Christmas   25–30
Sense of Guilt, A   71
serials, title sequence   67
set redesign, *Blue Peter*   64–5
Shackle, Freddy   135
Shannon, Martin   165
Silk   38–9, 42–3
Simpson, Ian   60
single drama, title sequence   68–9
Six O'Clock News   186, 191, 192
sketching   121–2, 124–5
Sky Sports   161
slit-scan technique   79–80, 82
'smarty ship,' animation   59
Smith, Terry   149, 150
Soldiers, title sequence   130, 132, 133
sound design   2, 3, *see also* ident/s
    BBC Two   41–3
    Charged   42
    experimentation   40–1
    Gripping   42–3
    Open University   143
    Paint   38
    Silk   38–9

Soldiers title sequence   132
'spangle' effects   79
synaesthetic correspondence   38–9
title sequence   53
Top of the Pops   2
Water   39
'spangle' sound effects   79
Sparkler   13
special effects   49, 52
    blur   75
    camera fly-through   49
    howlround   77, 78, 82, 84, 112
    slit-scan technique   79–80, 82
    starburst   80
    time travel   81
Spender   28
sport   5
    information graphics   162
    production teams   161
Sportsnight   103
    logo design   125
    title sequence   159
Spotify   56
starburst effects   80
stencil, Paintbox   124
Stephens, Maeve   156
stereotype   101
stills photography   68, 170, 174
Stills Store   181–4, 190
stop-frame animation   26, 132, 133, 156
Storm from the East   133
storyboard   74, 117, 124, 133–4, 138, 164, 175, 178–9, 190
storytelling   1, 10, 20, 52
strap easel   140
streaming   41, 76
Street-Porter, Janet   98, 126
Strevens, Matt   83
Studio TK4   77
style guide   184
summer school, Open University   138
Sunday Times, The   164
Superunion   41
surrealism   71, 72
Sutton, Dennis   132
Sutton, Sid   19, 31, 33, 75, 80, 81, 154
Sutton Hoo   80
Swinnerton, John   49, 118
symbolism, moth   71
symbol/s
    'the Mandala'   171
    map   173
synaesthetic correspondence   38–9

Talbot, Pauline   144, 157–9, 162
Tanton, Nick   109, 150
Taylor, Richard   152
Teather, John   154, 155
technology   45, 128, 138, 192, 194, *see also* artificial intelligence (AI); CGI; Quantel Paintbox
   colour television   31
   democratization   83
   digital graphic design   49
   digital revolution   113–14
   ident   30, 31
   motion control camera   69
   Virtual Globe   31, 32
television   111, *see also* Open University; video studio
   Canadian   86
   closed-circuit   137
   colour   113
   educational   138–9
   'flow'   9
   satellite link-up   112
   satire   90
   young adult market   98
Television Centre   169–70
Template Gothic   52
Tennant, David   17, 82
test card   37
Think of a Number   149
Thompson, Mark   23, 24
ticking clock   10
time travel   81
time-lapse photography   193
Tison, Hubert   91, 92
title sequence   67, 74, *see also* logo
   280 Useful Ideas from Japan   126
   2002 Commonwealth Games title sequence   166
   2004 Olympic Games   166, 167
   animation   81, 82
   Blue Peter   57, 60–4
   Breakfast Time   178
   budget   71, 126, 129–30, 132
   cel animation   130, 132, 133
   CGI   135, 136
   choreography   130, 133
   clip-based   162
   commissioning process   67–8
   copyright   68
   DEF II   98, 99
   Doctor Who   78–80, 82–3
   EastEnders   111
   editing   99, 101
   Euro 2004   166
   fan-made   82–4
   film editing   68

The Goodies   89, 90
Grange Hill   31, 130
howlround effect   77–9, 82
illustrative style   130, 132
The Lenny Henry Show   96–8
Match of the Day (MOTD)   157–9, 163, 164
multiculturalism   105
music   68, 71, 179
Nationwide   175
Open University   143
photography   69–71
serials   67
single drama   68–9
Sportsnight   159
title captions   68
Top of the Pops   45–9, 51
Top of the Pops 2   52, 53
The Two Ronnies   89
typography   79
Tomorrow's World   166
   animation   146, 147
   'Brain-Planet' concept   144
   virtual reality (VR)   146
Top of the Pops   3, 56
   audience   47
   branding   55
   guest presenters   52
   lighting   52
   logo   46–9, 52
   title sequence   45–9, 51
Top of the Pops 2
   logo   53–4
   title sequence   52, 53
Top of the Pops magazine   54
touchscreen terminal, General Election System   153
tracking dolly   80
training
   graphic design   190
   on-the-job   171
   Quantel Paintbox   185
transfer lettering   139, *see also* Letraset
Troughton, Patrick   79
Truly Madly Deeply   68
   end credits   68
   title design   69
Trumbull, Douglas   79–80
Tschichold, Jan   48
tuning symbol   19
Turk, Roy   114
Turner, John Nathan   80
Twitchin, John   95
Two Ronnies, The   89

Twombly, Cy 122
typography 3, 72, 111
    anti-aliasing 151
    Blue Peter logo 65
    Doctor Who title sequence 79
    Forsyte Saga 87
    Marber Grid 87
    Maseeley Press 112
    phototypesetting 113, 134, 178
    transfer lettering 139
    workshop 150, 152

Ultravox 46
Underbelly 74
University of Sheffield, Audio Visual Centre 177
Ure, Midge 46, 53

Vickers, Graham 79
video studio
    camera 140
    caption scanner 140
    caption stands 139–40
    display board 140
    OU programme-making 138–40
    roller caption stand 140
Video Tape (VT) editor 162–3
viewership, *Blue Peter* 62
Vince, John 135, 143
Vinnicombe, Ewan 63–4
Vinson, Robin 150
virtual reality (VR) 146
visual art 42
visual effects workshop 110
visual identity, Canadian Broadcasting Corporation (CBC) 91, 92
visual journalism 13
'visual music' 41
voice-over 40, 92, 174
Vora, Saz 122
VT80 150

Walking with Dinosaurs 15
Wallace and Gromit, idents 18, 19
Walmsley, Steve 153, 155
Walt Disney Studio 141
Walters, Mark 105
War in Korea, The 135
Warhol, Andy 53–4
Water 39
waterphone 39
Watkins, Karl 31, 118, 126
weather graphics
    Breakfast Time 183, 184
    maps 154–5
White Room, The 53
Whittaker, Jodie 83
Whovians 83
Wilde, Kim 55
Williams, Paula 26, 52
Williams, Raymond 9, 90
Willis, Magnus 13
Wilson, Francis 184
Wilson, Harold 137
Wimsey 134
wipe effect 79
wireframe 135, 143, 175, 179
Wiseman, Neil 150
working class 97
workshop
    Radiophonic 151
    typographic 150, 152
Wormleighton, Ian 190
Worthy, Sue 154
Wray, Colin 156
Wyatt, Jane 118
Wyatt-Brooks, Jane 18, 99

Yentob, Alan 14
youth
    culture 96, 99
    television 98
YouTube 82, 83, 86